Jackie

ACKNOWLEDGEMENTS

The publishers would like to thank the team at D C Thomson & Co. Ltd for all their help in compiling this book, particularly Martin Lindsay, Bill McLoughlin and Sandy Monks.

The publishers would like to thank the following sources for their kind permission to reproduce the pictures in this book.

Corbis Images: /Neal Preston: 63

Rex Features: /Andre Csillag: front endpaper; /Everett Collection: back endpaper; /Armando Pietrangeli: 192

Every effort has been made to acknowledge correctly and contact the source and/or copyright holder of each picture and Carlton Books Limited apologises for any unintentional errors or omissions which will be corrected in future editions of this book.

THIS IS A PRION BOOK

First published in Great Britain in 2006 by Prion
An imprint of the Carlton Publishing Group
20 Mortimer Street
London W1T 3JW

JACKIE is a trade mark of and © DC Thomson & Co. Ltd. 2006. All
feature material, illustrations and photographs (unless otherwise ascribed)
© DC Thomson & Co. Ltd 2006

10-digit ISBN: 1-85375-608-3
13-digit ISBN: 978-1-85375-608-5

Edited and compiled by Lorna Russell

Art Director: Emma Wicks
Design: Anita Ruddell
Production: Caroline Alberti

Printed in Great Britain

The best of Jackie
ANNUAL

Contents

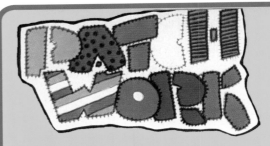

TV AND POP

Readers' True Experiences

FUN

Beauty

Features

Fashion

JACKIE KNIT·A·BIT PATTERNS

QUIZZES

Cathy and Claire Specials

On-the-Spot Interviews

Hello!

If you're reading this compilation of the best of the top-selling *Jackie* Annuals, I'm guessing you were a young girl back in the 1970s. You worshipped David Cassidy, Donny Osmond and The Bay City Rollers; you saved up for weeks to buy smocks and flared trousers from Girl and C & A; you experimented with make-up and agonised over boys; and your dream job would have been as a dancer with Pan's People on *Top of the Pops*.

Throughout the 1970s, though, I had my own dream job. I was privileged enough, and lucky enough, to be able to work on the best-selling teenage magazine, *Jackie*. I started on *Jackie* in 1972 and worked on everything from the Fiction to the Cathy and Claire page, before becoming Assistant Editor and then Editor.

And all during that time, and indeed, ever since *Jackie* began, 'way back in 1964, people had been asking us, "Why don't you bring out a *Jackie* Annual?"

We felt, however, that we would only bring out an Annual if we could match the same standard and value as the weekly magazine. We wanted the *Jackie* Annual to be something special, something to look forward to, something that was fun to read but had enough information and entertainment to keep you coming back to it time after time.

When we brought out that first Annual in 1975, we weren't sure what the response would be, but when you wrote to us to tell us how much you all loved it and how much you were looking forward to the next one, we

breathed a sigh of relief and knew that first Annual had been worth waiting ten years for.

From 1975, we produced an Annual every year, and I know that you looked forward to each one. I know, too, that you kept your precious *Jackie* Annuals year after year. There they were in your bookcase, ready for you to dip into and savour any time you felt like being amused, entertained, or maybe just needed a familiar friend to visit for advice.

You meant to keep your stack of *Jackie* Annuals forever, but then Life intervened, and over the years of growing-up and moving from school to job to marriage and motherhood, those faithful companions of your teenage years, along with the Donny Osmond badges

and the Laura Ashley smocks, somehow got lost along the way.

Now, though, you can renew your acquaintance with those old friends of your teenage years with this compilation, *The Best of Jackie Annual*. It's all here – from the famous *Jackie* quizzes to the pin-ups of your favourite pop stars. There are pages of fashion (some of which wouldn't look out of place in today's magazines!), beauty hints and tips, a Jackie day out with the Bay City Rollers and features and advice galore.

So for a moment, step back in time and once again become that young girl who would have walked miles for a smile from David Cassidy, who loved her platform shoes and her midi dresses, who worried about boys and that long-awaited, but scary, first kiss and who, on Christmas morning, hoped that the parcel from Auntie Joan, wrapped in the familiar green paper with the holly pattern, wasn't a box of hankies, but a long-awaited, much sought-after, *Jackie* Annual.

I hope reading this *Best of Jackie Annual* is like renewing an old friendship, and I hope you get as much joy and pleasure out of reading this compilation as you did from reading your Annuals in the 70s. I feel that you will, because, to borrow some phrases from my Ed's Letters in the *Jackie* Annuals I produced – these pages are crammed full of your favourites. There's loads to read, loads to look at, and it's packed with loads of goodies from cover to cover!

So enjoy this nostalgic look back to what was perhaps a gentler, more innocent age, when The Osmonds reigned supreme, when tank tops and hot pants were the fashion of choice and when Jackie magazine was around every week to advise and entertain and help you have fun.

Best Wishes,
Sandy Monks

A JACKIE GUIDE TO MAKING MONEY

(and we don't mean printing the stuff!)

ARE you, like the rest of us, feeling hard up? Well, there are lots of ways to earn extra money in your spare time and at weekends. So why not start making your first million now — and have some fun into the bargain!

GARDENING — This is a great job for warm summer evenings and weekends. You don't have to be a Percy Thrower, anybody can follow a lawnmower, but it does help if you can recognise the prize lupins from the weeds!

STABLES AND KENNELS — If you love animals and the outdoor life why not see if your local stables or kennels need evening or Saturday help? For anybody who eventually wants a career in animal care, this is marvellous practical experience. And you never know — you might discover you can't stand the beasts after all!

SHOP ASSISTANT — Lots of shops take on Saturday staff so you shouldn't have any trouble getting a job if you're thirteen and over. But you must get a working permit from your local education authority first. Choose the type of shop you'd like to work in if you can. You might be happier in the local corner shop than in a big department store or perhaps you'd prefer a trendy boutique. Whichever comes your way, you can have a lot of fun and learn a lot about human nature!

CAR WASHING — Hard work, but it's quite rewarding to find that a rusty old heap is actually a hot-rod Maserati once you've removed the layers of dirt! Put up an ad on your local notice board and you're ready to go. All you need is a bucket, some soapy water and a good selection of clean cloths — to look the real professional. 50p is a reasonable charge. You get extra if you polish the car as well. So get at that chrome!

BABYSITTING — It's the first job most people think of, and for a very good reason. How else can you earn £1 an evening for just sitting watching the telly and nonchalantly nibbling a few goodies while a baby sleeps soundly upstairs? Of course they do sometimes wake up — and it's as well to know how to change a nappy and bring up wind! (Luverly.)Always make sure you have a phone number where you can contact the parents in case of emergency too. Then you can 'sit' back with an easy mind!

WAITRESS — If you're sixteen or over then you can try this old stand-by (work permit required). Waitressing can be fun and is good for tips, but be warned, it is physically exhausting and not for those of a nervous disposition — you have to keep your cool when everybody starts shouting at once! Try central local cafes and Wimpy bars — they might well need help for busy Saturday morning coffees, lunches and tea-times. How much they pay varies, but you can normally make a few pounds in an afternoon.

DRESSMAKING AND KNITTING — For the nimble fingered, a golden opportunity to make your hobby pay. With the price of clothes these days, plenty of your friends will be keen to have really well-made clothes and hand knitted sweaters. Let them choose their own patterns, or design your own, make them up and you're in business. Well, that's how all the best dress designers started, you know!

DOG WALKING — This has always been a popular way of making money in the States and is catching on here too now as people get lazier! Offer to take your neighbourhood dogs for a walk (one at a time!) for 25p. an hour. That should mean you and the dog'll get lots of exercise!

SINGING — Don't laugh. If you're a good singer, why not let local groups know about it? They might be keen to take on a girl singer. Or how about forming your own group with friends to play at local youth clubs/old peoples' homes? (Why should they suffer? – The Ed.) You might not make much money but so what, you should have a lot of fun!

TOYMAKING — Boutiques and craft shops might buy stuffed toys made from scraps of material or felt, which are fun to make if you're good with your hands. Take a couple of samples round first and see if they're interested.

USHERETTE — Cinemas often need help on their matinee shifts. Great for film fans — you get paid for watching movies! If you like the idea, go and have a word with the manager of your local cinema.

HAIRDRESSER'S ASSISTANT — A good job for those of sixteen and over who fancy hairdressing as a career. You won't do much more than sweep the floor, wash brushes and towels and do the odd shampoo, but it's great experience and a clever way to get in with a good salon, too!

NEWSPAPER ROUND — All the best millionaires started this way! If you're thirteen or over, go along to your local newsagent and see if he has any vacancies for paper girls. You'll only be allowed to work an hour per day but most places pay at least 50p. The advantages are that as it's early morning work it doesn't interfere with school or social life. But it's not a job for those who don't feel human till eleven o'clock in the morning!

Remember, though, you need a work permit for certain jobs. Also age limits vary from area to area, so, before embarking on any part-time job, consult your local education authority.

The Sound Of Soul

ONE of the most exciting things to happen on the pop scene in 1975 was the new popularity of soul music. Suddenly, everyone seemed to be listening to the likes of Barry White, Stevie Wonder and The Three Degrees.

And it's easy to see why. Soul music is great to dance to, to sing along with, or just to sit and listen to, if that's how you feel. In fact, no matter what your mood is, the soul sound fits it perfectly!

Soul isn't a new kind of music — it's been around for years now. As far back as the early 1960's, everybody was raving about groups like the Four Tops, The Temptations and the Supremes. They were all part of the Tamla Motown sound, which originated from the city of Detroit, in Michigan.

And most of these people are still around today. Diana Ross, for instance, who in those days was a member of the Supremes, an all girl group, is of course a big solo star nowadays, and it was Diana who first discovered one of Tamla's newest star groups — the Jackson Five!

Back in the 60's, Tamla had another upcoming star — a very talented singer and songwriter called Little Stevie Wonder. The "Little" in his name was because at that time, Stevie was barely into his teens!

Nowadays, Stevie's become one of the world's best known and most brilliant soul artistes. He's no longer little — in fact, he's well over six feet tall! And over the years, his musical ability has grown and developed with him!

But although Tamla still has lots of big stars, it's no longer the only label around that's got soul. Recently, it seems that new soul groups have been appearing from all directions!

From America have come a whole host of names like The Tymes, The Stylistics, George McCrae, Al Green, and amongst the ladies, Gloria Gaynor, Betty Wright and that stunning group Labelle. But maybe the most popular of all are Barry White and The Three Degrees.

Barry, of course, is that very large (21 stone!) guy from Texas who makes really smooth, smoochy records — like his LP's, "Can't Get Enough" and "Just Another Way To Say I Love You." Definitely the kind of records to listen to when you're having a quiet, romantic evening by the fireside with someone you'd like to get to know better!

The Three Degrees on the other hand, are a group of ladies whose music is best for dancing to! Fayette Pinkney, Sheila Ferguson and Valerie Holiday, the three girls who make up the group, have had a string of hits in the last year. And not only do they sound great — they also look fantastic!

But America doesn't have the monopoly in soul music. Britain's been doing its bit too, turning out soul groups like Sweet Sensation and the Average White Band.

Sweet Sensation are an eight-piece Manchester group who got their first break when they appeared on the TV show "New Faces." Shortly after, they released their first single "Sad, Sweet Dreamer," and since then, they've just never looked back!

One of the things that gives Sweet Sensation their distinctive sound is the fact that they have four lead singers- one of whom, 17-year-old Marcel King, is quite a star in his own right!

Since they first made it, the group have toured all over Britain, and they've become a very popular live act.

The Average White Band are also a popular live group, both here and over in America, where they're very successful indeed. But the thing that makes this group unique is not so much their music — it's more that they're the only Scottish soul group in the world!

But listening to the authentic "black" sound that the boys achieve, you'd never guess that they come from Dundee and Perth instead of Detroit and Philadelphia!

So you see, soul really isn't one kind of music at all. Under the general title of soul, there are lots of different groups, all with their own individual sounds.

But whether you like going down to the local discotheque and dancing to the music of the Average White Band, or whether you prefer dreaming the night away with Barry White, the important thing is just to enjoy yourself, in your own way! ∎

Three Degrees

Average White Band

Barry White with his backing group, Love Unlimited

MY THREE THRILLING DAYS WITH DAVID

AND IT WAS WORTH EVERY BLISTER!

HOW would you like to meet David Cassidy? (Need we ask!)

For most of us, meeting David is just something to think about when we're alone with our dreams. But, for one "Jackie" reader, 1974 was the year her dream came true!

Sixteen-year-old Nicole Mutch was one of three lucky girls who won a trip to Los Angeles to meet David as first prize in a competition which involved doing a 12-mile sponsored walk around London.

Nicole says she was so determined to win that competition that she spent days going round from door to door in her home town of Ruislip in Middlesex, trying to persuade people to sponsor her on her walk.

And her tactics worked—because, altogether, she managed to get 1000 sponsors, which meant that not only did she win her prize, but she also earned £221 to aid people suffering from muscular dystrophy.

"I was absolutely thrilled when I heard I'd won," Nicole told me. "I've been a fan of David's for over three and a half years, and I have all his records. My bedroom's completely covered with pictures of him—at the last count I had 5640 different photos of him!

"I was keen to meet him because I wanted to find out what he's really like. He's always made out to be so perfect, such a goody-goody—and I wanted to find out if that was true or not. Now I know he isn't like that at all!"

Along with the two other prize-winners—Paula Howe, who comes from Barry in Glamorgan, and Nicky Price from Iver Heath in Buckinghamshire—Nicole was flown out to Hollywood, where the girls stayed in a hotel called the Chancellor, on Wiltshire Boulevard in Los Angeles.

The day after they arrived, the girls spent the morning being interviewed for the local radio station, and then, in the afternoon, they were taken on to the set of "The Partridge Family" where David was busy rehearsing for his last series with the show.

"When we got there, he was busily learning his lines for the next scene, so we waited till he was finished, and he came over to see us.

"At first, he seemed even more nervous than we were! He said, 'Hi,' and then paused, as though he didn't know quite what to expect—but after a few moments he was chatting to us as though we'd known him for years.

"At that time, I wasn't sure if I'd have the chance to see him again, so I gave him a toy dog I'd brought over from England as a present for him. He seemed pleased with it!"

Next morning, Nicole went to Disneyland for the day.

"It was fantastic! There's a place called 'The Haunted House' which is like a really scary ghost train. At one stage a ghost gets into the car with you and you can feel its clammy hand touching yours!"

Then it was back to their hotel for dinner, before going to bed and lying awake, looking forward to the next day!

"Next morning, we went to the head offices of David's record company, and met everyone there," said Nicole. "And in the afternoon, we were allowed to watch David at work in the recording studio!

"He took time off to show us all round the studio himself, and he explained how he records songs, how the different instruments are recorded on separate tracks, and how the final masters are produced."

But the three girls unanimously agreed that the next day—the last of their trip—was the best one of all!

"His record company laid on a chauffeur-driven Cadillac for us," Nicole told me. "We were taken on a guided tour of all the film stars' homes in the Hollywood hills, and we visited David's manager, Ruth Aarons, at her home—and, best of all, we went to David's house, where he showed us round!

"When we first went up to the house, we had to ask for him by name before the electronic gates would open. Because of the number of people who try the gates, he has special code names which he changes every week. When we went, we had to ask for William A. Bong! (Billa-bong, get it?)

"The house has about eleven rooms, and is E-shaped with a guest house at the back, where his mother sometimes stays. In the lounge there was a Union Jack painted on one wall, and I asked him why —and David said it had been there when he moved in so he had left it there.

"His bedroom is huge, and he also uses it as a studio—as well as his bed he has a large grand piano in there, four guitars, and a set of drums. It has built-in cupboards, mustard carpets and white curtains.

"His lounge is furnished very plainly with a striped suite, and a white-painted dining-room table and black chairs, with fluorescent lights, and all his gold discs, twelve of them, were framed and hanging in the hall.

"He had two bathrooms, both done out in blue and I had the impression that he seems to like cleanliness, but he's not too tidy! There are shoes and T-shirts lying around everywhere.

"He showed me what he calls his 'shirt collection'—over 400 different T-shirts, stacked away in cupboards in a separate room—and he introduced me to his dogs, Bullseye, an English setter; Sam, who's a hairy mongrel, and his cat, poor little Boots, who was sitting on a cushion with a paw bandaged, looking very sorry for himself.

"David told us he'd wrenched a claw away from his foot while climbing a tree that morning, and that he'd had to take him to the vet to have his foot bandaged.

"Then we sat in the lounge for a while, and he told us about the house he wanted to build in Hawaii. He said he really wanted to live there, because it was the one place where he could get away from everything. He said he liked the people of Hawaii very much, because they always left him alone.

"And when he noticed I had on platform boots, he laughed and said he didn't know how I could wear them, because he always fell over when he wore them!

"That's one of the nicest things about him—he's a natural joker. When I first met him I said, 'How's your dog?' and he put out his hand at about waist height and said, 'About that high!'"

All too soon, it was time for the girls to go—but not before Nicole got David to autograph two LPs she'd been given by his record company.

So, what did she think of him?

"He's lovely," she said. "He was very kind to us. He struck me as a very honest person, and he's very good-looking—but he likes to think of himself as just an ordinary guy.

"In fact, he was just as nice as I'd expected!"

That's me. Can you tell I'm shaking?

David

Slade laugh over some
incidents which weren't so
funny at the time . . .

No, dear, that's NOT part of the act!

WHEN you have a group made up of four crazy lads like Noddy Holder, Dave Hill, Jim Lea and Don Powell, you might expect that anything could happen—and it does!

During the years they've been together, Slade say they've had lots of hair-raising experiences—the sort of thing that is very frightening at the time, but can be quite funny when you look back on it.

"Some of our worst moments, as you might expect, have been on planes," Don told me. "None of us are actually scared of flying itself—but some of the planes we've travelled in would scare anyone!

"I remember once we had a really scary flight during a Scandinavian tour. We were flying from Copenhagen to Aahus, and the flight was delayed by snow.

"Then when it finally arrived we discovered the plane was very old—with an ancient propeller!"

The boys were a bit doubtful about the safety of the plane, but since it was the only transport available, they decided they'd just have to risk it.

"It was all right until it came to taking off," Don said. "Every time it tried to leave the runway, it hit the ground again! It did it four times—and each time there was a terrible bump.

"Eventually it did take off—and somehow, we got safely to our destination."

As far as the individual members of the group are concerned, Noddy says Don is the one who gets into trouble most often.

"I wouldn't say Don's accident-prone," he said, "but whenever he touches something, it breaks!

"For instance, I remember when we were in Holland, Don went round to Dave's room.

"He knocked on the door and Dave shouted 'Wait a minute.' So Don knocked again—and the door fell off its hinges!"

Dave says he's terrified of heights—and this led to one of his most frightening experiences.

"We were making a special film for 'Top Of The Pops' at a power station. I was wearing a silver suit, so they decided to film me walking along an overhead ledge, as though I was a spaceman who'd just landed.

"It was very high up, and I suddenly looked down at the ground. That was a mistake, because I just froze.

"I had this terror of falling and I just froze completely, like a cat does when it gets stuck up a tree.

"You know, you watch that cat and you know it could get down the same way it came up—but the cat's too frightened, and it just sits there till somebody rescues it.

"Well, that was exactly what happened to me. I've never been so scared in all my life!"

Another frightening moment for Dave came when the group were in the Bahamas a few years ago.

"There was a girl I really liked," said Dave. "I'd been trying to make a date with her for ages, and when she finally invited me to go snorkelling with her, I was really pleased.

"I didn't know what snorkelling was, but I was quite pleased to have a go, as long as I was with her. But I got a shock when I met her on the beach and she gave me all the gear she'd borrowed for me. You see, I can't swim!

"But I didn't have the courage to tell her that. I figured I'd be okay if I walked along the sea-bed, pretending to swim—and that did work, for a bit. But unfortunately, the sea-bed suddenly shelved away while I was going along, and I went down with it!

"Luckily the girl noticed I was in trouble and helped rescue me—but that was the end of my attempt at impressing her!"

Although all the boys love seeing their fans reacting enthusiastically at their concerts, they admit it can be frightening if this gets out of hand.

"We're always afraid someone will get hurt in a situation like that," said Jim. "It can be really frightening if you're going through a big crowd in a car, and they're all mobbing around you.

"When we played the Apollo Theatre in Glasgow in the spring, there were so many fans outside, we had to escape in a police Land-rover.

"That was scary enough, but the person who really came off worst was Swinn, our roadie. He had the job of acting as decoy in the Rolls Royce we usually travel about in.

"It took him ages to make his way through the crowd, and he told us afterwards he'd been petrified!"

Slade spent the early part of this summer in America and it was while they were playing in New York that Noddy had a rather nasty experience.

"While we were onstage, someone threw a firework on stage," he told me. "It landed right at my feet, and for a moment I just stood there in horror, wondering what it was going to do!

"It turned out to be a smoke-bomb, which of course brought us to a halt right in mid-act! There we were standing among great clouds of smoke. We couldn't see the audience, and they couldn't see us!

"When the smoke finally cleared, we noticed nobody in the audience seemed to be very upset by what had happened.

"But afterwards we found out why —they thought it was all part of the act!"

Do you remember your first kiss?

Moira Garland, Middleton, Leeds.
My first boyfriend took me to the fair for a special treat one night. We went on the ghost train and suddenly, in the dark, he kissed me — it was the first time he'd dared! I nearly screamed, because I wasn't sure if it was part of the horror show or not!

Marsha Dun, Liverpool.
We were walking hand in hand along the sandy beach, the water lapping gently over our bare feet, when David turned to me, kissed me passionately, and said, "I'm gonna make you a star!"
Then I woke up!

Tanya Saunders, Brighton, Sussex.
I'm afraid it was a great anti-climax! We were coming home from a lovely party, it was a beautiful starry night, the moon was full — and when he kissed me all I could think was, "Oh, is this what it's all about?" Now I come to think about it, though, everything else was perfect — he obviously wasn't!

Mick Robertson.
It was when I must have been about ten or eleven. I was cycling home from school with my little girlfriend. We stopped and I just kissed her. It was so nice I just kissed her and kissed her and kissed her.
Unfortunately, some friends of mine had been standing behind the trees — they told me that they'd counted up to 175!
In those days I believed in quantity. Now I've grown up I appreciate quality . . .

Sandra Pearson, Birmingham.
My first kiss was from a boy called — would you believe — Ivor Fowler! He was tall and skinny and he wore big, thick glasses. I didn't fancy him at all. In fact, I thought he was hideous. The worst thing was, after that first kiss, he followed me around for weeks.

Mary Butler, Stirling.
I think I'd rather forget it. I felt really chuffed when the boy next door kissed me on the way to school, but then my brother told me he'd only done it for a bet!

Geraldine Clarke, Exmouth, Devon.
My first real kiss was just like in the movies. There we were in a grotty old street under an even grottier old lamppost, then suddenly, at that first kiss, I saw stars and went all weak at the knees. That grotty old street suddenly seemed beautiful. It was unforgettable!

Alison Ross, Plymouth.
My first kiss wasn't really very romantic. I was at a party with six boys and only four girls . . . the boys decided we should play postman's knock, but I was terrified as I'd never been kissed before. I soon got the hang of it after the first one though!

Sheila Knox, Glasgow.
Last year, I had an enormous crush on this boy who'd bright red hair, glasses and loads of freckles. All my friends thought he was horrible, but I thought he was wonderful. He took me home from the school dance and kissed me outside my front gate. After that, I went right off him!

Martine Howard (Guys and Dolls).
I had my first kiss when I was 11 — it was horrible! His name was Dave and I was absolutely petrified. I thought he was going to eat me!

Sarah Roe, Chichester.
I went to this party, and about half way through, all the lights went out, and I got my first kiss. The only thing is, I don't know who gave it to me!

Rob Davis (Mud).
It was when I was 13. I had no idea at all what I was meant to do — so I stood there with my eyes shut and let her do the rest!

Dave Hill (Slade).
It wasn't bad. I was 9 at the time and on holiday in Rhyl in North Wales. I met this girl there who was also on holiday — she had lovely long blonde hair.
It was only a typical kid's kiss, but at the time I thought it was pretty hot stuff!

Moira McGrath, Glasgow.
First kisses are meant to stay with you forever, but I really can't remember mine, or even who it was. It was either the boy who lived near me at home, or the one in my Maths class at school. I went out with them both at once and can't remember which one kissed me first!

Alan Gardner, Grimsby, Lancs.
It was really romantic, actually. I was walking home with this girl, when it began to rain. It was a real downpour — thunder, lightning and everything. She was a bit scared, so I thought I'd be all protective and put my arms round her. She was soaking wet and her hair was all straggly but I thought she looked lovely — so I kissed her!

Andrea Maxwell, Newcastle-upon-Tyne.
My first boyfriend was dead nervous about asking me out, even though it was obvious he wanted to. So, eventually he managed to work up the courage. When I agreed, he yelled, grabbed me and kissed me! Then he went really scarlet, which made me feel even better.

Rosy Hanlin, Stockton-on-Tees, Cleveland.
Oh, yes! I remember it well! My first boyfriend tried to kiss me goodnight romantically at my door. The trouble was, he was about four inches shorter than me, so he couldn't reach! We soon solved that problem though — he stood up on the doorstep!

2

David Cassidy's idea of Paradise is Hawaii, where he owns a plot of land on which he's building a house.

"I'm building it myself, with the help of two friends who know a bit about building," he said. "I'm really looking forward to getting it finished, so I can spend as much time there as I like.

"I love Hawaii. When I'm there, I feel as though I'm in a world of my own, away from the music business and all that.

"That's why Hawaii's so important to me — when I'm there I can forget everything else."

MICK'S STAR

(Where you might just find you

3

Mick Robertson, as you know, writes a fortnightly column for 'Jackie' telling us about some of the exciting places he's travelled to during the time he's worked for Thames TV's "MAGPIE".

And his column is so popular we thought it would be nice if he, and some other stars, could tell us which are their favourite places.

Here's Mick to tell you more about it.

1

"In the time I've been with Magpie, I've been lucky enough to travel all over the world and see some places I thought I'd only ever be able to read about.

"Every country has its own special memories for me — but, at the moment anyway, my favourite place of all is New Orleans.

"The atmosphere there is incredible. New Orleans is the home of blues music, and the city is full of it — you can hear it coming from every café and bar you pass.

"The city is also beautiful to look at — the houses are all very ornate, and everywhere you go you find lovely flowers, thriving in the hot, humid climate.

"I think it's a very romantic city.

"Well, that's my choice of favourite place — but everyone has their own ideas on the subject, as you'll find out if you read on!"

4

The Bay City Rollers, who usually go on holiday together, spent a few weeks in Tunisia last year — and they loved it!

The highlight of the holiday, according to guitarist Eric Faulkner, came when the boys decided to sample the local night-life.

"We went to a big night club, where the cabaret was a company of belly-dancers," said Eric. "I don't know why they picked on us, but they came down into the audience and dragged us up on stage — and made us join in the belly-dancing!

"We must have looked a real sight, but it was fun, all the same!"

Bryan Ferry decided to get right away from it all this year — so he flew off for two weeks on the remote West Indian island of Mustique.

Mustique isn't a very big island — in fact, according to Bryan, it consists of one hotel, a few houses and seven sandy beaches!

"As you can imagine, I spent most of my time on one or other of the beaches!" said Bryan. "I also did a lot of swimming, and I played tennis — in fact it was quite an active holiday!

"The only trouble was, I really got used to the lazy pace that everyone lived at out there. I found it difficult to adjust to life in London when I came back again!"

5

Mott the Hoople spent the early part of this summer doing an extensive American tour. And when they finished it at the beginning of June, lead singer Ian Hunter and guitarist Aerial Bender decided that what they needed after all that work was a holiday in the sunshine.

"We were nice and near the West Indies," said Ian, "so we decided to fly down to Barbados for a few weeks, and have a proper rest.

"We had a super time, lazing about on the beach — it was just what we needed after a strenuous tour."

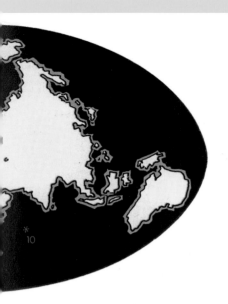

TREK

favourite pop star next summer.)

6

Ron and Russell Mael, that incredible pair who lead Sparks, say their favourite holiday place is Paris.

"We love the whole of France," Russell told me, "but Paris is, of course, the centre of it all.

"Everything about Paris is nice — it's a beautiful city, and the atmosphere is incredible."

Another thing the brothers love about Paris is the fashion scene there. They both love French clothes, and whenever they're in Paris, they like to have a look around the city's boutiques and clothes shops.

And there's one other thing Ron and Russell love about France — the food!

"We're both crazy about French food," explained Russell. "We could live off French bread and the gorgeous cheeses you get over there!"

7

Elton John likes to go to Los Angeles every July for his four weeks' annual holiday.

"I love going down to Malibu Beach," said Elton, "half an hour's drive down the coast from Hollywood. It's really nice there.

"It's very hot though, I'll tell you that! Step on the sand and you've got instant fried feet!

"One year I rented a house there which used to belong to Cole Porter. It was beautiful — you stepped out literally from the kitchen onto the beach and you could watch the sunset and people riding horses along the sands.

"I don't really like swimming in the sea very much, because I'm afraid of getting bitten by things like Piranha fish! But I did a bit of surfing while I was there, and that was nice."

8

During the 1960's, Alvin Stardust "dropped out" and spent a couple of years just wandering around Europe. And out of the whole of the Continent, he says his favourite city was Amsterdam.

"Amsterdam's a great place for young people," said Alvin. "The nicest thing about it is that you have the freedom to live just the way you want.

"If you want to rave it up, you can — but you can live quietly too. I used to love walking along the banks of the canals at night, where it was peaceful and quiet — but there were some great clubs and discos too!"

9

David Essex's favourite holiday area is the South of France.

"Apart from Britain, of course, my favourite place is the area around the Mediterranean," he says. "The South of France is particularly nice, because of the cool breeze called the Mistral which always blows through there.

"That means that, although it's beautifully warm and sunny, it never gets too hot. In fact, it's just right!"

10

Noel Edmonds and his lovely wife Gill spent their summer holidays in the Seychelles this year, and Noel liked it so much he got quite carried away just telling me about it!

"It was a real tropical paradise," he said. "The trouble with most of these places is that they're either very primitive, or, like Jamaica, they're totally commercialised.

"In Jamaica, you can go to a beach and there's likely to be a concrete factory just around the corner — but the Seychelles weren't like that at all.

"They were perfect — we could go and have a whole beach to ourselves during the day, but still come back to an air-conditioned hotel at night, where everyone was very friendly and only too eager to help us.

"The only thing lacking in fact, was any night-life — but we didn't mind that. We get enough of that in London."

11

David Bowie was very impressed with Moscow when he passed through it last year on his way back from Japan on the Trans-Siberian Railway.

"When I was there, the May Day celebrations were going on," he said, "and I was lucky enough to see the big parade, which is the highpoint of the celebrations. It's an incredible sight."

But according to a friend of David's, none of the Russians were watching the May Day Parade on that day — because they were all too busy gazing at David himself!

I can believe that!

David with his wife Angie just before he set off for Moscow.

THERE'S a new theory about choosing your ideal mate which has absolutely nothing to do with computers, signs of the zodiac or Chinese horoscopes. It's based on your age-position in your family.

Recent investigations show that most happy, secure marriages involve couples who are "complementary." The idea is that having older brothers, younger sisters or whatever influences your character, and likewise, your prospective boyfriend is affected by his place in the family.

We've simplified the theory and come up with this analysis.

N.B. We can tell you which category you fit into, give you a character analysis, tell you what your boyfriend should be. Afraid we can't find him for you, though. That's NOT part of the service!

SO—

If you are:

AN ONLY CHILD

Only children have absolutely no-one with whom to compete for their parents' attention. They're more used to adult company and can also be left a lot on their own.

You're likely to be shy and sensitive, yet self–sufficient. Chances are you're extravagant, generous and altruistic. You tend to lack drive, though.

You're constantly seeking attention, and you'll find it in a boy who has a natural inclination to spoil girls and shower them with gifts and affections.

Your worst fault, however, is that when you have a row with your boyfriend (as you're bound to do, occasionally, being rather self-centred) you tend to rush off in tears rather than have a fair quarrel. Most boys will find this infuriating.

So your ideal boyfriend is:

BROTHER WITH YOUNGER SISTERS

He's definitely the one for you. Having younger sisters of his own, he's something of an expert on handling rather spoilt females!

He'll give you the pampering and constant reassurance you need to be happy, whilst still remaining sensible and fair in his judgments.

He's not a loner, and will enjoy company of both sexes, but he's not only "one of the boys" — he'll be just as happy to spend a cosy evening with you, watching TV or having a chat.

His main fault is that he's not very

ambitious, but we'd say he was a reliable, steady, super boyfriend to have!

If you are:

DAUGHTER WITH YOUNGER SIBLINGS (THAT'S BROTHERS OR SISTERS!)

You're a friendly, but very responsible person, with a very practical streak. It seems to be your natural role in life to settle quarrels and calm other people's hot tempers!

You're good at making decisions and don't often change your mind, but this can become an obsession to the extent that you can become unreasonable over trivialities.

If you have more younger brothers than sisters, you'll tend to be calmer than someone with more sisters than brothers. Girls with younger sisters can be a little too dominant, if they don't get their own way, and have a tendency to sulk at the unfairness of life!

You need someone you can boss about a bit! Could be he's a couple of years younger than you, in maturity at any rate, but you'll soon straighten that out! So your ideal boyfriend is:

AN ONLY SON

Although he often demands more attention than is strictly necessary, and can be infuriatingly selfish at times, he's the one for you.

Being used to looking after younger children, you can dominate him when necessary, and soothe him when he's feeling low.

It's essential that he has someone to rely on, someone concerned about him whom he can turn to. You'll have to use all your patience with him occasionally!

On the brighter side, though, he'll bring out your maternal instinct and provide a suitable balance for your temperament.

He has a lot of affection and generosity to spare, and you'll probably find him so lovable you'll forget all about his faults — till the next time!

If you are:

DAUGHTER WITH OLDER BROTHERS

You're definitely a female female! You like to feel protected by a boy, and tend to go along with his opinion, even if you know at heart you disagree. This is probably a throwback from the days when you were teased by your elder brother(s) to the extent that you went along with their opinions rather than risk more teasing.

You're not over-ambitious, and may well decide to give up your career, if you get married, for a state of housewifely bliss.

The only thing you have to watch out for is that you treat your boyfriends like boyfriends, not as substitutes for your big brother.

You could become dominated by your boyfriends, if you let them, but as you don't really mind this, you should get on really well with your ideal boy, who is:

SON WITH OLDER SISTERS

He's your ideal male! He's a perfectionist, and can be a bit domineering at times, but he'll always try to see your point of view in an argument and will stick up for you if he thinks you're right.

As your "opposite number," so to speak, he understands what it's like to have elder siblings of the opposite sex, and has come through many of the same problems as you.

You'll find he's someone it's very easy to fall for — he's such a genuinely nice person. However, he has a tendency to be forgetful and unreliable, so don't expect him to turn up on time for a date!

If you are:

DAUGHTER WITH OLDER SISTERS

You're enthusiastic, adventurous and have a definite character of your own. This means you're very attractive to males and probably have lots of boyfriends but for one reason or another you never manage to keep them.

Either you begin to feel tied down and move on to pastures new, or the boy gets bored with your moodiness and lack of responsibility.

You tend to get wildly enthusiastic about things at first but can never be bothered to finish them — and unfortunately, this applies to boyfriends too! The idea of a new boyfriend appeals to you, but possibly because you're used to all these sisters, you tend to shy away from any deep relationships with the opposite sex.

You need someone with a remarkable degree of understanding to calm you down

fit in?

a bit! That's why the person most suited to you is:

SON WITH OLDER BROTHERS

Again, this is the case of someone with elder siblings of the same sex knowing how you feel.

He's imaginative and thoughtful, with a rare degree of understanding, which is great, as he'll need it all with you!

Having older brothers, it's unavoidable that he'll enjoy the company of male friends, but that only means he's doubly interested in you when it comes to romance — so make sure you always look your beautiful best for him!

If anything, he tends to be a bit over-romantic with his girlfriends, but we don't think that's a reason for complaining!

You'll be able to give vent to all your crazy ideas here without him taking you too seriously — he knows how fickle you are! He, too, likes freedom and independence, so you should make a super couple!

If you are:
DAUGHTER WITH OLDER BROTHER(S) AND SISTER(S)

Phew! What a mouthful! But despite the long-winded title, you have the distinction of being the most settled and happiest person of the whole bunch!

Being brought up with elder siblings of both sexes, you'll have had the advantage of a well-balanced childhood emotionally.

Although you probably argued with your brothers and sisters as a child, this actually served as a good basis for later life, when you're more interested in boys than toys!

Used to being with people of both sexes, you don't suffer from the inhibitions of shy people, or the selfishness of extroverts.

You tend to be rather middle-of-the-road in your opinions — but don't dare let anyone call you dull, as you're far from being that! You're the sort of girl the rest of us would like to be — happy-go-lucky, yet stable.

Although you would be suited to any of the boys previously mentioned, your ideal boyfriend is probably the one nearest to you in family placing, i.e:

SON WITH OLDER BROTHER(S) AND SISTER(S)

Like you, he has elder siblings of both sexes to contend with, so he is exactly on your wavelength as concerns family relationships.

Much of his character rating, of course, is just the same as yours with the same basic qualities of stability and fairness.

He's come from a well-adjusted family, too, so both of you are really ideally suited (do we hear wedding bells?).

Anyway, with two people as well suited as yourselves, you've no excuse for *not* being the perfect couple!

OUTRODUCTION (as opposed to Intro)

Of course, there are exceptions to every rule and you may find your ideal boy in entirely the wrong age-position. And there's also a four-letter word we haven't mentioned so far, which is rather important — love!

But it's really uncanny how one's character can unfold to fit into the categories once the family gets older and more settled — so bear our twosomes in mind next time you're stuck for something to say to that gorgeous guy sitting next to you on the bus. "Em, excuse me, I was just wondering — do you happen to be the middle sibling of three brothers?"

It's certainly a startling opening for a fascinating conversation.

Happy hunting!

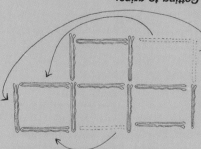

The Most Beautiful Man In The World...

... what would he look like?

That's what we were discussing the other day in the Jackie office. And though we all had our own ideas (!), we finally managed to agree on one man.

First of all, we decided he'd have hair just like RUSSELL MAEL, the lead singer of Sparks —his curly dark hair looks stylish, but still lovely and natural.

When it came to eyes, everybody wanted different people, so we gave the tea lady the casting vote, and she decided on DAVID ESSEX. And we had to agree—David has beautiful clear blue eyes that positively sparkle when he smiles!

Noses were a bit more difficult—I mean, there's not much you can say about noses, is there?! But everyone agreed that DAVID BOWIE'S is a very fine specimen!

The most beautiful man in the world, everyone decided, would have a mouth that was both friendly AND sexy. Like DAVID CASSIDY'S in fact— lovely!

Last, but not least, his chin would have to be just right— and we all agreed that one of the nicest chins around belongs to DONNY OSMOND.

So there's our choice for the most beautiful man in the world —he sounds gorgeous, doesn't he?

Well, with the help of some miracle-workers in our art department, we've made up a photo of him, and if you turn to page 93, you'll see what he looks like!

page 93

SECRETS OF

ALTHOUGH the Jackie office is a very happy place, we have been known to have little disagreements from time to time! But when it comes to our favourite T V show we are in total harmony. Our vote just has to go to "Top Of The Pops". The Top Thirty rave-up has been happily bouncing along since David Bowie was in short trousers and Gary had never heard of glitter. But the amazing thing is that it's still as fresh as a mountain stream. (This is beginning to sound like a cigarette advert!)

We thought you might like to know what goes on behind the scenes at "Top Of The Pops" so Pete donned his Sherlock Holmes hat and yellow woolly socks and set off to investigate . . .

I ARRIVED at the BBC T V Centre in Wood Lane, London, bright and early one Wednesday morning and soon found myself deep in conversation with Programme Director, Bruce Milliard. He told me the TOTP team had already been working on the show for 24 hours. On Tuesday mornings the new Top 50 chart gets the Hot Line treatment and Bruce knows the week's placings almost before the ink has dried on the new chart.

The next move is to decide who is going to guest on the show and a series of quick phone calls to various corners of the pop world let the lucky stars know they are wanted.

Every pop star wants to be on TOTP. It's the best possible way of getting across to millions of people and just one exciting appearance can make you a chart-topper overnight. Remember what happened with the Rubettes back at the beginning of summer?

Once the final list of names is ready, the backstage team can start to relax. Work starts again around eleven on Wednesday morning, when the stars start to arrive. Each group is given a separate rehearsal and the lighting is organised to make them look their best. As Bruce puts it "If someone has a big nose, we try not to make it too obvious. "They're very considerate people down at the T V Centre!

Everything is now ready for the dress rehearsal at five in the evening. The disc jockey is on the scene by this time and he runs through his introductions and now the show is getting very close to what you'll see on your T V screen.

THE TOP POP SHOW

Cameramen and floor managers scurry around and you have to be very careful where you step or you're likely to go flying over one of the curling black tails of cable that run in crazy patterns across the studio floor. The guys behind the cameras look very cool and professional and the only time they get a little hot under the collar is when Pan's People run through their latest sizzling dance routine!

The night I was at the studio, the rehearsal was over by six. Various stars chatted together and the scene was like an autograph hunter's dream! Then they wandered off to their dressing rooms in a long corridor running underneath the TOTP studio.

It's a long day for the stars and they pass the time by joking around in the dressing room, strolling over to the canteen for lunch and coffee (the chips are delicious!) or maybe popping into the BBC Bar for something a little stronger.

Boredom can set in during the eight hours from when they arrive to when the show is actually recorded, but as the big moment approaches a tingle of excitement touches the air and the stars suddenly come to life. Very soon they will be in front of the cameras. Like footballers before a big game, they feel the butterflies whirling and circling in their tummies.

Upstairs in the studio, it's seven o'clock and the audience are swarming through the doors. The first thing that hits them is how small the studio is. Cameras can play funny tricks. When you see the show at home you get the feeling TOTP is held in a huge discotheque but the studio is only about the size of an ordinary school gym.

The disc jockey of the week welcomes them and gives them a few friendly words of advice. The main thing is to watch out for the cameras. They whizz around like angry Daleks and it doesn't pay to get in their way. There are other hints and tips but the most important message is . . . have fun!

For half-an-hour, I joined the lucky 132 fans who had been given tickets for the show and we danced and laughed and almost forgot we were in the TOTP studios. It started to get very warm and

with the lighting dimmed, the atmosphere was great. Then, suddenly, it was seven-thirty and the show was on the road. The lights went up, the cameras started to move and the familiar theme music blared in my ears.

NOEL EDMONDS, surrounded by pretty girls and looking full of health and confidence introduced the first group and another successful show was being recorded. The programme seemed to whizz past at an amazing pace. No sooner had one group left one of the small stages spaced around the studio, than another appeared to get ready for their spot. Noel sprung around various cameras making his introductions and the dancers generally had a ball, while keeping a careful eye open for cables and runaway cameras.

The groups seemed interested in what they looked like and kept looking up at the monitor screens above them, while they sang their songs. Next time you

watch the show see if you can spot the stars gazing up at the roof. They're not admiring the ceiling, they're admiring themselves. Conceited lot!

Suddenly, before you knew it, the show was over. It had been a great experience seeing it all from the studio and you certainly get to know a few tricks of the trade when you are behind the cameras. Some of the best scenes never get on the telly.

"Gary Glitter was on the show once and we wanted him to stand on a little platform a couple of feet high," smiled Bruce. "D'you know, we had to have him lifted up there. If he'd climbed up by himself, he would have split his tight trousers!"

It's amazing what goes on . . . behind the scenes at "Top Of The Pops"!

If you want tickets for the show, you must be prepared for a long wait. It could be six months. But if you've got the patience, here's the correct address: "Top Of The Pops," B.B.C. Television Centre, Wood Lane, London W.12. Have fun!

JOIN THE MAGIC CIRCLE

ENEMIES · **WISHES** · **MONEY** · **SCHOOL/CAREER** · **TRAVEL** · **SOCIAL LIFE** · **HOME LIFE** · **LUCK** · **COMMUNICATIONS** · **FRIENDS** · **HEALTH** · **LOVE**

12 · 1 · 2 · 3 · 4 · 5 · 6 · 7 · 8 · 9 · 10 · 11

THERE are many methods of fortune-telling, from palmistry to peering into a crystal ball, but the easiest one to learn is by using playing cards.

It's easy — all you need is the basic meaning of each card and a little concentration. We'll give you one if you'll supply the other!

Cards were originally made for telling the future. It was only later they began to be used for playing the card games we know today. There are lots of different ways to read the cards. Our method is simple and needs only a little practice.

HOW TO START

Study the circle drawn here. As you see, it's divided into twelve sections, each section representing an area of your life. The card dealt on this section shows your future in that area.

First, remove the jokers and all cards under seven from the pack. Aces, of course, count high and they stay in. Shuffle the remaining 32 cards, cut three times, and deal them face up, clockwise, starting at "one o'clock" and finishing at twelve.

Unless you've a set of miniature playing-cards, it's better to draw your own magic circle on a really big piece of paper. Then, as you deal the cards, you can place them directly on your chart.

To interpret correctly, you must know the card's meaning and how this applies to the particular segment it lands in. Under "Card Meanings" you will see a list of what each card means, first in a general way, then its special meaning should it land on the particular section mentioned.

As an example, take the Jack or Knave of Diamonds which means "A stranger in uniform." If this lands on No. 3, "Travel," it looks as if you're taking a trip with hi▪

CARD MEANINGS

Court cards—Ace, King, Queen and Jack—represent PEOPLE in your life. The other cards stand for EVENTS.

General — SPADES — Special

ACE
Someone connected with music you have dreams about.

KING
Your boss or head teacher.

QUEEN
Mother or female relative.

JACK
A surprise compliment sets you thinking.

TEN
Young male acquaintance or relative.

NINE
You'll suspect a boy of deceiving you.

EIGHT
Arrangements you had been looking forward to may be changed.

SEVEN
The luckiest card in the pack!

WISHES
News of forthcoming visit has you in a tizzy.

SCHOOL CAREER
Punishment over a misdeed turns out to be less severe than you feared.

HOME LIFE
Temporary upset means more work for you.

LUCK
Stroke of good fortune for him has lucky repercussions for you.

ENEMIES
Someone you thought of as an enemy makes overtures of friendship.

LOVE
You have some heart-searching before making an important decision.

COMMUNICATIONS
A phone call brings a disappointment and a ray of hope.

***
Wherever this card falls it promises good news to come.

General—HEARTS—Special

ACE
A talented someone you have heard of but never met.

KING
Parent of older relative who has deep concern for your welfare.

QUEEN
Close friend or relative in same age group as yourself.

JACK
An admirer, though by no means a secret one!

TEN
A major change in your way of life.

NINE
Your bad patch will soon pass.

EIGHT
News of an old flame.

SEVEN
Danger from an unexpected source.

WISHES
Unexpected offer could have strong influence on your future plans.

MONEY
The outlook will soon be more hopeful.

FRIENDS
An annual event you are looking forward to could result in a long-lasting foursome.

LOVE
Information from a friend makes you view him in a kindlier light.

TRAVEL
Permanent move to another district possible.

HEALTH
Brief and minor health upset will be over shortly.

COMMUNICATIONS
Letter from a friend has interesting news of boy who may come back into your life.

ENEMIES
Unfounded rumour about you could cause a boy heartache.

General — CLUBS — Special

ACE
Attractive male who is the friend of a friend.

KING
A stranger, soon to come into your life.

QUEEN
Someone you disliked at first now proving to be a true friend.

JACK
An older boy at school or work.

TEN
Your second meeting with a boy takes place in very different circumstances from the first.

NINE
You're the subject of discussion among a group of girls.

EIGHT
You have cause to regret an impulsive action.

SEVEN
Be prepared to sacrifice a little pride to help a new venture.

COMMUNICATIONS
Phone call for you sends your hopes rising.

TRAVEL
A journey over water is indicated.

SOCIAL LIFE
Two late nights in succession for you.

LOVE
You're directly concerned in an exciting piece of gossip.

WISHES
You've longed for a second date with him and chances look bright.

SOCIAL LIFE
You'll be back in circulation and this could have surprising consequences.

LOVE
You would be wise to make the first move in patching up a quarrel.

HOME LIFE
You are given the extra freedom you wanted — and more responsibility too.

General — DIAMONDS — Special

ACE
Someone who attracts you strongly but is unattainable.

KING
Your dentist, doctor or some other person concerned with your physical health.

QUEEN
Girl friend at school or work.

JACK
A stranger in uniform.

TEN
You change your former opinion of a boy.

NINE
You regret an extravagance which proves unnecessary.

EIGHT
A disappointment is indicated.

SEVEN
As one door closes, another opens to you.

SCHOOL/CAREER
New turn of events leaves you with a difficult decision.

HEALTH
A visit to do with medical matters has a happy outcome.

ENEMIES
An unjust accusation angers and upsets you.

SOCIAL LIFE
A flirtatious offer is made to you.

FRIENDS
The group you have gone about with may soon split up.

MONEY
An emergency leaves you practically broke.

HOME LIFE
Some restriction or difficulty you hoped you'd resolved still persists.

SCHOOL/CAREER
You discover hidden talents in yourself.

Perhaps he's the bus conductor! If it lands on "Communications" that could mean a lonely soldier wants you a penpal. Or it could be that new young postman is thinking about you—the choice of interpretations is up to —

But if the Jack lands on Section 10 "Social Life" ''ll see the special reading "A flirtatious offer is made you." This is when you can start worrying if you see that French Navy are to pay your town a visit!

Are you beginning to see how it works? It's your judgment to decide what each combination means in the particular circumstances. If you become good at it, you could find yourself in demand at parties once the other girls find out about your powers!

But practise on your own for a while till you gain fluency. And remember to write down the results in your diary so you can look back a few weeks from now and see how many of your predictions came true!

WHAT DARK SECRETS WILL

YOU'LL need about half an hour to do justice to this Superquiz, so leave it for an evening when there's nothing good on telly and your tranny needs new batteries. It would also be a giggle doing it at an informal hen-party, as long as everyone is able to laugh at themselves! You never know which beastly side of your nature it might reveal to the others!

If you answer honestly, we'll provide a character reading which might surprise you, and add some hints about the career which would suit you best.

What You Have To Do

Just read the questions and jot down your answers on a piece of scrap paper. Don't write on the page — you may want to have another bash later on. We'll tell you what to do when you've finished. Remember, the more truthful you are, the more accurate will be the picture.

1. Imagine you get a book-token on your birthday. Which of these is your most likely choice?
(a) book of poetry?
(b) book on travel or adventure?
(c) book to help with study or hobby?
(d) historical romance or biography?

2. Your boyfriend is late and the rain is lashing down. Do you . . .
(b) listen to his explanation but secretly believe he was chatting up another girl?
(c) tear him off a strip, and hop on a passing bus before he can explain?
(d) forgive him on sight because you really didn't expect him to turn up anyway?
(a) wait for his explanation and if it sounds genuine, believe it?

3. You're shopping with a girlfriend and she's set her heart on a dress that doesn't suit her. Would you . . . .
(c) tell her she looks like Dracula's mother?
(d) refuse to offer an opinion?
(a) say you think another dress suits her much better?
(b) tell her you don't care for it, but she knows best what suits her?

4. Which of these would make you cry most?
(a) unkind words from your boy?
(b) peeling onions?
(c) you're given the sack or expelled from school?
(d) your beloved but elderly family pet has died in its sleep?

5. What appeals to you most about going steady?
(a) the romance and love angle?
(b) going out to interesting places?
(c) the envy in the eyes of girls still on the shelf?
(d) the feeling that someone understands you?

6. A boy takes you to a party then disappears for a few minutes. When he comes back, he has lipstick all over his face — the rat. Do you . . .
(a) say nothing but think he has very bad manners?
(b) start thinking how you'll get your own back?
(c) tease him about it?
(d) think he's only asked you for a laugh?

7. When you really dislike someone, do you . . .
(a) remain polite but keep your distance?
(b) find you can't help being rude?
(c) chat to them regardless in a friendly way?
(d) ignore them completely?

8. Friends arrange to meet you at the disco but don't turn up. Would you . . .
(a) feel awkward on your own but wait about twenty minutes?
(c) wait a few minutes then walk out in a temper?
(b) decide to enjoy yourself anyway and catch a nice boy's eye?
(d) feel too embarrassed on your own, so go outside to wait?

9. You're having a colossal row with your parents and have just threatened to leave home. What's the most likely cause?
(b) Their strictness. They won't give you enough freedom.
(c) Money. The pocket money you get, or the board you pay from what you earn.
(a) Boyfriend trouble. They don't like your latest, or think you're too serious.
(d) The state you leave your room in, or not helping enough around the house.

Right, that's all for this section, but you haven't finished yet. Score 1 for every "d" answer, 2 for "a's", 3 for "b"'s and 4 for "c"'s. OK?
If you're between 9 and 15, go on to section H.
If you're between 16 and 22, go on to section E.
If you're between 23 and 29, go on to section F.
If you're between 30 and 36, go on to section G.

SECTION E.

10. When you play Monopoly, what symbol would you choose?
(x) racing car
(w) top hat
(y) boot
(z) thimble

OUR SUPERQUIZ REVEAL?

11. The smashing new bus conductor has short-changed you by 10p. Would you . . .
(y) ask him in a jokey way if he's saving up for something special?
(x) point out the mistake immediately you notice it — with a smile?
(z) say nothing and hope it was a genuine mistake?
(w) ask in a quiet voice, just before you get off the bus, if he's made a mistake over the change?

12. At a wedding reception, you're dancing in a Paul Jones. After dancing with a big fat man, over twice your age, your next partner is much more your style and you'd like to get to know him. Chatting him up, you remark he's quite a change from the awful elephant who reduced your feet to jelly. He tells you the fat man is his dad. What do you do?
(x) say calmly, "Yes, I see it now — you both have the same marvellous smile!"
(z) pass hurriedly on to your next partner
(y) say "Well, you're lighter on my feet than your dad was!"
(w) say "Well, don't tell him what I said. I'm sure he didn't mean to tread on my toes!"

13. You ring up to answer an ad. for a job you like the sound of. Only when you put down the receiver you realise you've forgotten to ask for the address. Would you . . .
(y) ring up, pretending to be someone else?
(x) ring up and say *they* forgot to give you the address?
(w) ring up and admit you forgot to ask for the address?
(z) forget the whole thing?

14. A friend has a juicy piece of information but before she tells you, she swears you to secrecy. Do you . . .
(x) intend to keep the secret but know

you might blurt it out in a heated moment?
(y) ask her to keep it to herself as you never could keep a secret?
(w) make the promise and keep it?
(z) feel flattered that anyone should want to tell you a secret?

Finished? Right, which letter appears most among your answers? If it's W, your key letter is H; if it's X, your key letter is D; if it's Y, your key letter is K; and if it's Z, your key letter is S. Now turn to page 66 and look up your key letter to see what you can find out about yourself!

SECTION F.
15. There's an unexpected power failure one night when you're alone in the house. Then a knock comes to

the door, though you're not expecting callers. So you . . .
(w) pretend the house is empty.
(y) shout out "Go away or I'll set our vicious guard dog on you!" (you don't even have a pet goldfish.)
(z) rush to the door and hope it's a policeman with a torch.
(x) think it's probably someone collecting for charity, but light a candle and answer the door calmly.

16. Your joker of a boy friend puts his arm round you while wearing one of those hideous, hairy plastic hands with claws. When you've stopped screaming what's your likeliest reaction?
(z) tick him off, angrily.
(w) burst into tears.
(y) borrow it to frighten your mum or kid brother.
(x) laugh and forget it.

17. You've missed the last bus and in order to get home before midnight

and avoid a lot of trouble you must take one of these alternatives:
(x) take a short cut through the old haunted cemetery.
(w) ring for a mini-cab
(z) ask the police to get you home in time.
(y) thumb a lift.

18. When you come back after a week's holiday, your boy friend confesses he's been out with a girl or two. Would you . . .
(y) invent some dishy male conquests to show him you had just as good a time as he did?
(x) tell him you didn't expect him to stay at home with his knitting?
(z) smile sweetly and say you hope he had a good time but secretly hope he was bored stiff?
(w) cross-examine him on who and where and finally dissolve into tears or have a flaming row about it?

19. Money is taken from your pocket while you are having lunch at school or factory canteen. A girl you don't like very much has recently moaned about being hard up. Would you think . . .
(z) she must have taken the money and accuse her outright?
(y) she may have taken the money but you can't prove it?
(x) anyone could have taken the money and it's just as likely to be someone else?
(w) it's unimportant who took the money — it's your fault for leaving it carelessly around?

Jotted down your answers? Which letter have you written most? Ws take O as their key letter; Xs take P; Ys have M; and Zs, your letter is R. See what is said about you on page 26/27/28!

SECTION G.

20. **You and a girl-friend sneak into an X-certificate film for a giggle but get spotted by a neighbour coming out. Her parents think it's a joke, but yours throw a blue fit and ban you from seeing your friend ever again. It's unfair, but what do you do about it?**

(x) sulk and throw tantrums till the ban is lifted.
(w) argue constantly about it, trying to keep your temper and pointing out it was more your idea than hers in the first place.
(y) let the whole thing cool down before raising the subject quietly.
(z) admit you were wrong but say their reaction is stupid and refuse to give up your friend.

21. **Your girl friend is crazy about a boy she met at a party in a friend's house. He was only in town on a visit and lives 200 miles away. What do you advise?**

(w) keep in touch by letter and phone.
(x) go for a visit next weekend.
(z) forget all about him.
(y) get a job in the town where he lives.

22. **Your boy's supposed to be at evening classes and you spot him having a cosy cuppa with a girl who used to be at school with you. Would you . . .**

(z) pretend not to notice him till the last moment, then say "Oh, I'm glad I've seen you. I shan't be able to make our date tomorrow"?
(w) go up to the girl and ask what she's been doing with herself since she left school "five years ago, wasn't it" (although you know quite well it was only two)?
(y) wave to him and try not to torture yourself until you've heard his explanation?
(x) march in and "accidentally" knock a cup of coffee over the girl?

23. **An argument with your boyfriend develops into a blazing row. But after you cool off, you find out you had your facts all wrong. Later, when he calls round to see you . . .**

(w) you yell at him some more to cover your confusion and say he had no business shouting at you in the first place?
(x) you don't want to admit being in the wrong but make up the quarrel without really apologising?

(y) you make up first — admit your mistake later?
(z) you humbly admit your mistake and explain you must have got your facts mixed up?

24. **You're going to share a flat with three other girls and you agree to make a few rules everyone must stick to. Which of these rules would you put forward to make it easier for everyone to get along?**

(y) share everything, bills and chores.
(x) everyone choose a chore and stick to it.
(w) no borrowing other people's things.
(z) the one who makes the mess cleans it up.

Look over your answers. Which letter appears most? If it's W, your key letter is A; if it's X, your key letter is V; if you've more Ys than anything else, your key letter is E; and if you've two or more Zs, your key letter is T. Now look up your key letter on page 66.

SECTION H.

25. **Your boyfriend remarks how pretty a certain girl is. Do you . . .**

(x) take it as a challenge and really put yourself out to keep his interest?
(y) agree with him and say she's a bit like his sister (provided he has one)?
(z) admit she's prettier than you are?
(w) let it ruin your evening?

26. **On a long train journey, do you . . .**

(y) chat to fellow passengers if they talk to you first?
(x) get stuck into a magazine or paperback?
(w) start chatting to the person next to you?
(z) dream out of the window?

27. **You know for a fact your bloke dated another girl while you were out of town. So he's for it! How does he get the message?**

(w) face to face?
(x) by phone?
(z) via a friend?
(y) a "Dear John" letter?

28. **Imagine you have an older sister who is prettier, cleverer and more talented than you, but is nice with it. One day you overheard your mother telling a friend she wished you were more like your sister. Would your reaction be . . .**

(y) to go upstairs and tear something of your sister's into tiny shreds in an uncontrollable fit of temper?

(z) to burst into tears and tell Mum you wished you could leave home and never come back?
(x) to burst into tears, but keep it to yourself?
(w) to decide to ask your sister's help in making the best of yourself in future?

29. **If your boyfriend rings up to break a date because he has to take his mother to hospital, would you . . .**

(w) ask him to meet you when he IS free?
(y) offer to go along too for moral support?
(z) think it's an excuse & he's really meeting another girl?
(x) tell him all about the time YOU had to go to hospital?

Look over your answers for this section and see which letter appears most. W? Then your key letter is L. X? Your key letter is C. Two or more Ys means your key letter is G. If you've put down more Zs your key letter is B. Now turn to pages 26/27 to see a picture of yourself.

Elton talking colourfully.

I looked at the towel and thought "Oh no!"

AS you know, Elton John likes to look spectacular when he's on stage. And unlike a lot of pop stars, that doesn't mean he just wears outrageous clothes—for Elton also creates his own fashion in specs and hairstyles!

"Everybody wears beautiful clothes nowadays," explained Elton. "So I just take it a stage further!"

When I spoke to him, Elton's hair was looking a fairly normal fairish brown colour, except for a small green streak above his ears—but at various times during the last couple of years, he's had it about every colour of the rainbow!

"I think hair's such a boring colour normally," said Elton. "Why shouldn't it be orange or green for a change? I think hair that matches your clothes looks rather good!

"To get it done like that, they bleach it first of all, then they paint it the colour you want—they use Dulux.

"No, seriously, they do it with carpet dye or something like that. It fades out after a few weeks. I remember I once had it done in New York and they really made a mess of it.

"I decided I wanted it green, and they'd never done it before. They thought I was stark raving mad! After they'd done it, they told me not to wash my hair for three days to let all the green settle in.

"So there I was, walking round for three days with filthy hair. On the first hour of the fourth day I leapt in the shower and washed it.

"I came out of the shower and rubbed my hair dry. Then I looked at the towel—

green towel—and I looked at my hair—white hair!

"So I took it back!"

Now Elton makes sure his hair is done right by going to the same place every time.

"I always go to Smile in London," he said. "They're very good there—they know exactly what I want."

If you're looking at Elton's hair, you can't help noticing the other things that distinguish him at eye level—his specs!

"I first started wearing them when I was at school," explained Elton. "My hero at that time was Buddy Holly—and so I was thrilled to wear specs just like he did!

"Then I decided that if I was going to have to wear them, they might as well look interesting!

"My glasses are all my own creations. I think up the designs, and I get them made up for me at a place in Los Angeles called the Optic Boutique. I have about thirty pairs in all sorts of different colours, and my current favourites are a steaming hot pair that light up in the dark!",

BUT although his hair and specs are outrageous enough, what Elton really goes to town on is his clothes!

"I'm really into suits just now," he said. "Ties, jackets—the whole bit. In fact I have about six suits that I've just bought in Paris, in a place called the Box Shop.

"The jackets fitted me really well, but the trousers were a bit big, so my mum altered them to fit me.

"As far as my stage stuff goes, I get it all specially made up for me. I have several clothes designers who work for me, but a girl called Anne Meesey makes most of my clothes at the moment. She makes them all out of her own head.

"I'd rather designers did that actually, because I'm not much use. Anyway, they get more fun out of it when they can decide things for themselves!"

Every time we see Elton, he seems to be wearing something different! So, I wondered,

did he know exactly how many clothes he had?

"Actually, I've got a very good brain for things like **that**," he said. "I know what I've got.

"For instance, I have 300 shirts—but that's counting tee-shirts! I also have about fifty pairs of shoes.

"The only problem with my clothes is that I have a constant battle for space, so every few months I have a grand clean-out.

"Every time I have a clear-out, all my relatives gather—and then they all go to work wearing Lurex suits and platform shoes!"

Well, I bet it brightens up the commuters' Monday mornings!

A

IS FOR ALLIGATOR. Surprised at the description? Not as much as the people who took you for a harmless piece of floating driftwood and got the shock of their lives when they found out how you can bite. You're tough-skinned and though you don't go looking for a fight, when the occasion demands you're a match for most and don't care too much who you hurt.

Temperamentally, you'd suit a post with responsibility. You could make a capable, boss-shielding personal assistant, hold down a job in Public Relations or do well in the Police or Women's Services.

B

IS FOR BEAR. The Teddy type, rather than a fierce, snarling Grizzly. Maybe a little of Goldilocks' charm rubbed off, because boys find you attractive. You've strength in the things that matter most, without making a big thing about it, and you have a relaxed, cool, almost playful attitude which inspires confidence.

Jobs? You can adapt to many careers, but might be happiest in some branch of nursing. Other recommended jobs are in the domestic field — cook, waitress, nursery assistant.

C

IS FOR CHAMELEON. Do you sometimes feel invisible when trying to attract someone's attention? You're so good-mannered and good-natured you've got into the habit of merging into the background. But you have a brighter side under the surface and you're young enough to develop it. For starters now and then try unleashing that temper you keep under such strict control.

Career? If you're good with your hands, you'll find hairdressing or window display rewarding.

D

IS FOR DOLPHIN. You're sympathetic, intelligent and popular, although people don't always understand you. At the same time, you're a bit dreamy and idealistic, assuming people have purer motives than they actually do.

If you're keen on books, you could be an excellent librarian. You like meeting people and you'd also find job satisfaction in a bank or as a sales assistant.

E

IS FOR EAGLE. You're an unusual combination, someone with lofty principles who's a highflier in the career sense. Your main fault is being a perfectionist and trying to handle too much on your own. Popularity doesn't bother you, which is just as well. Ambition, capacity for hard work and desire for success could push you well up the Civil Service ladder, say. You'd make a respected, though, bossy, schoolteacher, but your real niche could be in an unusual job connected with long-distance travel. Air Stewardess, travel courier, Air traffic controller, perhaps?

G

IS FOR GOOSE. A highly-strung, excitable aggressive bird, according to those who know, often found wild or flapping about in rage or panic. Sometimes blessed with artistic talent, they are happy in the Art and Design field. They usually prefer a job without too much responsibility as they have a periodic urge to see what's over the next hill. But once the wanderlust is over they settle down contentedly. Well, you've heard of Mother Goose, haven't you?

— But you can only find out once you complete our Superquiz on page 38. Otherwise, shield your eyes, dear reader, and pass on.

L

IS FOR LAMB. You belie your fluffy appearance and people who try to mother or protect you can be taken aback when they find out you're tougher than you look. Over-conscientious in some matters, you tend to follow the flock and you wouldn't be fleeced so easily if there was more of the black sheep about you.

You'd be happiest working at an open-air job. If you have an affinity with animals, a vet's assistant or animal nursing auxiliary job would be right up your country lane.

H

IS FOR HORSE. A stable personality and often a thoroughbred, it's no wonder you're popular. If you bite or kick, it's usually with good reason. You take hurdles in your stride and come equipped with a fair helping of horse sense. You don't mind being saddled with responsibility, have the patience to be a good teacher and would suit most jobs where integrity and getting on well with people counts.

O

IS FOR OCTOPUS. Not by any means the sea monster from 100 fathoms with cruel beak and plastic suckers. Generally neighbourly and harmless, more scared than scary. But when she senses competition her instinct tells her to hang on for dear life. In the last resort a diversion of tears can be turned on at will. And when she gets a crush on someone, it can be fatal — for him!

A backroom job would keep her happy — scientific assistant or technician. She often has a knack with machinery and would make a good assembly worker or comptometer operator.

M

IS FOR MONKEY. A real swinger, aren't you! Playful, confident and a bit of a rebel, you're a terror to timid teachers. You have a following of what you take to be admirers but really they're only hanging around to see what new chaos will result.

If you've the talent, you'd perform well on some branch of showbiz. Jobs involving demonstration or interviewing the public would appeal to the exhibitionist in you.

K

IS FOR KINGFISHER. You're quick-witted, colourful, like to make a splash and there's an engaging cheekiness about you. Yet there's another romantic, dreamy side which only close friends get to know.

Work in a travel agency, busy hotel, newspaper office or any place which has an atmosphere of excitement would suit you.

P

IS FOR PLATYPUS. Look it up, then, and you'll find it's an incredible freak of nature which has a bill like a duck, burrows, lays eggs, yet suckles its young. The original mixed-up kid, in fact. But don't feel so sorry for yourself. All it means is that you haven't developed your adult personality yet. We can't advise on a possible career, either, so wait a few months before you tackle the quiz again.

HAVE YOU EVER MADE A MISTAKE YOU'D GIVE A YEAR OF YOUR LIFE TO UNDO?

On-The-Spot Interviews

My biggest mistake was having a row with my boy friend Larry. I thought we'd make it up next time we met but he'd already found someone else. Yes, I'd give more than a year of my life to get him back.
Christine Sanderson, Vine Ave., Sevenoaks, Kent.

I was going to this super party and knew the boy I fancied would be there. When I woke up that morning I had a little pimple coming on the side of my mouth. I made the mistake of squeezing it and by evening it was huge and my cheek was all red. I just couldn't go to the party, which I've always regretted.
Cindy Boycott, Vicarage Road, Croydon.

I had the chance to go to France for a year in exchange for a French girl coming to stay with my folk. I refused just because I couldn't bear the thought of some strange girl sleeping in my bed, reading my books, playing my records. That was two years ago and now I realise that an idiot I was and what a chance I missed. I'd give a year of my life, I think, to have the opportunity again.
Diane Crimp, Shelvers Gardens, Tadworth, Surrey.

I was helping Mum with my little brother's party. When the mothers came to collect their kids, one asked how they'd behaved. "Oh, they've all been good," I said breezily, "except for that little horror there." To my horror, it was her son!
Celia Cross, Addison Road, Kensington.

My big mistake was refusing to go out with Martin because he had spots. That was two years ago and now I do go out with him and he's great fun. I missed two years of fun and happiness, so I'd give one for my mistake.
Kay Millard, 12 Axes Lane, Salford.

After a big bust-up at home, I ran away to London and got fixed up with a shared flat and a job in a greengrocer's. Within a week I knew I'd made a mistake but I had too much pride to write home until six months later. I'd give much more than a year to turn back the clock. When I finally plucked up courage to go home I found my mother had died two weeks before.
Liz M., Whifflet, Coatbridge, Lanarkshire.

I went steady with Pete for three years and we planned to get engaged. Then I realised it was all a mistake, I didn't love him enough. I knew he was awfully hurt and that's why I' give a year of my life to undo the mistake of going steady at 14.
Sue Palmer, Cecil Road, Birmingham.

WELL, WHAT KIND OF ANIMAL ARE YOU?

T IS FOR TIGER. A strong, smooth relaxed man-eater, you know what you want and intend to get it. You're not immune from Cupid's darts, however, and if one gets under your skin causing you to lose your self-control, you could be your own worst enemy.

You're efficient and conscientious enough to make a go of most jobs but you're likely to end up in something out of the ordinary. Three suggestions in varying fields are physiotherapist, beauty consultant, receptionist/telephonist.

R IS FOR RHINO. Do you find life a series of angry confrontations? Do you tread on toes as you blunder along and cause upsets as you try to explain? Then welcome to the club. Your excellent intentions have a habit of not turning out as planned.

You do have a knack of getting things done, however, which is a consolation when thinking about a job. With your tough hide and boundless energy you could quickly make a supervisory grade. Remember, counting to ten is important in more jobs than a boxing referee!

V IS FOR VIXEN. Peope who think of you as cunning have the wrong idea. You're just impulsive with a fierce desire to protect those you love. To that end you'd tackle anyone or anything and your friends know better than to take liberties if you're in a fighting mood.

You're quick-witted and occasionally have ingenious ideas or flashes of insight. A normal nine-to-five job doesn't seem right for you. How does being a girl reporter, dress designer, circus acrobat, skating instructor or store security detective grab you?

S IS FOR SQUIRREL. Happiest amongst your own family tree or with a small circle of trusted friends. Apart from a hoarding instinct, you have a great sense of balance which will take you out of many a tight spot.

Jobs? You're neat and a hard worker so bank teller, office cashier and hospital technician are three jobs which suggest themselves. That's it in a nutshell.

WOOL DONE!

JACKIE FASHION

EVER thought of all the things you could do with those odd bits of wool? We got to thinking . . . and came up with loads of great ideas like fringing your woollies and scarves and making woolly belts and things.

All you'll need is some wool and a crochet hook . . . have fun.

Put it around the V-neck of your cardigan to make a super furry collar.

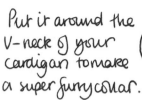

Put it around the wrists of your gloves

or around the cuffs of your jumper.

Put it on your shoulders or on the ends of a long scarf.

Buy 4 or 5 balls of double knitting wool and a crochet hook and put this furry fringing on your woollies. Choose bright colours!

Cut the wool into 12cm lengths. Pick up 4 strands and fold them in half. (1) Push your crochet hook into the garment you're adding the fringing to and underneath one strand of wool (2) Catch the folded strands with your hook and pull them through (3) Repeat this with the rest of the cut wool, fastening each one by looping the loose ends under the folded ends and pulling tight (4) Make each tuft about 1cm apart.

Put a big cluster on top of your hat, or around the edge.

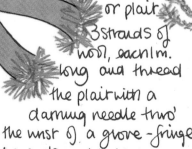

Plait a belt, using double strands of wool, each 2m. long, and sew fringing onto the last 5 cm.

or plait 3 strands of wool, each 1m. long and thread the plait with a darning needle thro' the wrist of a glove - fringe the ends and tie it in a bow.

AN OSMOND A DAY

Monday's child is fair of face,
Tuesday's child is full of grace,
Wednesday's child is full of woe,
Thursday's child has far to go,
Friday's child is loving and giving,
Saturday's child works hard for its living,
And a child that is born on the Sabbath
 day,
Is fair and wise and good and gay.

You're probably already familiar with this old rhyme — most of us in the Jackie office can remember learning it when we were little.

Of course, we've never taken it too seriously — it's really just for fun. But it occurred to us recently that there are seven singing Osmonds — one for every day of the week. So, just for fun, we decided to see if the family fitted the rhyme. And, to our surprise, they seemed to fit remarkably well — see if you agree!

MONDAY

The rest of the family may be handsome, but there's really only one Osmond who fits the description "fair of face"! Yes, of course, Marie the only Osmond sister.

Marie certainly does fit the rhyme! It's a safe bet that lots of girls would give anything to have her clear complexion, lovely brown eyes and long shining dark hair.

And not only is she blessed with those natural good looks that all the Osmonds have — she also knows how to make the best of herself. She has her own range of cosmetics specially designed for young teenage girls. They're produced organically, which means they don't contain any animal fats.

Marie says she likes to look casual when she's at home, but she still loves to dress up for special occasions.

One thing's certain though — whatever she's wearing, she always looks just right!

THURSDAY

"Thursday's child has far to go" — this just has to be Wayne! All the Osmonds enjoy travelling and meeting new people, but Wayne is undoubtedly the most adventurous. He loves exploring — both new places and new ideas. And he has a wide range of interests outside music.

Recently, he became interested in ancient Egyptian history, and when we last met up with him, he explained he had been reading all he could on the subject. Another of his interests is the geography of Europe — and he loves coming over to see for himself all the places he can otherwise only see in photographs.

Unlike his brothers, Wayne isn't content to settle down at home when he and his brothers have some time to spend on their ranch in Utah. He likes to get away — to explore the countryside surrounding the family home. And, to do this, he has his very own plane to fly around in — a Cessna 150. He's a fully qualified pilot, and says he likes nothing better than to take off for a few hours at a time.

So you see, Wayne has far to go — in more ways than one!

FRIDAY

"Loving and giving" — we think the Osmond who fits this description best is Jay.

When you first meet him, Jay seems to be rather quiet. As the drummer, he tends to be the man at the back, perhaps not noticed as much as the 'front-line' of the group.

But once you get to know him, you realise there are hidden depths to Jay's character. For instance, he's very affectionate — it's Jay who looks after the family pets, and he's always the one who's the most upset if a beloved dog or cat becomes ill.

In complete contrast, Jay is also the joker of the group. The others may groan and tell how awful his jokes are — but they know when they're feeling depressed, Jay will be there, cheering them again by making them laugh.

And we can't think of anything better to give than that — a happiness.

TUESDAY

"Full of grace" — in the rhyme, grace is used in the old fashioned sense, meaning good manners and politeness.

Of course, the Osmonds are all very polite, but since we've to pick out one person, we'd choose Merrill as Tuesday's child.

Merrill is the diplomat of the group — when you first meet the Osmonds, it's Merrill who's usually first to say hello and introduce himself. He's always pleased to tell you all about what he and his brothers have been doing — and if you're lucky enough to meet them again, Merrill's sure to remember having spoken to you before.

He's one of the quieter members of the family, with a soft, gentle voice. His manner suggests he can sometimes be a bit shy — and that's why we were all especially pleased when, in the autumn of 1973, we heard that Merrill had fallen in love with a lovely girl called Mary, and that they were getting married.

Don't you feel pleased that such a nice guy has the happiness he deserves?

WEDNESDAY

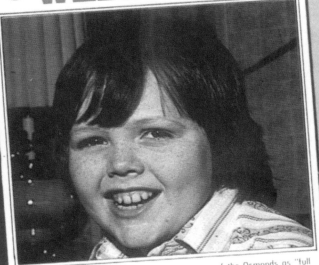

To be honest, we couldn't really describe any of the Osmonds as "full of woe" — because they are a happy family.

But if anybody fits the description, we'd say Jimmy does, simply because, up till now, he's sometimes had to be left out of things. He was just too young to join in everything his elder brothers and sister were doing.

And in a way that was good — because it made sure that Jimmy could be like any other little boy, with the normal boyish interests — football, toy cars and comics.

But now Jimmy is growing up and joining more and more in the group activities. As well as making his own solo records, he now tours with the group and appears on stage with the rest of the family.

So it looks as though he doesn't have much reason to be "full of woe" any longer!

SATURDAY

"Saturday's child works hard for his living" — although it's true that all the Osmonds work very hard, we reckon the hardest worker of all must be Alan.

He's the oldest of the group, so he tends to be the most responsible. He keeps an eye on his younger brothers, giving them advice when they need it, and making sure they keep out of mischief!

He's also the most dedicated musician in the family, and as well as lead guitar, he can also play the piano, saxophone, banjo and bass guitar.

Alan too is the main writer of the group, and the producer. When the brothers have finished recording a new song, he takes the tape to Los Angeles, and works on it until he's satisfied it sounds just right. The finished product is then put on record — and that's when we get to hear it!

On top of this, Alan now wants to involve himself more in filming. His big ambition is to direct an Osmond film.

We just don't know where he'll find the time!

SUNDAY

"And the child that is born on the Sabbath Day is fair and wise and good and gay" — well we're sure there are plenty of readers who'd agree that Donny is all of those things!

When you meet Donny, it's easy to see why he's so popular. Since he first began to capture girls' hearts four years ago, he's changed tremendously. He's grown from a rather shy boy to a self confident young man — and he's grown physically too. He's now tall and handsome and, we're sure you'll agree, even more beautiful than in the days of "Puppy Love" and "Too Young".

But Donny himself is basically still as charming and friendly as ever, with the same politeness that makes him so likeable. He always has a smile for everyone he meets, and if he gets fed up being asked the same questions over and over again, he never shows it.

Like the rest of his family, he really is a genuinely nice person — and that's why we love him!

How can you tell the difference?

As most girls probably know, you can love a guy without being 'In Love' with him. But what's the subtle difference that's really the great divide? Are you just a loving friend or are you fooling yourself and secretly in love with the guy? Answer these simple questions and find out.

When he walks into the room, do you
(a) Have to make a superhuman effort to appear normal, as your legs have gone weak and your head's so light you think you've just been deprived of your oxygen supply?
(b) Feel a pleasant sense of security and think it's nice to see him again?

When he makes a joke or a funny remark, do you
(a) Always laugh like a drain, just because he makes you feel so happy and bubbly you've got to let it out somehow?
(b) Laugh easily if the joke happens to be funny, but make a sarky comment if it isn't?

If your knees or hands accidentally brush, do you
(a) Leap away from the contact, as an electric shock has just zoomed through your senses?
(b) Feel warm and comfortable?

When somebody mentions his name in co[n]versation, do you
(a) Immediately leap out of the deepest som[nambulant] nambulant trance and take a sudde[n] enthusiastic interest in the conversation[?]
(b) Wonder what they're saying about hi[m] and make it your business to find out?

When you're out with your friends, do you
(a) Proudly tell them his opinions, as if they'[ve] just been handed down from the Ho[ly] Grail?
(b) Tell your friends what he thinks, but ma[ke] it clear that you don't always go along wi[th] his views?

If you see him dancing with another girl at t[he] disco, do you
(a) Think it would be worth twelve years' so[li]tary in Holloway for the pleasure of wrin[g]ing her neck? Tell the bouncers to te[ar] them bodily apart?
(b) Feel sure he'll come over to you when he['s] finished, and go off and dance with som[e] one else yourself?

When he comes round to your house for te[a,] do you
(a) Leap about, running after him, until yo[ur] mother's worried that you've undergone [a] serious personality change?
(b) Make him feel very welcome and expe[ct] him to help with the washing up?

When you're chatting with your friends, d[o] you
(a) Subtly keep dropping his name into th[e] conversation at every opportunity, un[til] they get up a petition to Somerset Hou[se] asking for his name to be struck off t[he] records and made illegal?
(b) Or do some of them have to ask what he['s] called because they're not sure who you['re] going out with?

If you walk down the street and happen [to] bump into him
(a) Does the whole day suddenly become gli[t]tery and sparkling and do you feel tong[ue] tied and very shy?
(b) Do you immediately feel more cheerf[ul] and ask him to have a cup of coffee wi[th] you?

If he mentions that he doesn't like skin[ny] girls, do you
(a) Drink a bottle of Guinness a day, pin[ch] other peoples' rolls in cafes, insist [on] chips with everything?
(b) Wear more clothes so he can't see wh[at] shape you are, buy a padded bra?

If he takes another girl home from the disco, do you
(a) Rush home and cry solidly for hours so that no-one's able to console you?
(b) Think you'll give him a row he'll never forget next time you see him. And gladly accept a lift from his friend?

If he says he hates fat girls, do you
(a) Go on a fast that Gandhi would admire?
(b) Promise yourself to diet next month and throw away your padded bra?

When you're out with him, do you
(a) Feel a tremendous exhilaration and excitement as if all life apart from him is just meaningless, drab, existence?
(b) Feel contented and happy, but sometimes wonder what other people are doing?

If you're going to a party together where your friends are going to be, do you
(a) Feel really proud and elated that they're going to see you together?
(b) Worry slightly about what their reaction to him will be, but tell yourself that you love him, so what does it matter what they think about him?

When he kisses you, do you feel
(a) As if the whole world is just made up of the two of you, and that nothing else exists except his kiss?
(b) Warm and cosy and romantic and loving?

CONCLUSIONS
If you've answered all A's, then yes, you're in love. You can tell the difference because all your senses are incredibly heightened. You're deeply aware of his every movement and feeling. Every moment that you're with him you feel on top of the world. You're a very lucky girl, because although your elation is often followed by deep depression, when things aren't working out, you're experiencing the most exciting emotion any human being can achieve.

All B's — You love your boy, but as you realise only too well, you're not in love. You need that extra excitement, that breathtaking tension that makes being in love so much less cosy and safe, but so much more rewarding!

A mixture of A's and B's — You're still not sure of your feelings. Although you love your boy you still don't feel ready to commit yourself totally and proclaim to the world that you're in love. At the moment you're playing it safe, but as time goes on you'll find your emotions taking over from your reason and your B responses turning into A's.

DO BOYS HAVE MORE FUN THAN GIRLS?
A JACKIE ON-THE-SPOT INTERVIEW.

Joan Curry, Hayes Drive, Barnton, Northwich, Cheshire.
Everything seems to be geared to boys having fun. Even at youth clubs there are lots of boys' games, like darts, and very little for the girls. There's not much to look forward to either. Marriage is the same idea, with the men going out to enjoy themselves, while women are tied at home with children.

John Lawless, Glebe House, Great Smeaton, Yorkshire.
I think it's about equal. Girls have a different idea of fun, that's all. Fellows like spending Saturday at a football match and sensible things like that — girls like to sit outside hotels all night hoping for a glimpse of the Osmonds. I think girls who complain about there not being equality are stupid — it's there if they want it.

Raymond, Penn Road, Wolverhampton.
Hard to say for sure, having never been a girl to test it out, but I reckon they have a far better time than us. They get taken out and paid for and bought presents. Then they can retire when they get someone to marry them, and spend their lives having fun, while the poor bloke has to slave away to support them!

Dianne Flynn, Purcell Road, Bell Green, Coventry.
You can't generalise. Life is what you make it, whatever your sex. I don't have any brothers, but my boy cousins don't get any more freedom than me and my sisters. I think you have to be sensible and come to an arrangement with your parents about where you can go and how late you can stay out.

Cathy McDonald, Mains East, East Kilbride, Glasgow.
Boys have it made before marriage, and after. They can ask up any girl at a dance or disco. All we can do is dance with friends or be wallflowers. And until kids come along, most girls have to keep on their jobs when they marry, as well as look after a house. If husbands are asked to dry dishes they think they're being hard done by.

Sue Brown, Lansdown Road, Bath, Somerset.
People are all different. I've known some girls who give you the impression of being very dull and stuffy but are great fun once the barriers are down. It's just that they get their enjoyment in more serious, introspective things. Certainly it's easier for a boy to have fun in a rowdy way than a girl — at least in this area!

Fiona Lawson, Easson's Angle, Dundee.
They certainly ought to — they don't have to sit around hoping someone will ask them out. That's one thing I'd really enjoy, being able to ask a boy I fancied for a date. All a girl can do is try to be noticed. The other week I was trying to catch the eye of a boy who worked in a newsagents. It cost me a fortune in magazines, with nothing to show for it.

Frances Connolly, Queens Drive, Liverpool.
No, I think girls have more fun. We're more light-hearted. I work with a crowd of girls and we never stop laughing, mostly about boys and their funny little ways. Boys are too intense. They turn any casual discussion into a heated argument, particularly if it's about sport.

Cathy Cleer, Parade Street, Passage East, County Waterford, Ireland.
Yes, boys get away with murder. If a boy has a dozen girls on a string everyone thinks he's great. If a girl acts like that, she is something unmentionable. I think things are getting better, though. Girls are getting not to feel so downtrodden.

Pauline, Greenbank Road, Darlington.
I enjoy being a girl, as the song says, and I don't think I've missed out on much fun. I think, though, some girls envy boys their freedom. A boy can walk into a pub or a club on his own and have a good time, but it takes much more nerve for a girl to do it. So girls tend to stay home if they haven't a boy to take them out.

CONFIDENCE
AND HOW TO GET IT!

PHOTO BY JEANY

IT makes all the difference between success . . . and failure, happiness . . . and despair, a full social life . . . and a diary of blank pages! It's CONFIDENCE. But never give up — even if you feel you haven't as much as a shred of the stuff to your name. Although some lucky people do seem to be born with it, ANYONE can acquire it!

Here's another good thing to bear in mind. A girl can't successfully PRETEND she's slim — when her hips are a robust 40 inches, plain for all to see! But *confidence* — or lack of it — is a personal, not a physical quality. You can PRETEND to a lot more confidence than you've actually got. In fact, if you keep on pretending long enough, you'll get so good at it, you will actually BE more confident.

So the first rule is — NEVER ADMIT HOW NERVOUS YOU FEEL. Not even to a best friend! It undermines what confidence you do have, and even best friends have been known to let you down. They'll maybe let slip, right in front of the gang, how you nearly didn't come to the party because you felt your knees knocking so much — and you'll feel so stupid, it will take a lot more courage to drag you out of your shell next time a party's in the offing!

For the same reason, NEVER UNDER-SELL YOUSELF. You know — none better — if your hair is like a hay-rick, face more spotty than a currant cake, etc.,etc. But most people will be far too busy worrying about their own looks to make a very close study of yours! So if you don't moan in public about the way your hair looks, and providing it's not actually three inches deep in grease, you'll get by!

DO THE BEST YOU CAN . . . AND THEN FORGET IT

OF course, some things are bound to nibble away at a girl's self-confidence. If you're worried that your breath may be a wee bit stale, or feel a wave of perspiration come on and wonder nervously if there'll be a wet patch under your arm . . . you can't look poised and calm!

So, when you're out to develop confidence, the very first things to tackle are the basic, simple things that affect you physically. People who are lacking in confidence and easily upset do tend to suffer more with bad breath and body odour problems than anybody else. It's no good leaving it and hoping things will be all right. Take precautions, first!

There are lots of products which deal efficiently with bad breath when nerves are the cause. You can get breath freshening tablets (Amplex), capsules, sprays (Gold Spot), liquids and mouth washes (Vademecum). Just try one or two, find which you like best for taste and performance, and use them regularly before nerve-racking personal appearances!

Of course, you must be CERTAIN that another cause of your bad breath isn't a tummy upset or dental decay, but the signs of either of those are pretty obvious, and in that case a fast visit to the doc. or dentist are called for!

Perspiration and body odour is easier to solve than suffer with. A daily all-over wash with a reliable brand of soap, either deodorant or a general family soap bar, is a must, plus a reliable anti-perspirant for under-arms, a spray for feet, and a third one for body use.

There are lots of brands available, and some work better for different people, depending on your body chemistry. We're sure you'll be kept cool and dry if you pick from Cool, Mum, Femfresh or Sure. Just remember that if the product is to work, it must be applied to clean, dry skin, and sprayed from a distance of eight to twelve inches, in a short, quick burst! Underarm hair should be removed 12-24 hours beforehand, too.

Spots can make you shy of taking your face out of doors — so do something about them, too. If you can't put a finger between them, you'd best see your doctor because there are now medically-prescribed treatments which might work wonders — he'll know what's best.

If there aren't THAT many, but still enough to make you wish masks were in fashion, follow a strict rule of spot treatment, being careful not to eat too many greasy foods, using a good spot-healing cream on your skin, and deal with a greasy complexion with an astringent solution such as in the Innoxa 41 range.

Practise, in spare time, until you can do a really good camouflage job on the nastier spots. Here's how! First dry out the surface by patting it with Innoxa 41 lotion, or TCP or even a dab of cologne (provided the spot isn't open or bleeding). Then put a tiny dab of spot cream in the centre, choosing a cream that matches your skin tone, of course.

Gently pat it outwards until it blends with your skin at the edges, but remains sufficiently thick in the middle to hide the spot. Let it dry for at least two minutes. Film on your usual light skin make-up, all over your face, spot and all. When THAT is set, dab a LITTLE transparent powder over the spot — it'll prevent any grease seeping through. But only apply this rather heavy make-up treatment to bad spots, and never leave it on for more than a few hours without thorough cleansing and a fresh make-up.

"Thank goodness — it's only measles!"

Hair a worry? If it's constantly a headache, get some advice from a sympathetic hair-stylist. If it is totally unmanageable, it means you are either using completely wrong products for the degree of dryness or greasiness your hair displays, or you have chosen a hairstyle which is unsuitable for the texture of your particular hair. A change — or changes — are called for!

Having sorted out the Big Four, and done the best you can for face and hair, don't give yourself a second thought. Force yourself to stop carrying a small portmanteau with your make-up needs in

it! Break the habit of looking in every mirror you pass, staring in shop windows for a glimpse of your reflection, dashing for the loo at every chance, and fiddling with your hair in between times.

If you've done the best you can, you won't improve things with odd dabs and touches while you are out, and you simply make yourself look more nervous and self-conscious, and draw attention to any teeny little faults! So . . . FORGET YOURSELF.

BOYS ARE HUMAN TOO!

THE main idea in developing confidence, of course, is to help you get and keep a boyfriend! If you're very shy, the very idea of being left alone with a BOY is enough to frighten you into fits, and you feel certain you'd never manage to say anything to keep him interested for five minutes, let alone a whole evening!

But there is truly nothing to be scared about. In fact, boys are usually much less self-confident than girls, only they hide it better! All you really have to remember is that most boys dislike extremes — the girl who never says a word, and also the one who never leaves off! And they don't like a false, insincere approach, either.

Also, they're totally against being made to look stupid, so you don't have to bash your brain to a jelly thinking of smart things to say, because the average chap would rather HE made the funnies!

In other words, all a boy wants is someone to boost HIS self-confidence — and that's very easy. Give him a nice, friendly smile, show interest in the things he wants to talk about, and you'll hardly need to open your mouth to keep the evening going nicely. If he's a boy who finds talking difficult, you may need to give him a starter, but again, you don't have to think of anything terribly clever.

Ask him how his football team is doing, or if his car is running well, or if he liked the telly programme last night, something like that. It's best to keep off anything which might be embarrassingly personal till you get to know him.

The problem may be that you don't seem to have much chance of talking to a boy . . . because you never get one to yourself. The difficulty here is working up enough confidence to make contact — but it can be done. Don't aim too high — try to get on friendly terms with any boys there may be, even if they aren't the sort you particularly want to date!

Smile at the paper-boy — exchange a few words with the milkman — have a greeting ready for the fellas who live or work nearby. Eventually, it comes naturally, and you'll find that when someone you WOULD like to date makes an approach, you have the confidence to answer back!

YOUR DAILY CHALLENGE

The important thing about confidence is that, like a precious plant, it must be tended every day! Then, showing a poised and confident face to the world becomes second nature. Make a list of all the things you would seriously like to be able to do, but feel you are much too shy to tackle. It might go something like this — put the list in order of difficulty, by the way, as it applies to *you*.

1. Speak up for yourself when ticked off in class
2. Go up to a girl you know by sight and make friends with her
3. Join a club or social group

4. Go to dances
5. Be more friendly with the boys in your group
6. Be able to talk to a boy in a natural way

Start with the easiest item on the list, and work at it. You don't have to plunge in and do the whole thing in one go! But each time a situation comes up when shyness in that department causes a problem, try to take one more step forward in overcoming it.

When you really feel you are able to deal with it without too much embarrassment, tick that item off and start working on the next one. The first two or three stages may seem to go awfully slowly, and it may seem impossible that you'll ever be able to tackle the more difficult things, but it really does get easier all the time, and suddenly you'll get the hang of the game, and swoop through the last ones quite quickly!

As well as this, make it a game to do SOMETHING to beat that nervousness, every day. There are perfectly ordinary things you can quite easily do which help to get you used to talking to people and standing up for yourself.

Go out on your own more, to shops, libraries and launderettes. When you have a job to do, you don't worry so much about confidence — it's not like going to a dance on your own, with nothing to do but prop up the wall! And the more you talk to people, the easier it will be, later on, to talk to BOYS.

Join in with school clubs as much as possible. Yes, even if the subject doesn't specially interest you! It's good to have a wide circle of acquaintances — lots of the girls will have brothers — and having more interests makes you a more interesting person. You may be glad you have a sketchy idea about stamp collecting some day, when you are on a date with a boy whose hobby this is, and there is a gap in the conversation!

Finally — BELIEVE IN YOURSELF. When you think seriously about the things that handicapped people can manage to do, you will realise that it doesn't take THAT much effort for you, with good health, a normal brain and the right number of arms and legs to do ordinary things like making friends, talking to people and going out to enjoy yourself.

You can do it . . . so why not start today? You can develop confidence more quickly than you can develop a perfect figure, and once you've got confidence, unlike people with figure problems, you never lose it! ●

I LET MY PARENTS RUIN EVERYTHING!

I WAS never one for saying goodbye, Pete, and I'm not proud of the way I said it to you. I mean, in the middle of the High Street, on a busy Saturday morning: it was a bit much really. I didn't offer any explanation, didn't give you a chance to talk about your side of things. I just dropped my bombshell and walked away from you.

By now you'll have guessed that my parents were to blame. You know they were never keen to meet you. I told you that, as I told you everything.

"Dashwood Road he comes from, you say? That's not a nice end of town, Margaret." I can hear my dad saying it now.

"Oh Dad, don't be ridiculous," I said. "I'm not going out with a road, I'm going out with a boy. And he's nice, you'll see."

Then he'd replied: "I can't pretend I'm happy about it, Margaret."

Mum was no better, although I'd expected a bit of support from her. "I know these Dashwood Boys have an exciting air about them, Margaret, and no doubt your friends think it's very daring of you. A sort of challenge to be dating one of them. But mark my words, these roughnecks just don't mix with our sort of people."

"Will you please stop judging Pete before you've even met him?" I demanded. "He's not a roughneck — he's a quiet, decent boy and he means a lot to me. You'll like him too if you'll just let yourselves forget that he lives in a council house!"

That was a bit underhand of me, because Mum and Dad used to live in a council house until, in Mum's words, they "bettered themselves" and bought the pokey little semi-detached we live in now. I knew what Mum meant by "our sort of people" — small-minded snobs who were always trying to "keep up with the Joneses" and thought they were better than everyone else. Well, I didn't want to be one of them.

And it wasn't as if I'd suddenly sprung the news of you on to them, Pete. I led up to it for ages. They knew we were in the same tutorial group at school; they knew we were both involved in forming the fifth-year Drama Society; they knew our friendship had gradually deepened into something more. But they wouldn't accept it.

I guess that, as long as they never actually met you, they could put you out of their minds. After all, it must be quite a wrench for devoted parents when their only child gets her first serious boyfriend. They probably torture themselves thinking that she's going to up and leave them all alone in their old age.

It's all so silly. I kept telling them that marriage just wasn't in our minds. Certainly not for years yet. We both want to go on to college, which means that we'd have to rely on parental support for quite a while yet! But right now we're in love, we need each other. Surely a mother would understand that?

I even tried talking to Mum about her own first love, trying to get things across to her. I told her that I realised our love might not last forever. I mean, it's real and serious while it's happening, like with you and me just now, Pete; but let's face it, most people go through the same sort of thing — at least a few times, before they finally settle down for life.

Not Mum, though. She swore that she'd only ever loved Dad — and that was since she was thirteen years old!

So I tried to explain instead about how good you and I were for each other, Pete. How you made me happy, helped my shyness disappear, kept me in fits of laughter with your crazy, happy nature! How they'd love your sense of humour!

But after a while I felt I'd tackled all the possible approaches. They listened, but they didn't understand. I really felt it was time they came to meet me halfway. So I invited you to Sunday tea. And then I told them what I'd done.

You'd have thought I'd stolen the crown jewels from the scene that resulted.

There were tears from Mum and a lot of, "Look here, young woman" stuff from Dad. In the end they had me crying, too.

"Look, I'm not asking your permission to marry him! I'm just asking you to have him to tea, to meet him, to get to know him. He's the person I love best in the world next to you two. You've brought me up — you've made me what I am — surely you can trust my judgement? Pete is a warm and good person."

"But think of your mother's feelings," Dad had replied. "The neighbours are sure to start talking. They'll say things to upset her."

"They'll probably say how pleased they are that your plain little daughter has got herself such a lovely boyfriend!" I retorted recklessly.

"But Margaret," Mum whispered tearfully, "a black boyfriend!"

THEY'RE so stupid, the labels we use to tag on people. Black is what coal is, Pete, it's not the lovely sunny colour of your skin. And is white any better a description of my wind-burned face?

But they just wouldn't understand the way I felt. They tore holes in all my arguments and talked me into the ground — cruelly, relentlessly, hour after hour.

Oh yes, they were cruel. They said some wicked, untrue things, and I knew I couldn't bring you here to have them verbally attack you the way they'd done me.

That's why I came to see you at your Saturday job and told you not to come to tea after all. And not to try to see me again either. Ever. Because when it came to a fight, I wasn't strong enough to defend you against my parents.

It wasn't their fault that we parted, Pete. It was mine. I should have been stronger — you deserved that loyalty from me.

They've got their opinions — wrong ones, I happen to feel — but none the less, they were true to their principles.

I didn't stick to mine. I let you down because I was too weak to stand against my parents. I just couldn't speak up and say that your colour didn't matter to me; that none of our differences mattered because we had so many much more wonderful things in common. I just sat there silent while they threw all their arguments at me.

And when I didn't fight for you, it convinced Mum and Dad that they'd been right all along. That you were a roughneck and I'd only gone out with you as a gesture of rebellion against them. They thought I wasn't arguing back because I'd realised that what they were saying about you was the truth . . .

Well, it's been two weeks now. It's the school holidays, so we haven't met, and although it's been painful, missing you, I've been able to get by, even think about day-to-day things.

I'm not angry with my parents any more — after all, they only wanted what they thought was best for me. And for their kind of person, mixing colours is an idea that takes a bit of getting used to.

But I'm not that sort, Pete. I want you to understand that. I was weak, I admit it; but having found out the truth about myself in time, I believe I can be strong in future when it truly counts. For many people, black and white don't mix — but for many others, they do, and I believe they could for us.

I'm asking you to forgive me, Pete, because I believe we had — and still could have — something special. I love you, and if I haven't hurt you too much, I'd like to try again at being the girl you love. I can only hope you'll let me, Pete . . .

●

SO FAR SEW GOOD
CHEAP & CHEERFUL FASHION IDEAS

Here's how to make this super tiered skirt. Buy 2 metres of one fabric, 1½ metres of another, and 60cm. of a third. Trim the 1½ metre length from 100cm. to 70cm. wide (use the left over strip to make the waistband) and trim the 60cm. length from 100cm. wide to 60cm. Cut each length of fabric in half and sew up the side seams to make 3 skirts, leaving 20cm. at one side for the zip. Now place the middle sized skirt outside the longest one and the shortest one outside that, zip openings all together, and run a gathering thread round through all 3 layers, to the size of your waist. Put on the waistband, put in the zip, check that the tiers are the length you like (if not, shorten one or more) and sew the hems.

Choose 3 really nice fabrics — 3 different flowery prints or silky rayon, or 3 different coloured satins or cotton voile.

three tiers!

APART from Christmas, birthdays are our favourite days. Your birthday is the one day of the year when everyone's nice to you, and you get all the attention—not to mention all those lovely cards and presents!

Every birthday's a nice occasion, but most people have memories of one special birthday that stands out as their best ever. Even pop stars like looking back on their happiest birthdays — and the presents they got . . .

Rick Driscoll of Kenny, for instance, says that his nicest birthday was when he was only six years old!

"I'd always wanted a bike," Rick said, "and I really envied all my school pals who had ones of their own.

"So for my sixth birthday, my parents bought me my first ever two-wheeler push bike. I was really proud of it, because it was newer and much more flash than all my friends' bikes!"

Dave Paton of Pilot is another person who remembers getting a very special present.

"It was my ninth birthday," he said, "and it was very special because I got a Robin Hood set. I'd been a bow and arrow fanatic for ages, and this set had a big bow and three arrows with rubber suckers on the end. It was great!"

Alan Merrill, the singer with **Arrows,** also has special memories of his ninth birthday.

"I remember I had a big party with 25 of my friends, lots of food and a big cake in the middle," he said. "In the other room, there was a huge object, all covered with brown paper, which I had strict instructions not to open until after tea.

"So when we'd finished eating, we all piled into the other room for the grand unveiling, and inside was an eight foot long spaceship.

"A commercial artist who lived downstairs had made it for me out of boxes, luminous paper, silver foil — everything. It was really impressive!"

Eric Faulkner of the Bay City Rollers (of course!) says his most memorable birthday was his 10th.

"That was the best," he said, "because that year, my mum bought me my first ever junior guitar!

"I learnt to play a few chords, and how to tune it, and I used to spend hours playing along with my favourite records."

HAPPY

Pete Phipps of the Glitter Band also remembers getting his first musical instrument — in his case a drum kit.

"When I was little I had piano lessons," he said, "but really I wasn't over keen, because I was always determined to learn to play the drums.

"I made my own kit from biscuit tins, boxes, lids, knitting needles and the like, and I used to practise on them.

"I think my parents must have taken the hint, because for my 14th birthday I received my first proper drum kit. I was thrilled with it!

"So that's a birthday I'll never forget!"

Andy Walton of Kenny says his happiest birthday was just two years ago, when he was 17.

"I've always wanted to drive," he explained, "and so my 17th birthday meant an awful lot to me, because my parents bought me a car of my own, and my dad took me out in it to teach me to drive.

"Within a few weeks, I passed my test. That was some present!"

All these people's memories were of birthdays which happened years ago, when they were still ordinary schoolboys, and no one imagined that they'd be stars some day.

BIRTHDAY ♫♪

I'm a bit vague, and I suppose I am most of the time. As I was sitting there, I thought, 'Oh, there's thingy', and, 'That's so and so', because I'm hopeless at names.

"Everywhere I looked there were mates of mine, and I thought that it was such a coincidence that they should all be there too. It never occurred to me that they'd organised it!

"But it turned out to be a fantastic party. Surprise parties are the nicest kind!"

Gary Glitter also had a surprise party last year, on his 30th birthday.

"I was in New York, feeling very depressed because I didn't know anyone,"

he said. "But when I went back to my hotel in the evening, my suite was absolutely full of people, a lot of whom were English.

"Without me knowing, they'd arranged a party for me with a huge cake, champagne, the lot. I had the time of my life!"

Brian Connolly of the Sweet is another person whose happiest birthday was spent abroad.

"It was three years ago," he said. "We left England on Wednesday, after doing 'Top Of The Pops', and arrived on the following day, my birthday, in the Seychelle Islands for the start of a tour.

"I can remember sitting drinking champagne in the blazing sunshine, and saying to the other lads, 'You know, this isn't bad for October 5th .'"

Another pop star whose birthday falls on the same day as Brian's is **Russell Mael of Sparks.** And October 5th, last year, was a very special birthday for Russell — his 21st.

"That was a good birthday, because I celebrated it on two TV shows!" he told me. "Firstly in the morning on 'Saturday Scene' in London, and then in the evening, on the Nana Mouskouri show in Paris. It was a bit strange, but it was good fun, all the same!

"The other nice thing about it was all the presents I got. I got lots of scarves with my name sewn on them, and lots and lots of homemade cards and drawings.

"Those are usually the best gifts — the ones that are hand-made. Even if it doesn't look all that good, it's nice to know that someone's actually worked on it. It seems to mean a lot more somehow."

But there were a lot of other stars whose happiest birthdays have been more recent ones. Of course, when you're a pop star, you can expect to get lots of lovely presents, and you can throw fantastic lavish parties — all of which goes to make a pretty exciting birthday!

Elton John, as you know, believes in doing things on a grand scale — and his birthday party of two years ago was no exception!

"We had a party on the 'Sloop John B', which was a boat on the Thames," said Elton. "It was a colossal event, with dozens of celebrities, including Rod Stewart and the Faces, The Who, Paul Simon and my mum and dad! (And the Ed was there too, folks!)

"It was a great evening, and a birthday I'll never forget."

Roy Wood was another star who had a party on the Sloop John B — but this time, he didn't organise it himself!

"A couple of years ago, my manager invited me out to dinner to celebrate my birthday," he said. "People tend to think

Your 21st is traditionally a very important birthday. But for **Donny Osmond,** like all other Mormon boys, another birthday was even more important.

Yes, of course, it was his 16th — because that was when he was allowed to start dating girls!

"It was a big occasion for me," said Donny. "I'd been looking forward to it all year! So when the big day came, I made sure nothing went wrong.

"I was a bit nervous about going on my own, so I took along Alan and Jay and their girlfriends for moral support. We all went out for dinner together, and we had a great time.

"Of course, I've been out with lots of girls since then, but that first date is still a special memory. It was one of the best birthday presents I ever had!"

So you see, whether you're a famous pop star or an ordinary person like us, birthdays are just as much fun!

DO YOU BELIEVE IN GHOSTS?

Before you shake your head and say, "Of course not," wait a moment! Have you ever considered that there might just be something in it?
We asked some of your favourite pop people if they believed in the supernatural and a surprising number of them claimed to have come face to face with a ghost at one time or another!
And here on this page are their answers — Tales guaranteed to send a shiver up your spine! So, to find out what they said, read on — if you're brave enough . . .!

Alvin Stardust

"One ghostly experience I had was the night some friends gathered at my house and decided, quite late at night, to have a seance.

"During the seance, we all heard footsteps coming down the stairs and towards the door — and then there was a knock at the door. But when we answered it, there was no-one there.

"There was one person there who'd been a total disbeliever before the seance and he told me that he'd completely changed his opinion. As for me, I've still got an open mind on the subject — but I'm sure something did happen that night!"

David Essex

"I didn't believe in ghosts until I moved into my last home, which was an old Victorian house in Essex.

"Often, when I was going upstairs in that house, I'd get the feeling that there was a little old lady beside me. She was a very nice, friendly old lady though — not at all frightening.

"I never saw anything, but I had a definite feeling there was something there!"

Bill Lyall—Pilot

"Before we formed Pilot I worked in Craighall Recording Studios in Edinburgh. My boss lived in a big house above the studios and once when I had to get up very early the next day, he invited me to spend the night there.

"Everything went okay until about midnight, when I was woken up by the sound of a chair in the corner creaking, as though someone was sitting in it. Then I suddenly felt my bedclothes being pulled off the bed — though, of course, there was no-one there to pull them!

"I later found out that this was caused by the ghost of a servant in the house who'd committed suicide."

Woody—Rollers

"All the others in the group laugh at me, but I really do believe in ghosts!

"When I was younger, I went on holiday to Inverness with some friends, and we stayed in a youth hostel which had been converted from an old castle. It was really creepy.

"One night I was walking along a corridor when I heard footsteps behind me. I thought it was my friends, but when I turned round to speak to them, there was no-one there!"

Noel Edmonds

"After doing a gig in a discotheque in Leicester, I had a minor dispute with the manager about my fee. I suggested that, to sort things out, we went upstairs to his office to look at my contract.

"To my surprise, he refused, then he agreed to go into the office only if I went too! I thought this was a bit odd, but I went in anyway.

"Once we were inside, he told me that he never went into the office alone because it was haunted. Of course, I laughed at this, but he said he'd prove it to me. He told me to let my mind go blank. I did and I got a real shock.

"Although it was a warm summer evening, and the sun was streaming in through the windows, I suddenly felt the room become icy cold, and I could see my breath condensing in front of me. I was absolutely terrified, I just couldn't get out of there quickly enough!

"Afterwards the manager told me that the building had previously been a funeral parlour, and his office had been the chapel of rest. All the staff of the disco had seen a ghost there at least once, and a medium who'd been there had seen no less than six ghosts in the room!"

Roger Taylor of Queen

"I once lived in Cornwall, in a 15th century house which was haunted by a poltergeist — an invisible spirit which throws things about.

"One night I was lying in bed when my bedroom door was flung open and all the hangers were jangling about. And another time, the entire contents of the attic were moved around and turned upside down!

"Someone told me that it was caused by the ghost of a person who'd died in the house in mysterious circumstances."

COVER-GIRL LOOKS FOR YOU

TWO fabulous model-girl looks for you to copy at home . . . we show you two completely different make-ups and tell you how to do them yourself.

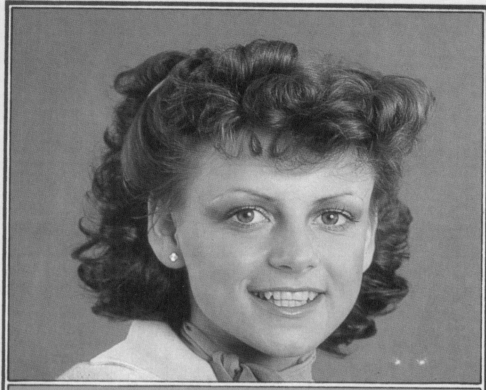

DAY-TIME

THE perfect day-time look is a healthy, glowing one . . . skin shou
be really clear and eyes should sparkle. Make-up should
subtle but very flattering, natural but very attractive.
Think of summertime when everyone looks so tanned a
healthy . . . then think of winter when everyone looks pale a
wan. We know which look we prefer and we're sure you agre
so here's how to look happy and healthy all year round.

STEP 1

Skin care is the first step to natural beauty, of course, so let's start from there. The latest cleansing theory is that regular cleansing with creams and lotions isn't enough because they don't remove the dead cells from the surface. So, even if you do cleanse, tone and moisturise religiously twice a day, there's still a good chance that your skin might be looking a bit dingy.

That's not the cue to go back to soap and water, though, try using cleansing grains and face packs more often to take away those top layers. Stick to your cleanse, tone and moisture routine as well and your skin should always look healthy.

Choose skin-care products according to your skin type . . . normal, greasy, dry or spotty. All the products are marked, so you shouldn't go wrong and there are always salesgirls to help you if you're stuck. Follow the directions on the pack and you're well away . . . if the product doesn't seem to agree with you try something else until you get it right.

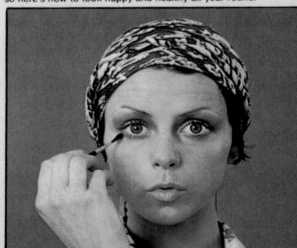

STEP 2

After a thorough cleanse, tone and moisturise, the next step is choosing your foundation. For day-time you'll need one that gives good coverage without being too heavy or too dark.

There are different types on the market, liquids, creams, sticks and even aerosol foundations, so choosing the right one can be difficult. Creams seem to be the most popular as they seem to be the easiest to apply and give good coverage at the same time.

For those people with skins that tend to shine after a while, there are the matte foundations which combine foundation and powder such as Max Factor's Sheer Genius, but these will be too heavy for girls with normal to dry skins.

Applying the foundation is quite simple, as long as you remember a few basic facts, like blending in under chin and around hair-line. The secret is to apply dots of foundation all over your face and then blend in with fingers for the best results. Foundation always goes on much better if your skin is soft and smooth, so moisturise well before applying.

STEP 3

Eyes come next and here's your chance to really make the m of yourself! Choosing the colour is always a problem, though, a where do you put it in the day-time so that you look nice witho looking tarty?

The secret of clever day-time eye make-up is choosing colours th go with the clothes you're wearing . . . not necessarily colours th match your eyes. Pearly highlights are out during the day, sa those for evenings when lights are low and you want to lo romantic. Stick to fairly basic colours on lids with a darker colour outline sockets and a very neutral colour on brow-bones, such shell pink or creamy beige.

Use a crayon to outline sockets (brown is good), then the colo of your choice on lids. Remember that cream shadows are best brow-bones, powder shadows for lids and the paint-on powd shadows last for ages and ages!

STEP 4

Blusher comes in all sorts of shapes and sizes, sticks, powde . . . even a roll-on kind from Rimmel, now, so choosing can prese problems. Day-time doesn't really call for too much blusher, thoug so choose your colour very carefully! Experiment with different area of your face, always keeping blusher well away from your nos Model-girls have a knack of applying it from ear-lobe level along t bottom of the cheek-bones and up towards temples.

Try all sorts of different ways until you find the one that sui you best and really makes the most of your face . . . blusher c make that vital difference that changes you from plain into rea fantastic! Remember to blend in at the edges so that you don't ha huge great circles on your face which can look really ugly.

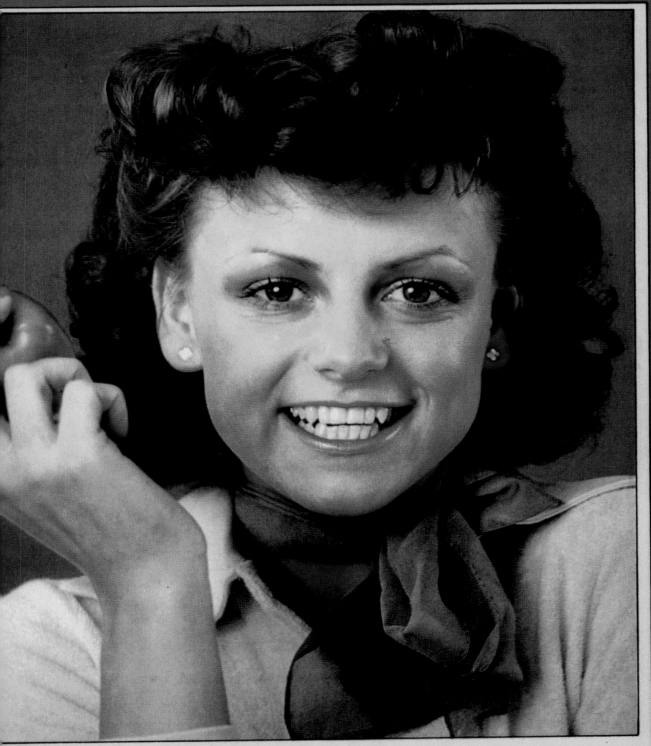

e finished look, complete with lipstick and powder. We find that slucent powder goes over everything and doesn't look caked itty in any way. Buy it in a compact with its own puff. Lipstick day-time should be light and bright, and sometimes even just a k of lip-gloss looks great on its own!

uge, scarlet lips don't look nice during the day at any time, so r clear! Stick to light, shiny colours, perhaps with a lip-gloss the top!

EP—BY—STEP

e used Boots 17 foundation, cleverly applied with fingertips all r face and neck.

2. Socket lines are outlined with brown crayons, also under lower lashes. Ginger brown cream shadow over brow-lines, out to the edges.

3. Green crayon all over lids and well into the outer corners of the eye to meet socket-line. One coat of browny/black mascara.

4. Pale pink blusher applied with a fat brush using sideways strokes from ear to cheek-bones.

5. Shiny pink lipstick from the Boots 17 range applied with a lip brush . . . lips are outlined first, then filled in with colour.

43

NIGHT-TIME

SOFT and romantic, that's the special night-time look w chosen. Soft colours don't have to look weedy . . . should be pearly so they'll shine in the candlelight (sigh!) and really romantic.

Night-time make-up can be heavier than for day-time, but doesn't mean just heaping on more of the same colours! Ge lasting looks so you won't go all streaky halfway through the eve and you shouldn't have to keep disappearing to powder your ne

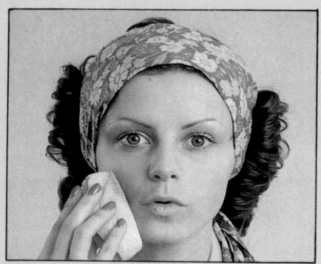

STEP 1

Evening foundation can be tricky. You want that flawless, soft glowing look without looking too heavily made up. Unlike day-time looks, night-time looks call for a pale, less healthy look . . . bright red cheeks don't look nice at all when you're trying to look elegant!

Stick foundations stay on for absolutely ages, especially if you use a moistened sponge to apply the colour. Surprisingly, you can choose a fairly dark shade if you're using a sponge, as the colour seems to be absorbed by your skin and looks several shades lighter.

You must cleanse, tone and moisturise thoroughly before you begin applying your foundation as it will go on much more easily if skin is soft and smooth to start with.

If you're prone to red marks and blushing, try using Boots No 7 Colour-Corrective Moisturiser underneath your foundation . . . It's a green cream which helps to counteract redness.

Sensitive skins need special attention, of course, so you'll need to choose a foundation from one of the ranges specially made for sensitive skins, such as Almay or Max Factor's Swedish Formula range.

STEP 2

Romantic eyes take time to perfect, so make sure you don't have to rush them. Pearly colours are best, of course, with fairly strong colours for lids, lighter ones for brow-bones.

Decide what you're going to wear first, then choose your eye colours to match or tone. Pinky lilac colours are great for night-time, along with silvery grey and light, shiny blues. Powder colours are easy to apply with a brush and last longest, especially if you use a fairly neutral cream shadow as a base.

Make sure eyebrows are nice, too. Not too thin and finely arched . . . that's out now, but shaped nicely without any stragglers showing!

STEP 3

Mascara is very important at night, 'cos you'll want those las to be extra long and fluttery! Try a mascara with built-in l lengthener, in a colour to tone with the eye colour you've chos You can buy all sorts of colours now, such as blue, plum, green a grey as well as black and brown.

Mascara's the last thing you do to your eyes, applying one c very carefully and allowing it to dry before applying the next. Wa out for bits that may get left behind on your cheeks . . . put a tiss underneath your eye as you put on the mascara if you think you likely to make a mess.

STEP 4

Night-time blusher should be light and pearly, applied high cheek-bones to make you look extra soft and romantic. Bright re won't do at all!

Powder blusher will be best for evenings, applied with a nice brush or a little puff. Stroke in from ear-lobe and over cheek-bone but not too near your nose as this will make your face loo unbalanced.

Powder is important at night, too, and this is when you can spla out on some loose powder and one of those lovely, feathery puf Max Factor make a splendid loose powder in their Swedish Formu range, it's translucent and has tiny sparkly bits in it . . . looks sup in candlelight! Always remember to dust off excess powder, though

STEP 5

Lips should be soft and shiny and oh-so-kissable, so choose a lipstick that's right for the occasion! Outline lips first with a lip-brush dipped in a deep colour . . . mulberry for instance . . . to give your lips shape. Then fill in with a lighter, toning colour that's really shiny.

Finish off with a slick of lip gloss if you like, but don't load up your lips with too much stuff . . . you don't want to leave it all on your glass or his face, do you!!

STEP-BY-STEP

1. We used Rimmel's stick make-up applied evenly and lightly with a moistened sponge, all over face and neck.

2. Pinky lilac shadow is applied with a brush all over lids and brow-bones, followed by a band of lilac painted straight across, just below the socket line. A pinky beige shiny highlighter at the outer edge of the brow-bone adds the finishing touch.

3. Two coats of navy mascara next, allowing the first coat to dry before applying the second. Wipe excess mascara off the brush to avoid bits.

4. Pearly pink blusher is applied high on cheek-bones and up temples to look extra stunning for evening.

5. Pale pink lipstick applied with a lip-brush adds the final touch, with a slick of lip-gloss (Max Factor's) over the top.

Both looks were created especially for Jackie by Claire of Boots 17, using the make-up that suited Belinda best. You'll find similar colours and products in various ranges such as the Outdoor Girl, Miners, Yardley, Boots No 7, Max Factor, Rimmel and Love make-up collections. Have fun shopping around!

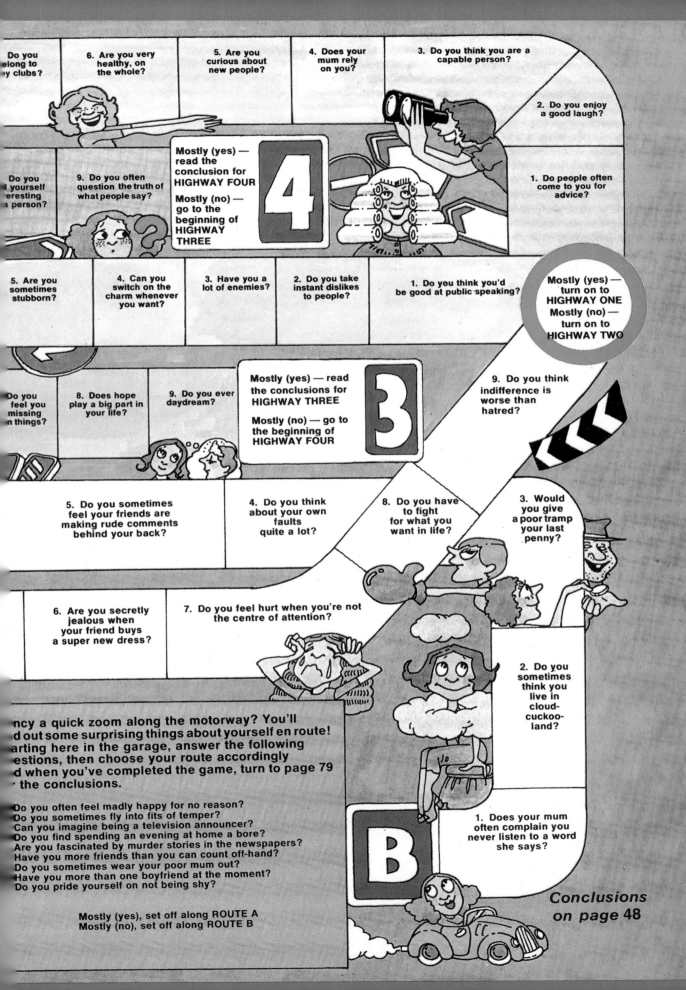

6. Are you very healthy, on the whole?

Do you belong to any clubs?

5. Are you curious about new people?

4. Does your mum rely on you?

3. Do you think you are a capable person?

2. Do you enjoy a good laugh?

Mostly (yes) — read the conclusion for HIGHWAY FOUR

Mostly (no) — go to the beginning of HIGHWAY THREE

4

1. Do people often come to you for advice?

Do you find yourself interesting a person?

9. Do you often question the truth of what people say?

5. Are you sometimes stubborn?

4. Can you switch on the charm whenever you want?

3. Have you a lot of enemies?

2. Do you take instant dislikes to people?

1. Do you think you'd be good at public speaking?

Mostly (yes) — turn on to HIGHWAY ONE

Mostly (no) — turn on to HIGHWAY TWO

9. Do you think indifference is worse than hatred?

Mostly (yes) — read the conclusions for HIGHWAY THREE

Mostly (no) — go to the beginning of HIGHWAY FOUR

3

Do you feel you missing in things?

8. Does hope play a big part in your life?

9. Do you ever daydream?

5. Do you sometimes feel your friends are making rude comments behind your back?

4. Do you think about your own faults quite a lot?

8. Do you have to fight for what you want in life?

3. Would you give a poor tramp your last penny?

6. Are you secretly jealous when your friend buys a super new dress?

7. Do you feel hurt when you're not the centre of attention?

2. Do you sometimes think you live in cloud-cuckoo-land?

ncy a quick zoom along the motorway? You'll
d out some surprising things about yourself en route!
arting here in the garage, answer the following
estions, then choose your route accordingly
d when you've completed the game, turn to page 79
the conclusions.

Do you often feel madly happy for no reason?
Do you sometimes fly into fits of temper?
Can you imagine being a television announcer?
Do you find spending an evening at home a bore?
Are you fascinated by murder stories in the newspapers?
Have you more friends than you can count off-hand?
Do you sometimes wear your poor mum out?
Have you more than one boyfriend at the moment?
Do you pride yourself on not being shy?

Mostly (yes), set off along ROUTE A
Mostly (no), set off along ROUTE B

B

1. Does your mum often complain you never listen to a word she says?

Conclusions on page 48

47

HIGHWAY ONE

You whizz fast and furious along the motorway without any regard for your fellow travellers. You're a bit of a road-hog, and can be very selfish at times, but you'll get where you want to go, all right! You are very ambitious, self-confident and determined. Many people envy your vitality and your powers of persuasion, and you have a way of getting people to do what you want, because you have a very strong personality. People can only take so much of you, but with your bull-in-the-china-shop approach to life, it's likely you don't care all that much what people think, anyway! You might be heading for a crash, though, so watch out. Try to consider other people a bit more, and your journey along the road to success will be enjoyable as well as rewarding.

HIGHWAY TWO

You speed along the motorway, enjoying the ride, and managing to consider others along the route, too. You are friendly, easy-going, and you enjoy the good things of life. You should be popular, because you are lively and fun, and get on naturally well with people. You are rather practical, and your sense of humour plus your intelligence will see you very nicely through life. You are a good mixer, you are good at solving problems, and you will be an asset to others wherever you go. You have the ability to spread happiness around you. Sailing through life is fine, but it would be worth your while to look beneath the surface a bit more. Do you really think you are making the best of your abilities and your talents?

HIGHWAY THREE

You are a danger on the roads — you wouldn't see a bright red lorry in front of your nose, because you'd be too busy dreamily admiring the pretty flowers along the hedgerows! You are a romantic, a dreamer and sometimes too emotional for your own good. Of course it's good to be sensitive and to feel things deeply, but you often tend to be *too* affected by events in your life, and too easily led by people around you. Try to get things into perspective a bit more — listen to your head as well as your heart. On the bonus side, though, you are sympathetic to others, you are loving and gentle, and although you are often depressed, you also have the capacity to be very happy. So go on living in your beautiful dream-world, but try to temper it with reality. Concentrate on the road-signs and get going — along the ground, not up in the clouds!

HIGHWAY FOUR

You drive cautiously and with great concentration. You're not in a hurry to arrive at your destination, but when you get there you'll enjoy it all the more. You are a complicated, thoughtful person, and, as a rule, things don't come easily to you. This is partly because you make mountains out of molehills, and partly because you tend to overlook the obvious in your quest to find great meaning and significance in everything around you. You are an individual, a bit of an intellectual really, and you tend to be intolerant of thickies; but perhaps they could teach you to relax a bit more. You'll wear yourself out with tension if you go on questioning everything and accepting nothing. You are very aware as a person, and your soul is always searching for something. Your journey through life will always be interesting because you will never allow yourself to park your car and doze off — your mind is always alert.

FIVE OF THE BEST!

If you could put together your ideal group, who would be in it?

We all have our own special favourites when it comes to pop stars. In every group there's one guy who stands out. No matter how much you like the others, he's the one you love — because there's something about him that makes him extra special!

And we thought it would be fun if we took some of our favourites out of their own groups, and put them all together in one big supergroup!

All you have to do is work out, from the clues listed below, who the members are — so get your thinking caps on!

And if you turn to page 71, all will be revealed in our magic photo of the boys all together!

THE LEAD SINGER

His birth sign is Leo.
He went to the Shipman County Secondary School.
He once worked for a scrap dealer.
One of his first groups was called The China Plate Blues Band!
His favourite food is Indian curry.
He has blue eyes.
He once had a horse called Zelda.
There are two women in his life!
His middle name's Victorian!
He once worked as Tommy Steele's understudy.

THE DRUMMER

He has blue eyes.
His birthday's on the same day as Mick Jagger's.
He was born in King's Lynn.
His family live in Cornwall.
He has blond hair.
He once went to dental college.
His group is very popular in Japan.
He can play guitar as well as drums.
He also writes and sings!
Cats are his favourite animals.
He once worked in Kensington Market.
He's 5 ft. 10 ins. tall.
He has a degree in biology.
His first group was called Smile.
He loves old clothes.

His first record was called "And The Tears Came Tumbling Down."
Football is his favourite sport.
December 18, 1971 was a very special day for him.
His grandfather was an Irish gipsy.
He loves dogs, and has two of his own.

THE LEAD GUITARIST

He has blue eyes.
He plays several musical instruments — including the violin!
He was born in the Elsie

THE BASS GUITARIST

He went to Liberton Secondary School.
He has blue eyes.
He's also a singer.
His dad's a singer too!
He once played with another well-known group.
He's very patriotic!
He has dark brown hair.
He wrote his first hit while he was working as a milkman!
He's also worked as a mechanic and an electrician.
His star sign is Scorpio.
His group went to America for the first time earlier this year.
He has a cat called Pussy.
He's 5 ft. 8 ins. tall.
He enjoys studying classical music.

Inglis Hospital.
He once played in his local schools' orchestra.
He's 5 ft. 7 ins. tall.
He has one brother, Alan.
He went to Morden Primary School.
His very first group was called Witness.
He worked for six weeks as a roof surveyor.
His birth sign is Libra.
He loves horse-riding.
His father's name is George.
When he was eleven, he met the Queen Mother.
He's the smallest member of his group.
He takes size 7 shoes.

THE KEYBOARD PLAYER

He can sing as well!
He has one sister.
He has brown eyes.
His birth sign is Sagittarius.
His middle name is Clark.
Red is his second favourite colour!
His favourite drink is orange juice.
He has a very useful hobby!
He was born in Ogden.
He has lots of nephews and nieces.
He's been going out with girls for two years now.
He's the third youngest child in his family.
He made his first TV appearance at the age of 5.
His brothers call him by his nickname, Corky.

Got A Minute?

Got a minute? Then here's a quick selection of fun games and puzzles to help you fill in some spare moments!

Just Picture It...

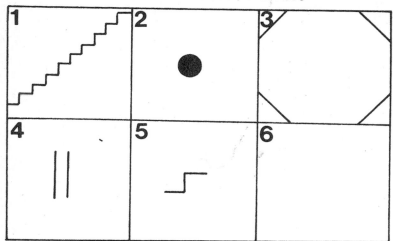

Here's a very simple picture quiz — but one which can tell a lot about you!

All you do is describe what you see in the diagrams.

Answers:

1. *If you treated the diagram as a flight of stairs, this shows you're conventional. As anything else this means you have a lot of character and will go far in life.*

2. *If you saw the dot as the centre of something, this means you're self-centred. As anything else, means you're open and generous.*

3. *If you saw the lines as a box, this means you're needing to widen your horizons a bit. Anything else, you're fine as you are!*

4. *If you saw them as matches, this means you're lonely and in need of company. If you see them as anything else, this generally means you're just doodling!*

5. *If you saw this diagram as part of an object, this means you have a practical, hard-working streak, and like to get problems sorted out quickly. If you see it as part of a design, you're moody and temperamental.*

6. *The answer to this is simple – the more complicated your answer, the more complex a character you are. If, however, you just answered "a blank space," you're a pretty boring person, I'm afraid!*

Penny For Them!

Play the penny game and astound your friends! Have someone blindfold you, and collect a dish full of one pence pieces. Ask them to pass round one penny — any one — and get them all to examine it so that they all know its date, etc. Then tell them to place it amongst the other pennies in the dish and hand the dish to you, lo and behold — you'll be able to pick out the "special" penny, every time! The secret is very simple — the "special" penny will be hot after everyone has handled it, and all the rest of the coins will be cold! Easy!

We've Got Your Number!

To find out someone's personality secrets, just add up his birthdate as follows. Take the month number (i.e. July is the 7th month, therefore its number is 7), then add on his day number (the 8th =8) + add the year number ($1960 = 1+9+6+0$)

Thus $= 7+8+1+9+6+0 = 31$.

Now reduce this to one number by adding $3+1=4$. Therefore 4 is the birth number. Now look it up on the column below!

1. Confidence, strength, reliability.
2. Sympathy, tact, artistic nature.
3. Always on the go, full of ideas.
4. Steady and unchangeable.
5. Impulsive, unrealistic, lives in the clouds.
6. Home-loving and generous.
7. Very talented, often musical or poetic.
8. Usually ambitious — and usually successful!
9. Has an unusual degree of understanding and intelligence.

Draw Your Own Conclusions

Here's a very simple way to tell the secrets of someone's personality — ask them to draw a flower! The type of flower they draw can tell a great deal about them — see below: —

Artistic and gentle, dreamy and inclined to be forgetful. A true romantic.
The details on the leaves and the difference of petals show a love of detail and an open mind to other people.

Secretive and withdrawn, can be reliable and moody. Doesn't fall in love easily.
The uneven lines represent someone whose life is unsteady and often worrying. The decreasing lines towards the centre mean someone withdrawn and secretive.

Acts on impulse — changeable, moody, restless by nature.
The spiky petals show a certain sharpness of nature and reluctance to give away any secrets. The fact that the flower is drawn from the centre shows selfishness.

Very much an individual, has her own ideas about everything.
A tulip, or other flower unlike the other five "usuals" shown, shows that this person is different and idealistic. She'll never be stuck in a rut!

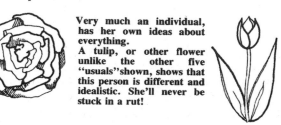

Very basic, down-to-earth character. Honest and reliable. The rounded petals here show a love of home life and a need for security. A business-like mind is shown by the straight stalk.

The five points show a sense of fun, an open mind with lots of interests. The simplicity of the drawing shows an unstable mind.
A bit childish, but full of fun, and makes the best of life.

PATCHWORK

Here's a very special selection of ideas to brighten up your life!

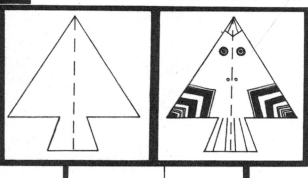

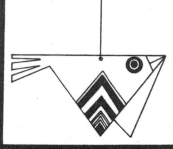

WATCH THE BIRDIE!

Make a hanging paper bird — cut the shape out of thin card (use a postcard if you want a little bird). Cut the tail to look like feathers and paint on a pattern (the same on both sides) Fold down the centre and suspend from the edges of your lampshade on a bit of thread. Make lots!

STICK TO IT!

Stick rubber suction towel holders on the back of your door and hang your scarves in them.

GETTING ROUND IT . . .

Buy some shiny windmills from a market stall or toyshop and put them in a jamjar covered in silver foil for a nice permanent flower display. Put them in a draught and they'll whirl, too!

ON THE SHELF

Ask a shoeshop for some empty shoeboxes and glue them together to make shelves. Paint them or stick coloured paper over them or cover with cooking foil.

HAVE A HANG UP!

Cut a heart shape out of thick card – cover it with red satin and stick suction hooks onto it to hang your beads from. Hang it from the wall, or put hooks on both sides and hang it with a pretty ribbon from the ceiling.

JUST PICTURE IT!

Ask all your friends for a photograph of themselves and stick them onto a sheet of coloured card, to make a friendly poster for your room. Screw the card to the wall with mirror screws.

A FISHY STORY . . .

Make a gloomy corner of your room cheery and bright. Buy a goldfish and bowl and some tiny tins of enamel paint. Paint trees and flowers round the outside of the bowl. Put a table lamp beside it to illuminate it prettily.

CHICKEN AND ALMOND SALAD

Chicken and Almond Salad.

You need some leftover chicken, a small green or red pepper, some toasted almonds, lettuce and mayonnaise. Cut the pepper into strips, lay it, with the chicken, onto the lettuce leaves, put some mayonnaise onto it and sprinkle with toasted almonds.

WHAT'S YOUR REMEDY FOR A BROKEN HEART?

Julie Thornton, Dewsbury, Yorkshire.
If ever I feel heartbroken over anything, I find the best thing to do is to shut myself away in my bedroom and have a really good cry, then go to sleep for a while, and when I wake up, things don't seem half as bad!

Pat Stewart, Hillhead, Glasgow.
Reading poetry. It convinces me there's nothing like being crossed in love to inspire the imagination, and also that however heart-breaking a situation may be, it's happened before, and the people involved managed to use it to develop a better understanding of themselves and others.

Clare Thornton, Portsmouth.
Read a very long, soppy novel, like "Gone With The Wind" or "Penmarric" — you'll get so involved, you'll almost forget your troubles — or at least you'll realise that you aren't the only one!

Steve Yates, Blackheath, London SE3.
Pick yourself up; dust yourself down — and start all over again! As the song goes! Pretty good advice, I'd say!

Julie Cave, Corby, Northants.
Fortunately this is something I've never experienced, but I think that if I ever did I'd try to make every effort to forget him and concentrate on finding happiness with somebody else. But if you've been really serious about somebody, everything you possess, records, presents, photos, anything at all is bound to remind you of him for a long while, so you have to be very strong willed and make up your mind that you're going to mend it again. But as I've got such a fabulous boyfriend I hope I'll never be in this position.

Crazy Mary, New Addington, Surrey.
Stick it up with sellotape — then no-one will know it's broken and you can recuperate in peace!

Jackie Nicholas, Bemerton Heath, Wilts.
Oh, if it was me I'd get a new boyfriend as quickly as possible. One that's much better-looking than the last. It's a good way to restore your confidence! And of course I'd get out and about as much as I possibly could.

Sharon Gillingham, Harlow, Essex.
I don't take boys as seriously as most girls do, so I don't ever suffer from having a broken heart. So having never been in this position I find it difficult to answer. But if I ever did have a steady relationship with a boy and suddenly it ended I'm sure it would be a very long time before I'd want to go out with anybody else. I think it's just true to say that 'time heals' and you just can't rush it.

John Lumley, Bury, Lancs.
Work. I have a market stall, and work is not only hard graft to me, but also my hobby and way of life. It may not mend a broken heart — I wouldn't know about that — but it can be guaranteed to ensure you don't go broke financially as well. And that must be some comfort.

Suzie Lofthouse, Swindon, Wilts.
Fall in love again as soon as possible — it may be superficial, but it works.

Lindsay Fraser, Northampton.
Write a long, beautiful, sad poem, telling the world your unhappy story. If it got published, it might help to cheer you up!

Ray Stiles (Mud)
I think you should try not to worry about it and go out and make new friends. Don't linger on the broken romance, make a big effort to find new friends. Who knows, you'll probably meet somebody better.

Sharon Mackenzie, Cambuslang, Lanarkshire.
The only real cure for a broken heart is time. But it's possible to speed up the cure by finding interesting things to do, so that time seems to pass more quickly.

Helen Boyd, Largs, Ayrshire.
The sea. Walking along the sands, or sitting quietly by myself, looking out over the water, always soothes me and makes me feel more philosophical about things. So does the rhythmic sound of the waves, and the beauty of a west coast sunset.

Diane Wilson, Huddersfield, Yorkshire.
The only time I was really heartbroken was when my old dog died, but we got a new puppy straight away. I know it sounds a bit hard, but we were so busy with the new puppy that we didn't have time to cry too much over the old dog, although we were very upset at the time.

Christine Compton, Salisbury, Wilts.
Just keep away from boys in future!

POP CROSSWORD SOLUTION

T		J	A	C	K	S	O	N		P	A	G	E
H	E	L	L	O		O		O		E		I	
R		O		H		L		N		I	S	L	E	Y
E		W		N		I		N		L		O		P
E			A	N	D	Y		A		S	T	E	V	E
D	A	N	N	Y		A		S		L			T
E		O			W	O	O	D		L	O	Y	E
G	R	E	E	N		N		L					
R		L				R	O	B		A	D	A	M
E		M			A		O		I		U	
E	N	G	L	I	S	H		I		B	E	C	A	U	D
S		O		C	I	A	N		B		N	
	R	O	C	K		T		Y		C	A	L	E
		D				G				Y	
B	R	I	A	N		B	L	A	C	K		L	A	N	E
A		E		A			R		E		E	
Y	E	S		N	O	D	D	Y		N	A	S	H

HEAD LINERS

A Jackie Special

YOU'VE asked for them! So here they are — the idols who've hit the headlines in the past year, for their looks, skill, determination and sheer ability to gain an admiring public!

Here's all the information on the kind of people they are; how they've achieved success, what they've done and what they want to do with their lives. So read on for everything you've always wanted to know!

John Conteh

JOHN CONTEH is 6 ft. tall, 12 st. 13 lbs, with a glistening body in the peak of condition — undeniably handsome, tough, dedicated and single-minded.

The boxing superstar from Liverpool was 24 on May 26. The fourth child of ten, he left school at 14, and he's boxed every evening since his father sent him to lessons at the age of 10, to keep him out of trouble!

John Conteh's earned himself a bit of a playboy reputation, though, with his cool self-assurance and his unashamed liking for the glamorous things in life. He's had a luxury house built in London's Hampstead. "I've made London my home and I love it," he says. He buys hand-made shoes and silk shirts as the fancy takes him, and has been known to order, in one week, six new suits at £150 each!

His interests range wide. He takes guitar lessons, watches films (goes in for war documentaries and cartoons) likes listening to soul, reggae and blues, and reads anything people tell him he should!

Nothing stops John Conteh. "I'm a positive thinker," he says. He also applies the rules of boxing to life. "Keep your head down and let nothing from the outside interfere with your target."

If success seems to have come easily, it's only because he's given himself to it, 100%. "There's nothing I won't do to get what I want," he explains. And that's how John Conteh's got so much of what he wants!

Michael Crawford

MICHAEL CRAWFORD'S the one who's taken 16 years to become an overnight sensation — he gets rediscovered with every new role!

He's 5 ft. 10½ ins. tall, weighing 9½ stone, with sandy brown hair and blue eyes. He was born in Salisbury, Wiltshire, on January 19, 1942, and spent most of his childhood in London and Kent, leaving school when he was 15.

Michael reckons that all in all he's had about 500 parts, including TV and radio, as an actor and singer!

His first London part was over 13 years ago. That was in something called "Come Blow Your Horn." Currently of course, "Billy" is the word that's been on everyone's lips!

Gradually, Michael Crawford's developing wider popular appeal, not only because of his success in musicals but also in TV, particularly with the hit comedy series "Some Mothers Do 'Ave 'Em!" where as the accident-prone Frank Spencer he's sailed unscathed through many stunts! People are always asking him whether the real Michael Crawford behaves like Frank Spencer — to which he answers emphatically, "No!"

His spare-time interests are reading (mostly paper-backs, anything from classics to detectives!), theatre (of course) and he also likes listening to pop records.

But more than anything, Michael Crawford's working hard to become accepted as a serious dramatic actor. And he's bound to make it with the next "discovery"!

Bjorn Borg

HIS father gave him a tennis racquet when he was nine, and he's never looked back since!

Swedish Bjorn Borg — 19 last June 6 — with a typically handsome Scandavian face and seemingly ice-c confidence, hit Wimbledon two ye ago, and as far as he's concerned, ten is his job and his life. He's got a straig forward approach to professio tennis — and enormous drawing pow as the girls who cheer him on and off courts agree!

But for a stubborn, tough, int national champion, Bjorn Borg lead surprisingly unexciting life off courts. Tennis comes before eve thing, so it's no late nights, no smoki no drinking — and "there's no way going to become involved with wom If I were emotionally tied to a girl, I'd finished as a top class tennis playe he says.

He's travelling constantly ten mon of the year, but when he's not playing tournaments he gets out to discos and loves eating in restaurants.

The films he likes best are cowboy war ones — preferably starring C Eastwood and Steve McQueen!

Long term ambitions? Bjorn's set tennis for several years yet, but h always had ideas about teaching g when the tennis scene's worn out him — or when he's worn out every else!

And when he does have time for t girl? "She must be honest; and, ab all, enthusiastic about tennis!"

Roddy McDowall

RODDY McDOWALL was a child s in the "Lassie" films when was five, and since then he's had o 80 films to his credit!

Many of them have been British, a in fact, it was the Academy Awa winning, "How Green Was My Valle that first made him a star. After th Hollywood kept making him offers couldn't resist!

5 ft. 10 in. with brown hair and brown eyes, London born, Roddy McDowall now lives near Central Park, New York. Films still figure largely in his life. His very favourite occupation is watching movies, and he can sit through two or three a day (the highest figure he ever reached was six!). He's a talented photographer himself, and has published his own photo-illustrated book.

He's appeared in four "Planet Of The Apes" films to date, and for each one his face is insured for £400,000 against damage from the make-up, which takes three hours to apply!

Roddy loses weight easily while "Planet" is being filmed. Because of the thick make-up, all he can have is liquids through a straw, and those have to be cold, as anything hot would melt the ape-mask!

Robin Nedwell

TV'S handsome, competent doctor, Dr Duncan Waring, is in reality intelligent, extroverted Robin Nedwell.

Born in 1946 in Birmingham, he lived in Cardiff from the age of four, and it was here that he started his acting career — working as general dogsbody with the Welsh Theatre Company, for nothing but the love of it!

In 1966 he went to the Central School of Speech and Drama in London, and was offered his first part in the "Doctor" series before he'd even finished!

After he'd filmed the first series, he got more varied experience — including arranging the fights for the film of Macbeth.

Fight arranging's quite a hobby with Robin. Sword fights fascinate him, and as he's really interested in Japanese culture, he's made a collection of Japanese swords.

All things Japanese interest him, in fact, including the women, though he says he certainly doesn't want to get married before he's 35. He's a happy bachelor, even doing his own housework, and his life of pubs and pals suits him fine!

He's also keen on reading science fiction, likes watching TV and prefers a game of darts and a chat with friends to extravagant nights out on the town. When it comes to acting, he admits he's not the dedicated type, but he'd like to try romantic parts. Otherwise, his main ambition is just to enjoy living!

Ben Murphy

AMERICAN BEN MURPHY bewitched the hearts of many when he became TV cowboy Thaddeus Jones. But in his real life, Ben leads a cosy bachelor existence in a small Hollywood flat, littered with books and sports equipment.

Born on March 6, 1942 (he's a Pisces!) in Arkansas, he drifted his way through more universities than he likes to remember, but eventually came out with two B.A. degrees!

He got into acting because he "felt the need to express himself." But I bet you couldn't spot him in his first film role — a one-line part in "The Graduate"!

He has little spare time, but whenever he does, it's taken up with tennis, playing guitar, reading, doing karate and ski-ing. He's a great fan of all sports, and likes travel, too. Another passion with him is health foods — he tries to eat only the "right" things. Even tea and coffee are out!

Ben's always learning, seeks inner peace, and is also looking for someone to love! Chief quality in any girl for him must be honesty, and it's important she's a very positive type.

Well, the 5 ft. 11 in. of blonde, blue-eyed heart-throb shouldn't find it difficult to get someone to love him!

Robert Redford

ROBERT REDFORD'S everybody's idea of rugged masculinity — and the private life of the 38-year-old Californian star bears out the legend.

He says he's been a rebel since his childhood, never bright at school, he went for art and sports and thought of becoming a baseball player when he left!

Instead, though, he took to painting. He left California, worked his way across the United States, often hitching and living very rough indeed. Then on to Europe — sketching in Paris — and over to Britain where he got as far as Scotland. He returned to the States depressed and unsettled, till he met Lola, the 17-year-old Mormon girl he married and has lived happily with for the last 17 years!

Between films, he and his family (there are three children now, Shauna, Jamie and Amy) take off and wander round Greece, Crete and the Aegean Islands. He's also built his own house, a retreat 8,000 ft. up in the mountains of Utah. There, in natural, rugged, unspoiled surroundings, Robert Redford can be himself. By nature he's aloof, controlled and completely independent. He loves to ride horses, ski and go off trekking and camping for weeks.

He doesn't neglect filming though: most recently he's made "The Way We Were," "The Great Gatsby," and "The Great Waldo Pepper." So it seems, whatever he does, Robert Redford's a winner!

Telly Savalas

CHEEKY, sarcastic Detective Lt. Theo Kojak's won everybody's heart. And Telly Savalas (the name's short for 'Aristotle'!) is himself natural, single-minded and involved a lot in public affairs.

Born in New York on January 21, he grew up in a large lively family and went to school in Connecticut and Long Island. He spent three years in the American army in the second world war, then went to Columbia University and got a degree in psychology. Then he worked for the Information Service of the State Department.

He started acting, when he couldn't find an actor for a theatrical agent who wanted a special European accent. Telly went to the audition and to his astonishment, got the part!

Telly Savalas had only appeared in three television shows when he was signed up for a role in the film "Birdman of Alacatraz." For that, he was nominated for an Academy Award as the best supporting actor of the year!

6ft. 1 in. Telly Savalas, brown-eyed and weighing 14 st. 4 lbs., is a busy man between films and television. He plays golf and travels the world, often on goodwill missions on behalf of the State Department. He's kept almost as busy as Kojak!

YOUR LIFE IS IN YOUR HANDS

Heart line

Life line

Fate line

WILL I be lucky? What kind of romance will I have? Will I travel?

The answers to all these questions and many more are in your hand.

So read on to discover the secrets of your personality. We reveal the luck, health, happiness and romance in your life — through the mystic art of palmistry.

HEARTLINE —
Tells you most about your love life.

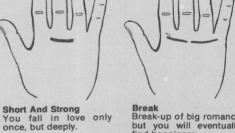

Starting Under First Finger
Luck in love will be yours.

Starting Under Middle Finger
You must try to be less selfish towards those you love!

Normal Length And Curved
You have a warm, pleasing, romantic nature.

Short And Strong
You fall in love only once, but deeply.

Break
Break-up of big romance but you will eventually find happiness.

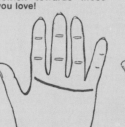

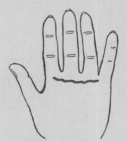

Starting High Up On Base Of Index Finger
A short romance and sudden marriage.

Long And Curving
You like to put your boy-friends on a pedestal.

Normal Length And Curved Upwards.
You're willing to sacrifice everything for love.

Wavy
You're a fickle, flirt-atious girl!

Star
Happy marriage.

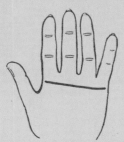

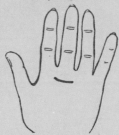

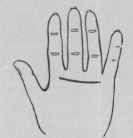

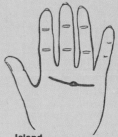

Starting Between Index And Middle Fingers
You give your heart away without thinking!

Long And Straight
Your heart controls your head.

Short And Thin
You have little interest in romance.

Faint
You have a faint heart in romantic matters!

Island
An unhappy love affair!

Continued overleaf

54

YOUR LIFE IS IN YOUR HANDS

LIFE LINE —
Health, length of life, events affecting health and life.

Long and Clearly Marked
Good health, vitality, normal life span.

Short But Strong
Vitality, good chance of normal life span.

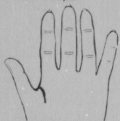

Short And Weak
Another person will control your life!

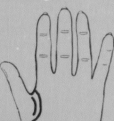

Doubled
A double dose of good health! A very lucky sign.

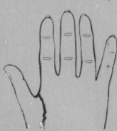

Weak and Wavy
Health problems and many changes in your life!

Swooping
Strong health.

Cramped
You're timid and shy especially in love!

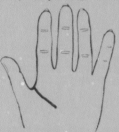

Sloping Towards Centre Of Palm
You will travel a great deal during your life.

Chained
Many emotional problems! But you'll never be bored, you love adventure in life.

Break
Sudden change in life.

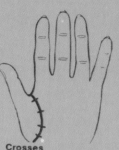

Crosses
Worries, but if the line is strong you are self-reliant and able to overcome setbacks.

Star
Crisis

FATE LINE-
The effect that other people and events have on shaping the course of your life — your destiny.

Strong And Deep
You'll have a very secure life with no money worries and you will make your name at whatever you choose to do. Fate will be kind to you.

Joined To Life Line At Start
To achieve what you desire in life you'll have to make many sacrifices at the beginning, but eventually you will have a very successful life.

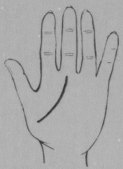

Starting On The Fleshy Pad Of The Thumb
Relatives will help you a great deal in reaching your goals in life.

Starting At The Heel Of The Palm
Destiny will bring you before the public. You will be a famous personality with a large following!

Breaks
Every break is a change of career or a big change in your life, such as emigration, a money windfall.

Branch From Fate Line To Heel Of Palm
A romance will influence your destiny for good or ill.

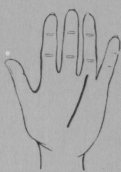

Fate Line Rising To Ring Finger
Success in your chosen career, probably something artistic.

Rising To Index Finger
Your career will place you in authority over others.

Rising To Little Finger
A career in some field of communication.

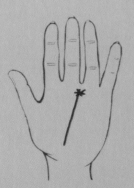

Star
Fame will come to you.

A Cathy & Claire Special on having that certain something....

REAL charm is a natural quality no-one can ignore, and some people can charm their way through life. People flock round them, and good fortune seems to come their way, almost as though they carry some sort of magic secret wherever they go.

Research has proved, for instance, that good-looking, charming children are more likely to do better at school than the ordinary and not-so-appealing kids.

The charmers may not be cleverer or more hardworking, it's just that they get more attention and more favoured treatment from teachers and examiners.

It seems awfully unfair, but people aren't even aware of favouring the charmed ones. It's just an automatic reaction.

Linda, aged 16, is one of the specially charmed people. All the boys fall for her, even though she's not always the most stunning girl at the party.

All the neighbours say what a lovely girl she is, although she's no more lovely than most girls.

She wasn't specially brilliant at school, yet she's just walked into a super job as P.A. to the boss of a small record company, where she was picked out from hundreds of applicants.

"I don't know why I got the job," she says modestly, "I think I'm very lucky that things usually seem to work out well for me. I must have been born under the right star, or something."

In fact, she was just born to be a charmer, and one of the ingredients of real charm is to be modest and natural with it.

People with natural charm are always noticed in a crowd. They seem to have some inner quality which shines out and spreads confidence.

People are magnetised by them and even insincere charm-power can be devastating till you see through it. How many women in history, and out of it, have given away fortunes to men who charmed them out of every penny?

BUT insincere charm can be very sickly indeed.

The cute kids who use insincere charm to get their own way are simply transparently calculating. You might be taken in by them at first, but you'll soon see through the act and realise that they're using their charm for selfish motives.

Sue, sixteen years old from Leeds, laughs when she recalls her early schooldays. At eight years old she had an angelic face, golden locks and large, beautiful blue eyes.

"I knew I was teacher's favourite," she says. "I knew how to get round grown-ups just with a smile. Well, I got rather fat when I was twelve and had my hair chopped off, and I found my charm didn't work on people any more.

"I guess it was a bit of a shock. I became very self-conscious because I felt I'd grown ugly and people didn't like me any more.

"It made me realise you can't go through life relying on being charming if you're not willing to put in the same work and effort as other people."

In fact, Sue's still very charming, it's just that she's stopped using her charm as a weapon. She realises that she is a far happier and more genuine person as a result.

If you're thinking you've missed out on all this beautiful charm, you can begin right now. Everyone has charm, it's just that most people don't develop it.

It has nothing to do with good looks, although good looking people find it easier to be charming because they usually have extra self-confidence.

Charm, you see, is really an attitude to life. If you feel good in yourself, you can be good to others.

The first important thing is to genuinely like other people, and take a real interest in what they are saying.

If you're always too busy worrying about the impression you are making on others, you can't be charming.

If you are suspicious and untrusting you can't be charming.

So charm begins by having sympathy for other people and being genuinely warm-hearted and open-natured.

SHYNESS is often an obstacle to charm.

Shy Sal envies the charmers and would like to be like them. She wants to talk and be friendly, but finds herself tongue-tied. She'd like to give a warm, sunny smile, but can't bring herself to commit herself for fear of being snubbed.

The will is there, and if Sal could control her shyness, she could be a real charmer.

It takes time and practice to overcome shyness, and the best thing to do is to practise little by little. Talk to people in shops and bus queues, talk to lonely old people and gradually build up to joining a club and getting on with boys and girls of your own age.

It's well-known that the less practice at meeting people you have, the more difficult it is to become at ease with people. And remember that if you really like people and want to get on with them, you'll manage it in the end.

Awkwardness in conversation is another problem. When you meet someone new you can make them feel at ease by talking about yourself and letting them know what sort of person you are. Then they will relax and begin to thaw through.

People with charm usually have to go more than half-way towards meeting others.

You don't have to make brilliant conversation to get along with people.

Even if you smile sweetly and embark on a boring description of the weather or the terrible 157A bus service, at least you're showing warmth and friendship, and others can't help responding.

The charming person has to have a strong enough personality to be able to cut across barriers of shyness and uncertainty.

A simple thing like a smile works wonders. Haven't you ever noticed that when someone smiles at you, it's almost impossible not to smile back?

Even when you're in a grumpy mood and you're walking down the street with a scowl on your face. Then a friend breezes up and gives you a glowing smile, and you suddenly find, quite without realising it, that you're grinning like a Cheshire cat.

So smiles and laughter are infectious and set a happy mood. **The charmers, above all, make others feel happy and at ease.**

MANY people cover their shyness by acting cool and casual. Instead of trying to overcome shyness they make it worse by refusing to admit it even to themselves and building up barriers between themselves and the rest of the world.

Wendy, aged 15, admitted being cool in self-defence against her shyness.

"I'm getting a bit better now," she said, "but a year ago I'd snub people at any opportunity. When someone spoke to me and tried to be friendly, I'd be as cool and off-hand as I could, just to show them that *I* was OK, and I didn't need *them*.

"Being honest, I was just petrified of being made to look foolish, in case I'd start stammering or blushing or something.

"So I pretended I didn't want friendship. Looking back I'm sure I hurt people often, specially shy people who needed courage to make the first move to be friendly."

Wendy discovered the secret of charm for herself, and she needed a lot of courage to drop her cool couldn't-care-less-act and show her real feelings for people.

The charmers are people who can show warm feelings towards others without fear of losing face.

Charmers have a good effect on other people. They never make people feel small or embarrassed. This means being easy-going and tactful, considering the other person's feelings and being sensitive to their moods.

Of course, natural courtesy and politeness are part of charm, but charm is often confused with social etiquette.

The rich young ladies who go to Charm Schools learn how to behave at a cocktail party, how to make small-talk at the races, and which cutlery to use for which course at a banquet. But that's not charm! You could be a charmless beast and still be an angel at a wedding party or a school open day!

Charm isn't an act. It's a way of life. We all have the natural charm there, and if we make a habit of using it more, we'd have lots more fun.

You can't learn it in a charm school; you just have to practise it in your everyday life. Don't go overboard on the fatal charm all at once, though. People won't know what's hit them!

Are you a real charmer?

CLEVER CLOTHES

PLANNING a wardrobe's a difficult job. You can end up with all sorts of colours that don't match and some things that you can't wear at all because they don't go with anything you've got!

We've divided you up into two groups . . . the casual 'jeans' look for those of you who love wearing trousers day and night and the dressier look for people who prefer skirts and dresses. There's a day-time look for each group and a night-time look, so there's something for everyone.

DAY-TIME THE DRESSED-UP LOOK

Some girls like to wear skirts and dresses, others have to for work where trousers may not be allowed. The secret of a useful 'everyday' wardrobe is simple . . . make sure that the basic colour is a plain, fairly dark one. You can always brighten it up with coloured shirts, jumpers and scarves so choose something like black, brown, dark green or the grey we've chosen here.

Our day-time wardrobe consists of a grey suit with A-line skirt, which is the most flattering kind for most shapes. The jacket is simple, too, shaped at the waist and single-breasted.

The cotton shirt is in a plain colour and has a tailored collar and long sleeves. The total look is smart without being over-dressed, it will

take you anywhere and will last for ages, especially if you save up for a suit in good material that will wear — jersey is excellent as it keeps its shape and lasts for ages.

Stage two shows a really useful wrapover cardigan, that's warm and flattering for most shapes and can be worn indoors or out on warmer days. It's really a second sort of jacket, not just a cardigan that needs another jacket over the top.

Next comes a pinafore in the same colour as the skirt and jacket. Wear it with the jacket on top and the shirt underneath and you've got a completely different look. We chose a simple v-necked style rather than a scoop neck, v-necks are much more versatile.

When it's chilly you can pop on a polo-neck under the pinafore or the suit, or under the cardigan.

Accessories like bags, belts and shoes should be plain, we chose black to go with the grey but choose brown ones if your basic colours are brown or green.

Scarves can be plain or patterned . . . it's nice to have some of each so you can ring the changes. Buy different shapes, too, some long and thin, some square so they all look different.

LEVER YOU!

Jeans don't always have to be ragged and tatty, you know. We've chosen a very simple pair for our casual look, with two pockets and zip-up front. They're slightly flared and you can make them look how you want, very casual or dressier with smocks or jackets.

The first, everyday look we chose is made up from the jeans, plus a bright, plain shirt and a plain, round-necked navy wool jumper with long sleeves.

Buying a jacket the same colour as the jeans is a great idea, like this button-up bomber jacket which is warm but very casual. Pop it on over a sleeveless T-shirt like this scoop-necked one.

For a dressier look you could pop on a smock over a shirt, great for disguising unwanted layers around your hips and bottom! Buy a plain smock so you can brighten it up with patterned shirts, scarves etc.

The complete look is simple and very, very useful. Just jacket, jeans and a plain shirt, not at all fussy, but not tatty either.

Accessories should be simple . . . a pair of laced-up shoes and matching bag were our choice, plus one matching scarf and one other patterned.

The jeans look seems to have got itself a bad name, but there's no reason why you should keep it going by looking scruffy in yours.

Take care with accessories and always make sure that your clothes are clean with the right number of buttons, etc. and absolutely no hems hanging down!

NIGHT-TIME ALL DRESSED UP

Night time's always difficult when it comes to clothes, especially if you go to a regular club or disco every week. It's impossible to buy different things so how can you make what you've got go further?

Easy, invest in a really plain dress like this blue one that we've chosen. It's straight, but not too tight, sleeveless with a round neck that isn't plunging and isn't too high, either.

Now, the obvious thing to do next is to pop on a really super blouse underneath . . . this one's got a tie-neck and wide, floaty sleeves. These will cover up any extra flab on upper arms, should you have any!

Then there's always the over-shirt like this

one that's got long sleeves and is nipped in at the waist. It can serve as a sort of evening jacket, too, to save you carting along a thick coat that doesn't go with the dress. Choose your colours carefully, though, plain colours will look smartest together.

A floaty smock looks great over the dress, too, and can disguise figure faults. This one's really floaty with short, wide sleeves and a round neck . . . remember it should be high enough to cover the top of the dress, though, otherwise it will all look awful!

Ring the changes with different evening accessories, black shoes and bag are best and you'll probably find that cheap 'silver' jewellery looks much nicer than cheap 'gold', so go for stainless steel bangles and chokers.

Buy scarves in all sorts of colours to tie round your neck, long silky ones look great. Invest in a shawl, too, to pop round your shoulders when evenings are chilly!

Sometimes you just can't get away with wearing your jeans to everything and you feel you have to try and dress up! No point in putting on a dress if you're going to feel silly in it, so invest in a really good pair of black trousers. Black's a flattering colour for heavyweights, too, so they're just right for everyone.

Grey and black look great, so we chose a soft grey bomber jacket in silky material with long sleeves. Put a shirt underneath or just wear it on its own, zipped up of course!

Really dressy is a super jacket, like this sequinned one we found, black velvet would be great, too. Buy a plain grey sleeveless T-shirt to go underneath, sew sequins on it one week if you want, your name on it the next.

Same jacket and trousers again, but this time with a plain shirt, with ties at the waist . . . just hang up your jacket when you're ready to dance!

Smocks are great for evening, in soft materials with wide sleeves. Make sure they're not so see-through that your bra shows through, though, and remember that a flesh-coloured bra won't be half as noticeable as a white one.

If you're going to a disco where they might have those ultra-violet lights that pick out everything white, don't wear knickers with a white lace trim if there's the slightest possibility of it being seen and check for white labels on the insides of things that might look very odd when picked out by those lights!

Black shoes and bags are best with black trousers, of course, and choose wide, shiny belts and pretty scarves to cheer everything up!

We haven't given you prices (because they change so quickly) or manufacturers' names as they can't guarantee that particular clothes will be in your area at the time you're reading this.

But these are the looks to aim for, so follow our fashion pages every week in Jackie and have fun shopping around!

NIGHT-TIME THE TROUSERS LOOK

what's your nature?

WHY does a storm excite some people, and frighten or depress others? Well, even without realising it, we all respond to nature, and the way in which we respond reveals a lot about our personality.

So study each of our illustrations carefully and decide which statement is closest to the way you feel. Then count up your score and turn to the conclusions to find out the hidden personality secrets you've revealed!

1. A light rain in the forest.
a) It makes you want to run barefoot in the grass.
c) You hope it stops soon so you can plan a picnic.
b) You want to walk beneath the dripping trees with the boy you love.
d) It's fabulous to stay at home with a good book.

2. Sunset on a south sea island.
a) You'd like to lie in the sand and let the surf lap over you.
d) You excitedly explore your surroundings.
c) You fall asleep lulled by the soft tropical breeze.
b) A suntanned boy plays a song specially written for you on his guitar.

3. Venice in the fog.
c) It depresses you and you imagine the city is closing in on you.
a) You feel a tremendous sense of excitement, mystery and suspense.
b) It is an ideal place to arrange a secret meeting with the boy you love.
d) You long to seek out all the most fascinating corners.

4. Storm over the city.
a) It makes you feel totally exhilarated.
b) You rush into the comfort of your boyfriend's arms.
d) You're glad because it will clear away the smog.
c) What a drag! All that rain.

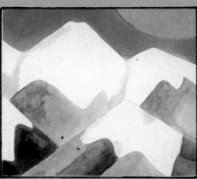

5. The sun shining on snow-covered mountains.
a) You cover your body with freshly fallen snow.
c) You feel bored.
b) You're enchanted and dazzled.
d) You take a brisk walk.

6. The moon over a desert oasis.
c) It makes you sleepy.
d) You feel like writing the most beautiful love poem ever.
b) A handsome sheik passes by and carries you off on his camel!
a) You lie down on the sand and bathe in the moon's rays.

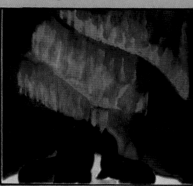

7. Light shining on the North Pole.
a) You shiver — not from cold but from intense excitement.
b) You feel amazed to be actually there.
d) You're interested in the reflection of the light on snow.
c) It doesn't particularly affect you.

CONCLUSIONS

If you had mostly (a): You have a full appreciation of nature. You are alive, receptive and gifted with a passionate temperament. In the city, you can't stand the restrictions of open spaces, fresh air and lush country of the country. You like to feel at one with nature because it frees you from everyday cares and allows you to be totally yourself.

If you had mostly (b): You are a serious girl with profound views on life. You are sensitive and delicate. You don't like to be alone and you have a constant need for company, for someone to reassure you. You love to be petted and caressed. You're inclined to dream, to use your imagination and you tend to try to escape from the real world.

If you had mostly (c): You don't enjoy life to the fullest, and tend to be narrow, poetic in your outlook. You hate flights of fantasy. You don't see how it will materially benefit you. If you free yourself from this attitude, you'll find your life more complete.

If you had mostly (d): You are gifted with acute powers of observation and with you, reason and facts come before imagination and emotion. But you also look deeply into superficiality and always exploring your own motives and judging them. In this way you sacrifice acting impulsively on a whim, but every sensation you do experience makes a lasting impression on you.

DOWN ON

IT'S the sort of scene you've probably dreamed about. It's springtime, the sun's beating down, and you're alone in the country — alone, that is, except for the Bay City Rollers!

It all happened earlier this year when the Rollers were staying at a health farm deep in the heart of Hampshire. They came up to London for a day to record a spot for for "Top Of The Pops," and while I was chatting to them in their dressing room, they invited me to go down and visit them at the farm.

As you probably know, only four of the five members of the group went to the health farm. Les decided instead to go home to Edinburgh — for a very special reason!

"I'm taking flying lessons!" he told me. "I went down to see the people at Edinburgh Flying Club, and they've agreed to give me lessons. I've to go down to Edinburgh Airport tomorrow. I can't wait!

"I really want to learn to fly a helicopter, because they're more useful than planes. They can take off and land anywhere. But it takes ages to qualify as a pilot!"

In fact, Les turned out to have a natural flair for flying, and within a few months he was able to act as pilot for the rest of the group, and fly them from one town to another in the small private plane you see in the photo!

Although Les with his usual endless supply of energy, was spending his holiday racing about all over the place, the rest of the group were taking things much more quietly.

They told me that the health farm was the perfect place for them to relax and recover, away from the stresses and strains of the pop world. And when I arrived there the next morning, it was easy to see why they liked it!

To get to the farm itself, you have to turn off the road and drive for what seems miles up a drive which winds through thick woods. Then, just as you think you're never going to reach it, you turn a corner, and suddenly, there it is — a large, rambling building, with beautifully kept lawns leading down to a boating lake.

Driving round the edge of the lake, David the photographer, who'd given me a lift down to the farm, drove into the car park and parked our Mini between a Daimler and a Rolls Royce!

Then we went inside the building, where the receptionist told us to go straight up to the boys' bedrooms. They turned out to be right at the other end of the building, through a door marked "Men's Treatments" (ladies go through "Women's Treatments"!) which led into a corridor of rooms, all containing strange-looking machines that looked suspiciously like instruments of torture!

Then it was up a flight of stairs, past the sauna baths and the beauty salon, until at last we arrived at rooms 21 and 22 — the Rollers' bedrooms!

JUST at that moment, th first door opened, an Derek looked out, smilin in his usual friendly wa

"Hello there," he said, "I thought I hear voices. Come on in!"

Inside the room, I discovered Er kneeling on the floor, carefully ironing pair of jeans.

"Hi," he said. "You've come just in tin for lunch. We'll go down as soon as I'v finished this. I won't be long!"

While I was waiting, I sat down on one the white-covered twin beds and looke round the room. It was big and airy with colour T V playing silently in one corne

"We're sharing this room," Derek sai "and Alan and Woody are in the room ne door."

Just then, right on cue, Alan and Woo appeared. Like the others, they we dressed in the health far "uniform" — very smart, royal bl tracksuits.

They told me that, that afternoo everyone but Woody intended to horse-riding.

"As you know, I'm allergic to horses," told me. "They bring me out in a rash! It' real shame, because I love horse ridin But it's just not worth it. I might enjoy it the time, but I suffer for ages afterwards

Instead, Woody was intending to out a very exotic skin treatment that he seen advertised on the clinic's noti board.

"It's supposed to vacuum your skin a deep cleanse your pores — or somethi like that!" he laughed. "So you wo recognise me when I come back, I'll be sparkling and clean!"

By this time, Eric had finished ironing, so we all trooped down to t dining room for a lunch of deliciou healthy salads.

As we ate, Eric and Woody took gr delight in leaning over the table and telli us in whispers that the man at the ne table was a millionaire, and the old la sitting by the window in dressing go and slippers was a duchess!

AFTER lunch, the boys chang into jeans, and saying goo bye to Woody, everyone pi into our car and we set to the stables, which were over the oth side of the lake.

"The man who runs the stables is friend of ours," Alan told me. "He used run our local riding stable in Edinbur before he moved down here."

THE FARM...

That's me and Pampiano in the foreground!

At the stables, the stable boy, John introduced us to our horses. Mine was a [ni]ce quiet one (thank goodness!) called [Pa]mpiano, Derek and Alan were riding [da]rk brown horses called Florinda and [Se]norita, and Eric was riding what he said [wa]s "the best horse of the lot," a very [fri]sky grey called The Pickler.

When I remarked that these were quite [un]common names, Eric explained that [th]at was because these were no ordinary [ho]rses!

"They're all very valuable," he told me, [b]ecause they've been specially trained as [po]lo ponies. You'll soon discover that for [yo]urself, actually. Be careful when you [pu]ll your horse up, because they're used [to] stopping dead in the middle of polo [m]atches. If you're not careful, you find [yo]urself bumping all over the place!"

As we rode out into the field, Derek told [m]e that they often held polo matches at [th]e stables.

"They're holding one this evening in [fa]ct," he said. "We might come down to [w]atch!"

"We also have lots of shows here," [a]dded John, who'd come out to keep an [ey]e on us! "On average, we have about [th]ree a week. And we get all sorts of [fa]mous people coming down for the [sh]ows — Princess Anne and Mark [P]hillips, for instance!"

The Rollers decided to ride down to the [l]ake, so the five of us set off together down [t]he track, with poor old David following on [f]oot!

The boys were all good riders, but out of [t]he three, Alan seemed to be the most [e]xperienced.

"I've been riding for years now," he told [m]e. "I used to look after the horses at our [l]ocal dairy in Edinburgh, and I also used to [g]o up to the common and ride the ponies [t]hat belonged to some gipsies who lived [t]here.

"Of course, I don't have much time to go [r]iding these days, but I still love horses."

Derek meanwhile, was impatient to let [h]is pony canter. He obviously liked riding [f]ast! When I suggested he should have [b]een a cowboy instead of a pop star, he [l]aughed and agreed.

"I would have loved to have seen the [W]ild West as it was in the olden days," he [t]old me. "I love cowboy films. It must have [b]een a great life!"

Eric, on the other hand, had ambitions [t]o be a show jumper.

"I've done a bit of jumping," he said, "but I haven't had much time to practise. At one point, I was intending to buy myself a horse that I could jump, but I haven't had a chance to so far.

"Still, I'll maybe get round to it sometime. I'd love to have my own horse."

At the lake, the boys decided to take their horses into the water for a paddle. Senorita and Florinda splashed in happily, but The Pickler wasn't so sure. First of all, he wouldn't go in the water, and then, once Eric had persuaded him to go in, he wouldn't come out again!

Finally, everyone arrived safely back on dry land and despite all the splashing about that had been going on, nobody's jeans had even got damp.

"Now you know the real reason why we wear our trousers so short!" laughed Eric.

Going back through the woods towards the stables, Eric told me he was sorry we hadn't time for a longer ride.

"Sometimes we go off into the hills for two or three hours at a time," he told me. "You can ride right up to the top of the hill behind the farm. It's beautiful up there."

AT the stables, we put our horses back in their boxes, and then, waving goodbye to John, headed back up to the health farm.

At the door, we met Woody, all clean and glowing from his skin treatments!

"It was great!" he told us. "My skin feels really good."

The treatment also seemed to have given Woody an appetite!

"I'm starving!" he said. "Come on, let's go and have tea."

Tea consisted of slices of wholemeal bread and butter, a piece of the most delicious home-made fruit cake, and a choice of Indian or China tea —without sugar.

"That was a bit of a shock to us at first," said Alan, "because we all take sugar in our tea normally. But it's surprising how quickly you get used to the taste."

After tea, Derek went off to his daily yoga class, and Alan and Woody decided to go for a run in the woods. Eric, meanwhile, offered to show us round the games rooms.

First of all, he took us into the billiards room which was in a separate building across the drive.

"We spend a lot of time in here," he said. "We're getting quite good at it now. The other night, we got so involved in the game

that we forgot what time it was. And when we went back over to the main building, we discovered they'd locked us out!

"We'd to stand and bang on the door until someone came to let us in!"

Along the back wall of the billiards room was an amazing set of photos of stars who'd spent some time at the health farm. There were hundreds of film, T V and pop stars there — and every single photo had a signed message written on it, thanking the staff of the health farm for their help.

"We're going to get a photo of us and get it put on the wall as well," said Eric. "That'll be great, won't it?"

Then he took us upstairs to the exercise room which contained things like weight-lifting equipment, medicine balls and two cycling machines.

I had a go on one of the cycling machines but I have to admit, I didn't get very far! After pedalling for ages and ages, I'd still only managed to clock up three tenths of a mile on the metre!

"Oh, that's nothing," said Eric. "We have to do at least 10 miles a day!"

As we strolled back across the drive, I asked Eric what he liked most about the health farm.

"Well," he said, quite seriously, "the main thing is that it's relaxing!"

Well, it may have been the Rollers' idea of relaxing, but it certainly wasn't mine! By this time, I was beginning to feel I'd done quite enough for one day.

So, leaving the Rollers to make their plans for the evening, I headed back up to London — feeling quite relieved to be getting back to some peace and quiet!

IT'S OUR CHRISTI*

Princess Caroline of Monaco — because we're masochists — and because Alan fancies her!

Linda Lewis — because she's a super, fun, bubbly person — and because Alan fancies her!

Fanny Craddock — So she could do all the cooking, of course.

Princess Anne — Just to add a bit of class — and to make sure her brothers came along, too.

Pan's People — Well, we have to have some girls. And it would be nice to see them as they used to be on Top of the Pops.

Mae West — Because she's so witty and dynamic. And because she'd be able to tell us all the secrets of Hollywood in the Thirties . . .

John Curry — Who better to break the ice at a party?

Lee Majors — Because Dorothy fancies him — and she wants to see if he's really bionic . . .

Bing Crosby — Did you know that he's sold one million copies of "White Christmas?". It'd be nice if he could do it one more time just for us.

Jack Nicholson — Because we've always wanted to get our hands on an Oscar — and an Oscar winner!

Bryan Ferry — Because Nina's met him twice at parties before and she's hoping it'll be third time lucky!

Muhammad Ali — Well, we have to have a bouncer, and who better to get rid of unwanted gate-crashers?

Bianca Jagger — Alison would invite her, then tell Mohammed Ali she wasn't invited, so he'd throw her out.

Telly Savalas — Mary reckons he could provide the other blokes there with a lesson in how to treat a lady. Also, she fancies older men . . .

Stavros — He could cook delicious real American hamburgers for us. And Mary thinks he's cute and cuddly . . .

Gordon Jackson (Mr Hudson in "Upstairs, Downstairs") — Everyone in here's too lazy to go round all the other guests with crisps and peanuts and drinks and things . . .

Prince Andrew — Alison and Sandy agreed that if one of them gets off with Prince Charles, the other can chat up his young brother.

Tom Baker (Dr. Who) — If the party got boring, or if too many people turned up, he could whisk the bores and the extras to a different time zone where they couldn't bother us any more . . .

IS PARTY!

And, as you can see, we've invited all (well, almost all) our favourite people. Our reasons for inviting them are all very personal (and very different!) and we didn't all agree on some of them! But, after a lot of argue . . . em . . . discussion, we finally decided that these guests would make any party go with a swing . . .

Leonard Nimoy (Mr Spock of Star Trek) — He can try the Vulcan mind probe on us any time!

Vincent Price — If things look like getting too hot, he can always chill our spines!

Robert Shaw (Captain Quint in "Jaws") — Can you imagine the size of turkey we'd need to feed all the people at this party? Quint's the only guy who'd dare take it on! Maybe they could film it and call it "Gobble" . . .

Paul Newman — Because we all want to stand and gaze into those incredibly blue, blue eyes . . .

Prince Charles — Because we all reckon that if he could only see us and talk to us, he'd fall instantly in love with us and then we could get to be Queen. Also, we all (at least, Alison and Sandy) think he's lovely!

Paul McCartney — Because he's lovely and everyone except Cheryl fancies him like mad, so while they were all chatting him up, Cheryl would be free to work on Prince Charles.

Dad's Army — We think they're all sweet (especially Godfrey) and since Mary fancies older men, there should be plenty here for her . . .

Les McKeown, Midge Ure of Slik, Yan from Kenny — To see if all three get on as well as the groups say they do. And if the record player broke down, we wouldn't be short of music.

The rest of the Rollers and Slik — Well, it wouldn't be a party without them, would it?

Brian May of Queen — Because Una, one of our artists, says she won't come unless he's there.

Mike Yarwood — In case nobody else turns up!

Mick Robertson — He's super and he's got such a fantastic voice. Jenny thinks it would be nice to have a quiet conversation with him (preferably in the broom cupboard) when she didn't feel like dancing.

Mick Jagger — So Alison could take him on a guided tour of the office buildings — including the filing cabinets —

Elton John — Because he's the star of any party — and he could bring along all his famous friends. We wouldn't mind a few extra people . . .

Robert Redford — Because . . . well, just because he's Robert Redford!

The Wombles — Everyone else is too lazy to clear all the mess up afterwards.

Fred Astaire — Because he's the best dancing partner anyone could possibly have!

HAVE YOU GOT WHAT IT TAKES?

WELL, have you? Do boys stop and stare when you bombshell by and generally stampede to get you under the mistletoe? If not, why not? Perhaps you're the original Ice-Maiden, all snowed-up inside, freezing them out, and leaving a trail of broken hearts behind you? To find out exactly what kind of appeal YOU have, answer our fun quiz and we'll tell you just how with it (or without it!) you are.

1. You're at a party and there are lots of lovely males around. What's your first reaction?
(a) Super! Which one shall I have first?
(c) That one over there looks nice.
(b) You fancy one in particular, but you aren't going to let him know it.
(d) So what?

2. Your long-lost cousin traps you under the mistletoe. He's very good looking. What would you do?
(b) Kiss him of course, but not by any means passionately.
(d) Give him a cousinly peck on the cheek.
(c) Keep still and let him do the kissing.
(a) Show him just how much you've learned about kissing!

3. What do you think about kissing in general?
(a) It's the best thing since nail varnish!
(c) Not sure yet — you'll have to get some more practice in!
(d) It has to be over-rated.
(b) Lovely — with the one and only boy for you.

4. How do boys usually react to you?
(b) They're very protective towards you.
(c) They don't know quite what to make of you.
(d) They're a tiny bit frightened of you.
(a) They hang about making suggestive suggestions!

5. You see that special boy walking along the street and you feel —
(b) amazingly, crazily, happy,
(d) all warm inside,
(a) like you're tingling from top to toe,
(c) half thrilled, half afraid.

6. A gang of workmen start to whistle at you. How do you feel?
(c) It depends on the workmen!
(d) Annoyed.
(b) A bit embarrassed.
(a) Delighted! At least they've noticed you.

7. What's most likely to be your favourite party outfit?
(b) A long floaty feminine dress.
(c) Something bright and beautiful.
(a) A figure hugging T-shirt dress in soft velour or velvet.
(d) An elegant and classic dress with a high neck and long sleeves.

8. Given the chance, who would you most like to change places with?
(c) Linda McCartney.
(a) Bianca Jagger
(b) Marie Osmond.
(d) Angie Bowie.

9. What's your favourite party game?
(a) Postman's knock.
(b) Sardines.
(c) Murder-in-the-dark.
(d) You don't have one. You think they're a bit silly actually.

10. What's the nicest thing he could possibly say to you?
(c) You're the most beautiful thing that ever happened to me.
(b) Marry me?
(d) I only want you for your mind!
(a) I think you're the sexiest thing on two legs!

11. What's your favourite bath routine?
(d) A sparkling shower and rub down with cologne.
(b) Lots of bubbles — and "Jackie" to read.
(a) A long, hot steam, with amber oil.
(c) A sauna.

12. What do you really think of boys. Are they —
(a) a lot of fun,
(c) some pleasure, some pain,
(d) a challenge,
(b) the ones who wear trousers *all* the time?

13. When he looks at your for the very first time, what's he most likely to notice?
(b) Your face.
(d) Your eyes.
(c) Your general expression.
(a) Your figure.

14. The lights go out at a party and suddenly someone grabs you! Do you —
(a) grab him right back,
(d) deliver a neat karate chop,
(b) scream (then giggle),
(c) just plain scream?

15. How much energy do you have?
(c) If you're happy, you've got tons; if not, none!
(a) You're always bubbling over with it.
(b) You mostly seem to have it when you need it.
(d) Basically, you're a bit lazy really.

QUIZ CONCLUSIONS ►

MOSTLY A

You've got it, all right! Tons of it – there's no doubt about it! Wherever there's fun to be had, you're generally there, too. Boys find your bubbling nature truly irresistible and usually they don't put up much resistance! Nor do you, if he's as easy-going and nice-to-be-near as you are yourself. But you can run into trouble when some boy mistakes your freewheeling attitude for something more serious.

You have to know how to say No, and nicely, without him thinking you really mean Yes! It's best to make it quite clear where your heart really is, as you're the kind of girl they used to fight duels over - and they could be back in fashion! So be very careful where you flutter your eyelashes - or you could be fighting them off on the doorstep!

MOSTLY B

Warm, cosy and lovable, that's you! You're everybody's pet person. You have the kind of appeal that makes a boy think about firesides and slippers and apple-pies. It might sound very old-fashioned, but get him as relaxed as that and you've got him well and truly hooked! You're the sort of girl who makes him feel comfortable and protective. He'll want to look after you almost from the start. You stand for all the nicest things about being a girl. He loves you because you're deeply romantic and truly affectionate, because you care about people, about animals, and most of all, about him. And so he should, he's a lucky guy! Just make certain he's the right one, and you have the best chance of all of living happily ever after!

MOSTLY C

Completely unpredictable, changeable as the ocean, broodingly moody and, occasionally, even mean – that's what they say about you! Boys find you absolutely fascinating because they haven't the faintest idea what you're really like. (Often, you haven't either, but that's your secret charm.) You're a mystery, even to yourself.

If you say Yes today, it's likely to be No by tomorrow! You don't mean to be maddening; you just can't help it! Your feelings seem to go up and down like a yo-yo, and you never know whether the day will end in smiles or tears. Sometimes it's a bit difficult for you to know whether you really love or trust someone, but whether you're going to have the chance sooner or later, because you can't string him along forever!

MOSTLY D

Ice-cold princess, that's you! You have the enviable ability to scare the fellas stiff whenever you feel like it and only the bravest and best will take on the challenge. It'll be well worth it when someone does, though, because, although there's precious little sign of it on the surface, there's fire beneath that ice! The really intelligent ones (and that's the only kind that interest you) will bring their own ice-pick!

You have the kind of attraction that enslaves forever; it's simply the amazing allure of the unobtainable! But sometimes, you're the one who misses out because, really, you actually want to be obtained!

So try to let a little of that hidden fire into your eyes and, show some more warmth and behave less like the Snow Queen. It could have interesting results!

20 WAYS TO BE IRRESISTIBLE

1. Always look as if something wonderful is about to happen, and with any luck — it will.

2. Go out with a price ticket attached to the back of your coat or jacket. Nobody will be able to resist telling you about it — and it's a great way to start a conversation, especially if you make the ticket a nice big price.

3. Be fun to be with. Sing in the rain, yodel in the snow; if nobody laughs with you, someone's sure to laugh at you.

4. Become very rich. A wallet full of twenty pound notes makes anyone irresistible.

5. Cultivate becoming one of those people who always seem to say and do exactly the right things at exactly the right times!

6. Sit by yourself in a corner or on a park bench looking lost and tearful. No boy can resist a damsel in distress, even in this day and age.

7. Use musk- based scents, which are derived from the musk glands some musk deer use to attract their mates. It's supposed to work on human males too, only you'd best not visit the zoo at mating time — you might be in for a few surprises!

8. Try to be nice to everyone, and not just the people you care about.

9. Look dark and mysterious — if not irresistible, you'll certainly be interesting.

10. Find out as much as you can about anything you can think of. At least you'll be able to impress everyone with your conversation and general knowledge.

11. Find something nice about everyone.

12. Take a party of boys to the Hampton Court Maze, and hide yourself in the middle. They won't be able to get away from you — however hard they try, they'll keep coming back!

13. Work in a sweet shop. Sooner or later, everyone falls for something soft and sweet.

14. Soak yourself in expensive French perfume. (At least the chemist will love you.)

15. Enter, and win, the Miss World contest. That way you're sure to be irresistible to at least half the population of the world.

16. Start carrying a machine gun around with you. You'll find that people suddenly become very willing to obey your every command — whatever it might be.

17. Never take the power of a kiss for granted — develop your kiss into a deadly weapon, guaranteed to knock any boy flat on his back.

18. Smile a lot at everyone you meet. You'll often get a smile in return. (Don't smile *all* the time though, or someone's sure to come up to you and say, "All right, clever clogs, what's so funny!")

19. Impress everyone with your great sense of humour and sparkling personality. These often count much more than looks, so don't worry if you're not exactly a cross between Racquel Welch and Susan George.

20. Don't act as if you *are* irresistible!

ARE you one of life's beautiful dreamers, making quick getaways from the same boring old routines, faces and places to dreamy, faraway worlds of glamour, gaiety and glitter? Or are you one of those down-to-earth, hard-headed realists who have both feet always firmly planted on the ground? To find out the kind of stuff your daydreams are made of, and exactly what your daydreams reveal about your personality, follow our fascinating quiz . . .

HOW DREAMY ARE YOU?

1. When a boy hasn't looked at you, let alone smiled at you for a whole month, do you daydream that you're —
(d) Miss World,

(b) a fashion magazine cover-girl,
(c) sought after by legions of fanciable boys,
(a) the girlfriend of some handsome American millionaire?

2. You know for sure that the letter lying on the mat is just another bill for Dad, but in your daydreams it's —
(a) to tell you you've won the pools,
(d) to tell you a famous film producer wants to groom you for stardom,
(c) from an anonymous admirer to tell you how much he loves you,
(b) to tell you you've won a competition — and the prize is a night out at your local cinema with David Essex?

3. When you begin to wonder if you'll ever find someone to love, which situation seems dreamiest to you?
(a) To have a famous on-off relationship like Liz Taylor and Richard Burton.
(b) To be married five times.
(c) To have one glorious, steady love of a life-time.
(d) To have a tragic, secret and forbidden romance, full of heartache and joy.

4. When you feel you're just a nobody, do you dream of seeing yourself —
(a) on a 'wanted for bank robbery' poster,
(c) on a huge billboard with your name in flashing neon lights,
(b) on telly, advertising soap suds,

(d) immortalised by a famous portrait artist in the National Gallery?

5. When you go to deposit a few measly pounds in your post office savings account, do you dream of investing in —
(c) an Indian tea plantation,
(d) a chain of luxury hotels in Florida,
(b) a metal foundry in Huddersfield,
(a) a diamond mine in South Africa?

6. Waiting at a cold, dreary bus stop in the pouring rain, do you dream you're —
(a) lazing on a private beach in the South of France,
(b) eating chips on the prom at Bognor,
(d) eating scampi in New York,

(c) lying beneath the waving palm trees of a beautiful desert island?

7. When you've disgraced yourself, failing exams and getting rotten reports, which great honour do you dream of having bestowed upon you?
(b) To have a book written about you.
(a) To have a ship named after you.
(c) To have a song written to you.
(d) To have a street in your town named after you?

8. When you go to the disco and no-one asks you up to dance, do you daydream —
(a) that all the boys are queueing up to dance with you,
(d) that you look so beautiful and cool, none of the boys dare ask you,
(c) that a boy across the crowded room has fallen instantly and desperately in love with you,

(b) that none of the boys are good enough for you, and you've turned them all down anyway?

9. Listening to smoochy music, getting yourself all depressed and feeling lonely with just your radio for company, which dream boy do you imagine you're dancing with?
(a) A super-sophisticated boy who's in with the jet set.
(b) A particular real-life boy you've always fancied.
(d) Your favourite pop star.
(c) A mysterious, romantic stranger.

10. When you feel you must be the dullest, most ordinary person in the world, do you dream that —
(c) you're actually the nicest, most beautiful girl in the world, only you can't tell anyone in case they get nasty and jealous,
(d) you're actually related to the Royal Family and were found by gipsies when you were a baby,
(a) you're actually the richest person in the world, but you have to keep it a secret for your family's sake,
(b) you're a genius with an IQ of 250 but you can't let anyone know until you pass your O-levels?

11. It's Saturday night but you've nowhere to go and nothing to do. You're feeling a bit miserable. Do you start to dream that you've been invited —
(b) to a friend's birthday party rave-up,
(c) to a romantic dinner for two,
(a) to a private party on board a society yacht,
(d) to a mad round of jam-packed fun, first the speedway then the disco, and after that there's dawn sausage and mash at the all-night transport cafe?

12. When you look in the mirror and groan, do you dream you had the money/courage to —
(c) go platinum blonde,

(d) have extensive plastic surgery,
(a) go to an exclusive health and beauty farm for a month,
(b) buy and use the best, complete range of make-up on the market?

13. Everything goes wrong: you quarrel with your boyfriend; your friends gang up on you; mum nags you; no-one loves you, and you feel life just isn't fair. So you think everything would be so different if you were —
(b) Marie Osmond,
(c) Linda McCartney,
(d) Princess Anne,
(a) Aristotle Onassis's daughter.
Now count your score, mainly (a), (b), (c) or (d) and turn to the conclusions

how dreamy are you?

Quiz Conclusions Continued from page 70

Mostly (A)

You're the million dollar girl whose daydreams centre around money and the good life. Never mind if you haven't got a penny in the bank, your daydreams take you round all the rich, jet-set centres of the world — from luxury hotel, to casino, to millionaire's private beach and island.

You're a bit of a sophisticate: you have good taste and appreciate good things, and for you, money *does* buy happiness. You're a big spender at heart, though, which shows that you're basically an open-hearted and generous person.

You're extremely sociable and have a magnetic personality and few doubts about yourself, because you have a basic self-confidence and faith in yourself. You'd like to be at the centre of a sophisticated and fun-loving crowd of friends and you're motivated by a desire to impress other people. This goes with an ambitious nature — you want to get to the top of the ladder of success and you're not afraid of hard work if you think it will achieve your goals. You'll probably choose a fairly glamorous career and you won't be content with being second-best.

An ordinary type of existence isn't good enough for you — you want something a bit special. Basically, you want a life of comfort, ease and luxury, and really, you should have been born rich. If you weren't, well, never mind, because you've got the go and determination to get what you want and work to make your dreams come true.

Mostly (B)

Of all the dreamers, you're the one who's best able to face up to reality. Daydreaming's all right in its place, but you don't take it seriously — it's just a laugh for you. You don't believe in your daydreams partly because you just can't see all those fabulous things happening to little old you, and partly because real life is pretty nice anyway, so it doesn't matter much if your dreams fall on barren ground.

You're the type who makes the best of things as they are. You can accept things and enjoy life without wishing too much for the things you haven't got. You have the ability to be realistic about yourself, and you're mature enough to be able to come to terms with your faults as well as your good points. This gives you a strength which many other people lack. Because you're realistic about yourself, and you don't expect miracles, you cope much better than most.

You don't expect too much from life. Your attitudes are sane and practical; you can be quite tough when you have to be, and you have a clear-sighted view of your surroundings and your relationships. In fact, you're so well-adjusted to life, you hardly need to daydream at all — though it's relaxing when you're in the mood!

Mostly (C)

You're a romantic dreamer — all your daydreams are centred around love and romance, and your deep sensitivity of feeling. Your dreams are full of the most wonderful romantic situations, of deep relationships, and mad, passionate love affairs!

Everything in your dreams is centred around your emotions, and there isn't much room for ordinary feelings or any dull, routine happenings. How can real life possibly match up to your beautiful visions? You must guard against living in your dreams too much, though. Because you expect so much from life, disillusion may set in unless you ration the dreams a bit and come to terms with the hard unromantic world.

Basically, you're a loving sort of person, gentle and emotional. You're very aware and very sensitive to others — often too sensitive for your good. You feel everything very deeply and the most important things in your life are always to do with relationships with others. You have the ability to give a lot and to get a lot of satisfaction in return, and if you can find a boy who's as loving as you are, you'll have a wonderful relationship. But you must come to terms with the fact that not everyone in the world is as loving and genuine as you are, so be careful not to get hurt.

Mostly (D)

Your daydreams are wild, wonderful and far-fetched and you want the best of everything — riches, fame, beauty, adventure, excitement and all the best things life has to offer. You throw yourself into your daydreams and you really enjoy imagining yourself in the most romantic and glamorous situations, but deep down in your heart you know that the dreams are only stardust and are unlikely to come true.

So you cleverly have the best of both worlds — you can wallow in wonderful daydreams, and you can also face up to the harsh realities of everyday life! Basically, you're very outgoing and impulsive. You're great company and you have great energy and enthusiasm for life, coupled with a great sense of humour.

You don't brood over things for too long; instead you go into action, sometimes stirring things up and creating havoc. You have an open nature and a generous spirit. You look for adventure and excitement in your life and you tend to rush into situations without thinking what the consequences might be. You occasionally lack understanding in your relationships with others — this is because you often fail to realise how insecure other people are.

You have few doubts about yourself and it's difficult to appreciate other people's problems and panics when you're able to cope so well. You genuinely enjoy life. You get a kick out of your extravagant daydreams, and you get just as much pleasure and excitement from life itself. Aren't you lucky?

ALL OUT—IN STRIPES!

Warm up to winter in the brightest woollies around! Our stripy ribbed scarf, leg-warmers and matching drawstring bag are *the* things for winter, and the brighter the better! They're quick to knit and great to wear, so get out those needles and start knitting, right away!

OUR really simple pattern has been specially designed for Jackie by Gillian Green, with Sirdar Superwash DK wool, used double for quickness and extra warmth! We chose Gorse and Roman Pink from a huge range of 45 different shades which includes almost every shade and tone you can think of. You'll also need a pair of 6 mm (No. 4) needles, available from almost any wool shop.

STRIPED KNITTED SCARF, BAG AND LEG WARMERS

MATERIALS: Of Sirdar Superwash DK: **Scarf** — 7 (25 g) balls Gorse (shade 124) and 5 balls Roman Pink (shade 144); **Bag** — 3 balls Gorse and 3 balls Roman Pink; **Leg Warmers** — 9 balls Gorse and 5 balls Roman Pink. You'll need 18 balls Gorse and 12 balls Roman Pink for the complete set. Two 6 mm (No. 4) needles.

Sizes: Length of scarf, 180 cm (71 ins.); length of bag, 28 cm (11 ins.); length of leg warmers, 57 cm (22½ ins.).

Tension: 8 sts and 10 rows to 5 cm (2 ins.) with rib slightly stretched.

Abbreviations: K – knit; P – purl; sts – stitches; beg – beginning; rep – repeat; yrn – yarn round needle to make a loop stitch; tog – together; cont – continue; G – Gorse, RP – Roman Pink.

Note: USE YARN DOUBLE THROUGHOUT.

SCARF

TO MAKE: With 2 strands of G cast on 32 sts. Working in k2, p2 rib, work in stripes of: 12 rows G, 8 rows RP until 18th G stripe is completed. Cast off in rib (k2, p2). Sew in ends.

BAG

TO MAKE: With 2 strands of RP cast on 48 sts. Work 6 rows in k2, p2 rib.

Holes Row: (K2, yrn, p2 tog) to end. Work 1 row more in k2, p2 rib. Still working in rib, work (12 rows G, 8 rows RP) 4 times then 12 rows G again. Break off G and cont in RP only. Work 1 row in rib.

Holes Row: (K2 tog, yrn, p2) to end. Work 6 rows more in rib. Cast off in rib (k2, p2). Fold bag double and join side seams.

Cord: Cut 6 strands of RP 300 cm (118 ins) long and knot at each end. Place one end over a door handle and a pencil through other end. Spin pencil until the strands are very tightly twisted. Place ends tog and allow cord to twist itself. Smooth out cord and thread around holes at top of bag. Join ends of cord.

LEG WARMERS

TO MAKE: (Knit 2 alike). With 2 strands of G cast on 64 sts. Working in k2, p2 rib, work in stripes of: 12 rows G, 8 rows RP until 6th G stripe is completed. Cast off in rib (k2, p2). Join side seam.

Sirdar Superwash DK is available from wool shops and stockists throughout the country, but if you have problems send an s.a.e. to Direct Enquiries, Customer Relations, Sirdar Ltd., PE 31, Alverthorpe, Wakefield, WF2 9ND asking for the address of your nearest stockist.

EYE~OPENERS!

Who says blue eye colours don't go with brown eyes (or vice versa)? Model Vivienne says she can wear any colours she likes and she always matches up her eye colours with the clothes she's wearing. You can do the same thing too . . . so eyes down for the latest ways to make up *your* eyes, just like Vivienne!

Beauty Box

DON'T BE BROW-BEATEN!

BEFORE you begin to apply eye colours, you have to make sure that your eyebrows are neat and tidy and make a good frame for the whole eye area. Shaggy brows will spoil the whole look and you'll get the colours all mixed up with them!

Plucking your brows becomes a quick and simple habit after a while, although it can be a bit painful at first. The simplest way is to buy a good pair of tweezers with slanted edges and cover your eyebrows in cold cream so that the hairs will come out easier!

Never pluck away the straggly hairs from the tops of the brows because this will alter the shape completely and ruin the arch of your brows for ever!

If you do find plucking painful (even with cold cream) you could try dipping cotton wool into fairly hot water (*not* boiling) and holding it against the brow to be plucked for a few seconds. This opens the pores and allows the hairs to slip out quite easily!

Once you've neatened up your brows, you're ready for your eye make-up, but do decide what you're wearing *before* you choose your eye colours. You don't have to match up the colours with your clothes exactly, just make sure they tone nicely.

If you're wearing a patterned dress, or several colours at once, you can pick up two of them. Always choose colours that look good together and don't be afraid to try something really different and a bit daring.

Vivienne always uses powder shadows in basic, primary colours — they look good on their own or she can mix them to make more delicate and unusual shades.

WHAT YOU SHOULD CHOOSE

Vivienne's powder shadows are bright "primary" colours made up by Cosmetics A La Carte Ltd., 16 Motcomb Street, London SW1 8LB. They cost £1.50 each plus 20p for postage and packing, and come in clear pink, blue, rust, green, etc. You can find bright colours in your own town, too, from ranges such as Boots 17, Rimmel, Outdoor Girl, Miners, Evette, Maybelline, etc.

Powder shadows usually last longer on the eyes and look soft and pretty. **Eye Pencils** are simple to use and are great for shading small areas and drawing fine lines. **Cream** shadows are easily applied with the fingers but may crease after a short while, unless you choose one that claims to be creaseproof!

Powder shadows are best applied with a small eye brush or sponge applicator if one is provided with the shadow you choose. Loose powder shadows are a good idea because they come in plastic bottles with sponge applicators set into the caps. Try Rimmel and Boots 17 mascaras, especially, and try Outdoor Girl Special Mascara Refill which you simply squeeze into the container you have already!

Don't make the mistake of getting stuck in a rut, using the same colours in the same way month after month. Take time off every now and then to sit in front of a good mirror and experiment with different colours used in different ways. You could be really surprised at the range of colours that will suit you!

PINKS AND BLUES

TAKE a look at Vivienne's pretty flowered top and you'll see that the main colours are green and pink! But clever Vivienne decided to pick up the pink and the little *blue* flowers for a really super look. Here's what she did.

1. Using a bright blue powder shadow, Vivienne started from the middle of the lid and coloured the outer section, sweeping the colour past the end of the lashes to the outer corners of each eye and also round the corner and underneath the first few lower lashes.
2. With the same blue, she then started from the inner corner and coloured the socket-line of each eye, taking the colour down to meet the blue at the outer corners.
3. Changing to a bright pink powder shadow,

she coloured in the remaining space on the lid, from centre to inner corners.
4. Vivienne then used the pink to colour the final section from the middle of the brow-bone out to the end of the brow, as shown.
5. Mascara came last, using navy blue swept *down* over top lashes, *up* under lower ones, then *up* under top lashes, *down* over bottom ones.

RUSTS AND BROWNS

BRIGHT yellow looks great on Vivienne, but bright yellow, green or blue eye colour would have looked all wrong. So, instead of matching her eye colours to her clothes exactly, she chose a pretty, clear rust as the main colour, with light brown to tone. Here's how she did it.
1. First of all, Vivienne used the rust powder shadow to colour lids from centre to outer corners just past the outer lashes, and round the corner just under the first few bottom lashes.
2. Using the same rust, she then coloured the brow-bones, shading quite lightly at the inner corners, heavier at the middle and outer corners for deeper colour.
3. Next came a light brown shadow on lids from middle to inner corners and just below lower lashes

from middle to inside corners.
4. Finally, Vivienne

used black mascara applied as for the pink and blue eye make-up.

PARTY PIECES

It's those original touches that make you stand out from the crowd at any party! Here are some really stunning ideas . . . and they don't require a lot of effort!

Wear a cobwebby, lacey petticoat *over* a bright flouncy skirt. Search around jumble sales or second hand shops for a lacey petticoat. Sew pretty coloured ribbons to the top of the skirt and leave them trailing over the petticoat — (just like the lovely grass skirts of last summer!).

Make yourself a little rag doll, from odd scraps of wool and material. Attach it to a piece of plain cord and wear it round your neck.

Steal an idea from the chic French, who originated the idea of carrying perfume bottles around on cords! Tie your favourite perfume to a length of cord and wind it round your waist several times to make a really original belt. (He'll know which perfume to buy you as a present too!)

Carry your make-up around in a pretty drawstring bag.

We made ours from 18 rectangles of printed cotton (each 3 x 2 inches). Sew all the patches together, so that you have one large rectangle. With the wrong side facing you, turn down a small hem along one of the longer sides. Run a piece of cord through this, half an inch in from the top edge, sew on a Broderie Anglaise lace trim, fold the rectangle in half and (wrong side facing you) stitch together along the bottom and side, leaving the top end open.

Now you have a super drawstring bag, which is not only useful, but looks great hanging round your neck or dangling from your belt!

Wear tiny paper flowers in your hair. Cut yours from fairly stiff paper, then paint them in pretty colours. Stick the flowers to kirby grips, with a strong glue, such as Copydex (available from most large stores and stationers). Use them to pin your hair up . . . simply lovely!

This lovely peasanty apron is really cheap and easy to make.

You'll need three dishcloths — buy yours cheaply at any chain store (like Woolworth, Marks & Spencer or Fenwicks).

Cut one of the dishcloths in half and sew the halves to the other dishcloths, to make two large rectangles.

Sew four lengths of broad ribbon to each dishcloth — two for shoulder straps and two for ties at the waist. Try it on first, so that you get the waist ties in the right place.

Tie it on over cotton camisoles, and be a pretty peasant!

Carry the peasant look through, right down to your watchstrap! Buy a piece of embroidered braid, wide enough to fit your watch and sew snap fasteners on. Looks really original!

THEY'VE GOT STYLE !!

MANY pop groups nowadays, such as the Bay City Rollers and Slik, as well as having their own individual sound, have also developed their own original look. And their distinctive gear helps to make them easily recognisable as well as giving them an instant impact onstage.

Pop stars have always appreciated that they need to look good and wear interesting, exciting, (and sometimes outrageous!) clothes and costumes, especially when performing live. And that's why the creative talents of top fashion designers are so much in demand.

Bambi Ballard, for instance, is currently working for a whole list of famous names, including the Bay City Rollers and Sweet.

"I enjoy working with the Rollers," she says. "At the moment I'm working on some new trousers for them and they know exactly what they want! Their basic look won't change, they just want to use better materials and feel more comfortable onstage.

"Andy Scott of the Sweet is also always full of good ideas. I did most of the band's clothes for their American tour and as they've had a complete change of image it was quite a challenge.

"They wanted to get right away from the high heels and glitter so their new wardrobe helps to mark them out as individuals and gives each of them a different look."

So, as you'll realise, thought, time and money are all important factors in the making of even the simplest clothes for a pop star!

Bambi thoroughly enjoys all the hard work she puts in though, especially when she gets the opportunity to see all her creations being worn by the stars.

"It's very satisfying when you see your clothes at a concert or on television. I always think that I could have done a better job, but I suppose that's natural!"

SLIK'S sensational look, too, baseball shirts and tight, drainpipe jeans, was their own idea and stemmed from the groups' interest in the music and style of the fifties. Those special

shirts were mainly designed by Glaswegian artist, Ed Smith.

"I've known Slik for a few years now as we share the same building in Glasgow," he said. "I have a studio on the top floor and they rehearse in the basement. The boys decided to design their own shirts, and the idea was that we should get together and pitch in ideas about the colouring of the shirts and the words that should go on them.

"Each shirt has different wording on it," said Ed. "For instance, Billy's has 'McIsaac Park' on the back, and one of the others says 'City Slikers', which I think is a great slogan!"

In contrast to Ed, Len Wilton, who works for Bespoke Tailoring in London, has been involved with show business fashion for quite some time now. He was the person responsible for the wonderful bump suits Kenny wore when their record, 'The Bump', was in the charts.

"The first suits we made were fairly dressy," Len says. "They looked fantastic but the boys found them a bit restricting onstage when they wanted to

move around.

"Kenny like a loose cut but all the groups have different ideas. Slik, for example, want a completely opposite look to Kenny. We've just made some velvet trousers for them and they're very tight indeed!"

Another person who has a very distinctive style of dress is Bryan Ferry, who's well-known for being a very smooth, extremely dapper dresser. He has very definite ideas about his image and likes to discuss the design of all his stage clothes with designer Anthony Price.

He's been friends with Anthony for some time now and between them they come up with the looks that really appeal to Bryan.

For the suits he wears both on and off stage, Bryan goes to David Chambers.

David's another perfectionist and will spend ages getting the cut, the cloth and the colour just right — which is very important to Bryan!

ANOTHER person who sets a very high standard in the world of fashion is Tommy

Nutter, who lives and works in London's Savile Row. He doesn't design many stage costumes for the stars but concentrates mainly on their private wardrobes.

Many of Tommy's clients have become personal friends and one of the closest is Elton John.

"I first met Elton about two years ago and he's always quite happy to leave the design of his suits entirely up to me," Tommy said.

"When he first came I did him some suits with padded shoulders, very wide Oxford Bag trousers and double-breasted jackets with no vent at the back. He ordered about eight suits at one time!"

Tommy has some very illustrious names on his client list, besides Elton. Gilbert O'Sullivan, Paul Simon, Paul McCartney and Mick Jagger are just a few of the more famous visitors to his shop.

Tommy's world is certainly very glamorous. He's forever buzzing about all over the world on business trips, especially to America and Paris. Obviously he's a very talented person who gets the most out of life but he also puts a terrific amount of hard work into his business, which is why it's so successful.

"It's not easy," he says. "Sometimes you can find yourself working till midnight. But I wouldn't give it up for anything — it's a wonderful life."

Tommy aims, and succeeds, at giving personal service and the same goes for well-known fashion designer Zandra Rhodes.

Zandra designs stage clothes for Queen and once managed to help them out of a right royal jam!

Queen were touring in the United States and Brian May lost the outfit Zandra had designed for him. He was terribly upset and immediately rang her up in London and asked if she could possibly send him a replacement. Unfortunately, the original designs had gone missing, but Zandra took the trouble to recreate her masterpiece, with the aid of a large photograph of Brian onstage.

And it's that kind of dedication and attention to detail that has got today's pop fashion designers where they are today.

So, the next time you see your favourite group all dressed up in their special onstage (and offstage!) clothes, just remember the people behind the scenes, who've helped make them look the way they are today! ●

Fashion do's & don'ts

1. Wrong Short, skirt, strappy shoes pale tights all make fat legs look fatter.
Right Skirt just below the knee, darker tights, plain shoes help to camouflage.

2. Wrong Single-breasted jacket with side pockets makes thin girl look even more stick-like.
Right Double-breasted jacket with wide collar and deep pockets takes away that skin-and bones look.

4. Wrong Calf length skirts, coloured tights and huge shoes with no fronts make legs and ankles look like sticks.
Right Skirt just below the knee and pale tights help to accentuate fattest part of the leg, shoes with high fronts make legs look more substantial.

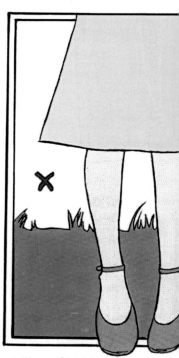

5. Wrong Short legs look ridiculous in calf-length skirts and ankle-strap shoes.

The right choice of clothes can make all the difference to your figure and help disguise faults. We take a look at some of the most common problems and how to cope with them.

3.Wrong Opposite of No. 2. Double-breasted jacket makes broad girl look vast. Padded shoulders make the whole thing even worse.
Right Slimming single-breasted jacket in a dark colour gives the impression of length instead of width.

Right Knee-length skirt and plain, uncluttered shoes give the impression of length.

6. Wrong Dumpy girl looks podgier when jacket breaks her up at the waist and patterns draw attention to it.
Right Longer, plain jacket is slimming and gives the impression of height.

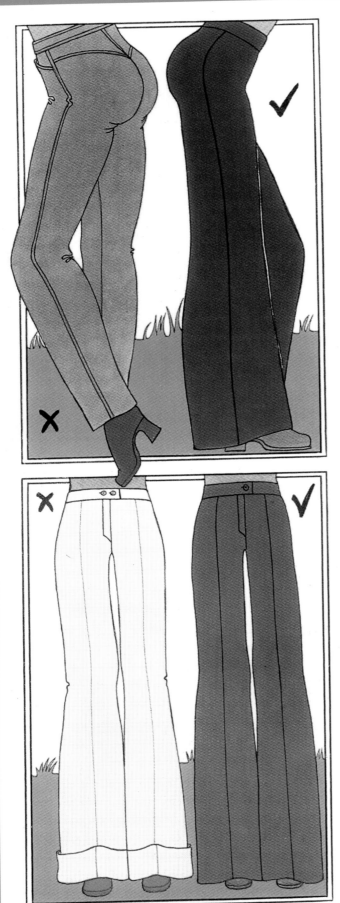

7. Wrong Big bottom looks really grotesque in tight jeans which are straight or tapered.
Right Trousers that fit well and are the right size are the only answer, preferably with flared or wide legs.

8. Wrong Being short from waist to neck isn't helped by high-waisted trousers which make the gap even smaller.
Right Trousers with a thin waist-band, or none at all, give more length to body.

9. Wrong Short legs look even shorter when trousers have large turn-ups.
Right No turn-ups help give a long, slim look.

AND NOW FOR SOME QUICKIES

10. Horizontal stripes make fatties look wider than ever.

11. Fussy prints, buttons, frills and bows make fatties look bitty and lumpy.

12. Scoop-neck T-shirts and tops accentuate skinny shoulders and lumpy collarbone.

13. Tight waists make large hips and bottom look worse.

14. Short skirts make busty figure really top-heavy.

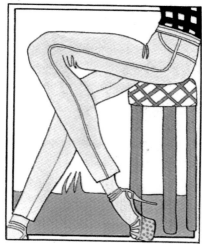

15. High-heeled, dressy shoes rarely look sexy with tight jeans.

16. Wide expanses of back, unless brown and beautiful, look horrid, especially if there's any flab about.

17. Spot the difference! No prizes for guessing that the clean, tidy girl looks better than the dirty, sloppy one.

EVER wanted to find out what your boyfriend is really thinking? Well, you can quite easily become clairvoyant, read his mind like a book, discover his very deepest thoughts and exactly how he feels about you. How? Merely by getting him to sit down, and then studying the way he arranges his feet/drapes his legs/and, altogether, occupies the chair. For the way he sits tells you all you need to know to truly understand your boy . . .

The way this boy is sitting speaks louder than volumes of words. He's poised on the verge of flight and is ready to spring into action at any moment. His feet are ready to run and he looks restless, as though he feels confined just sitting in a chair.

A boy who sits like this is not giving *you* his full attention, as he's so full of pent-up energy that he longs for freedom. It might be that he's thinking of leaving you to search out new adventures and experiences, and even if he doesn't do anything about getting up and going, be warned, because it's in his mind.

When you see your boy's in this mood, it's up to you to interest and stimulate him — suggest some exciting excursion, even take him for a run round the block — anything to keep him occupied and to dampen his restlessness.

If this is his most usual sitting position, you've got trouble on your hands. This boy is very lively-minded and aware, and he needs constant excitement in his life. He's the type who gets really enthusiastic over something, but very quickly loses interest and latches on to something else. He's very sociable, he loves parties and being with lots of people, but he's also a bit of a flirt.

He's not easy to pin down as he hates any form of set routine. It's up to you to be so fascinating that he'll never lose interest and his desire for freedom will take second place to you. He's a wild character so good luck to you if you think you can tame him!

This way of sitting suggests that the boy is a bit arrogant, and likes to be in complete control of a situation. If your boy sits like this he's definitely intrigued by you, but although he's keen to get to know you better, he's not going to go overboard — not yet, anyway.

He likes to play it cool and to preserve his independence as long as he can. He doesn't like the idea of being tied down to a steady relationship on anything but *his* terms. He's a bit wary of what you want from him so the best thing to do is not to rush your fences but let him take his time. Show him that he's the boss all right, and that you're just an adorable weak female!

If this is your boy's most usual sitting position you can be sure that he's very self-confident and knows exactly what he wants from life. He does tend to be a bit critical though and his ideal girl

would really have to be nothing less than perfect. He's strong-willed but he's fair — he always weighs up a situation very carefully before committing himself.

He also wants to be proud of you and for you to feel proud of him. The best way of catching this boy and holding his attention is to be subtle, and pander to his every need, but don't appear too weak or he'll walk all over you!

Poor little boy, he's scared! Look at the way he's sitting, with his knees together and his feet turned inward, as though he's petrified that you're going to eat him alive! When a boy sits like this, he's feeling very insecure and lost.

All his self-confidence has drained away and he just doesn't know what to do. His sitting position is a kind of cry for help. He desperately wants your love, but is frightened of being rejected: he desperately wants to confide in you, but is scared about what your response will be.

When he's in this kind of mood try and put him out of his misery by mothering him and telling him what a marvellous person he is. Be kind to him, coax him and, above all, flatter him, so that his faith in himself is utterly restored. Give him all the love and comfort he needs and you'll have a man, and not a mouse!

If this is his most usual sitting position, he's a bit unsure of himself and finds it very difficult to express his feelings. In fact, he's got plenty of feelings, the trouble is that they're all hidden away inside. Underneath he's generally very kind and understanding and, if you can help to put him in the right mood, he'll be very sympathetic and romantic. But he's a shy type and finds relationships difficult.

It takes time and patience to get to know him properly, but once he really trusts you, you'll find he's a very warm person with a lot to give. Make him feel manly and appreciated and he'll soon come out of his withdrawn moods. You can be sure of one thing — this boy really needs you, so don't let him down!

Arrrgh! What a wreck! This boy looks permanently as though he's just crawled out from under a stone after a very hard night on the town — either that, or he looks like he's about to go down with some deadly disease. But it's far more likely that he's out of his mind with worry — he carries all the problems and burdens of the world on his own shoulders.

When he sits like this you can be sure he's a very worried boy. Perhaps you've done something to upset him; maybe he's worried about his relationship with you and would like to talk about it, but doesn't know where to begin. Or it could be that he's so wrapped up in his own problems he probably wouldn't notice you even if you pranced about in front of him wearing nothing but a grass skirt and a few flowers!

However, you can soon get him out of this state of mind if you persevere. First of all, try to make him talk about all his worries and tell you what's getting him down. Once he's got it all off his chest and out in the open he should feel much better and start being human again.

If this is his usual sitting position, he's frankly well on the way to worrying his life away. He takes life and himself extremely seriously and consequently reads far too much into everyday situations and takes little things much too much to heart. He succeeds in complicating everything around him and is very liable to get his love-life hopelessly tied up in knots. He's an over-emotional

EALLY LIKE?

type and, all in all, he sounds rather a dead loss, but he does have a saving grace — he's a very clever bloke. He's the intellectual type who's hopeless on relationships but utterly brilliant on Einstein's Theory of Relativity. In fact, he's mentally alive and interesting, and if only you could stop him worrying, he'd be a terrific boyfriend to have around!

You only have to glance at this boy to see that he's all tensed up, with every nerve in his body on edge and anxiety oozing out of every pore. When he sits like this, you immediately know that he's not happy about the situation he's in.

His way of sitting reveals that there's something wrong with your relationship and, to help put his mind at rest, it would be best to get it sorted out right away. He's withdrawn into himself and unless you can establish contact with him again, this could well be the end of your beautiful friendship. What you've got to do is to have a real heart-to-heart and, hopefully, start watching those tortured limbs untwisting!

If this is his most usual sitting position, he's a naturally tense, shy sort of person who's very sensitive and easily hurt. He feels he has no control over his life and goes in for a great deal of soul-searching in an attempt to find out just where his destiny lies. He hasn't really "found himself" yet and, because of this, is inclined to get very depressed.

He needs lots of patience and understanding, but at the same time be careful not to pander to his moods too much as he does tend to be selfish. He's got to learn that it's up to him to make the effort to unbend and relax. He's an emotional type, and you could have a great relationship with him if only you can make him loosen up and enjoy life more. He may need dynamite to get him going but it'll be worth it!

Sunshine boy himself! A boy who sits like this is feeling incredibly happy and relaxed, amazingly lazy and he hasn't a care in the world, as life has never looked so good before. For this optimist everything is permanently coming up roses and things always seem to work out well for him.

He's enjoying your company, he's completely happy about your relationship and he also feels very sure of the situation. You've got the knack of making him feel utterly at home and at ease and although he's not in an incredibly romantic or passionate mood, he's feeling very warm towards you and is probably very fond of you indeed.

If this is his most usual sitting position he's a very out-going, sociable person who finds it easy to get along with others and is always pleased to meet new people and take up new interests. He has a happy nature, usually very con-

tented and relaxed, and life holds no problems for him.

He's a confident person who doesn't like compli-

cation so he does make an effort to keep things running smoothly. He's also understanding and considerate, although he doesn't really enjoy deep, soul-searching discussions about your relationship too much. He's got a very open and natural personality and he'll always be popular.

If all this sounds too good to be true then we have to admit that he does have one slight drawback — he's such a natural charmer that you'll have to keep a close eye on him as every girl for miles around is almost bound to fall for him, too!

When a boy sits like this, legs spread out in abandon, feet firmly touching the ground, he's feeling in top form. He loves you and wants to express his feelings for you. All his reserve is gone and he's extremely happy.

To him, every word you utter is a gem and he's watching you with rapt attention. He feels emotionally warm and close to you, and he has a great deal of faith in your relationship as he regards you as a very special person.

If this is his most usual sitting position, it shows that he's a very active, masculine type with bags of energy and always on the go. He enjoys outdoor activities — rugged, masculine sports like rugby, football, climbing etc.

He's fairly ambitious and usually succeeds at anything he puts his hand to. He's sociable too, and he really enjoys being "one of the boys." He'll always be a good sport and whatever activity he happens to be engaged in, he puts his heart and soul into it.

Altogether, he's a great guy, with lots of personality. He makes you feel very feminine and secure and wherever he goes he seems

to inspire confidence and admiration, in other people as well as in you.

He's kind-hearted, too, especially to anyone he feels is a bit of an under-dog and he's generous, particularly to those he's fond of. So if this boy's yours, hang on to him — he's too good to let go!

Any boy who sits like this, with his legs stretched out and his feet curled round, is a real humorist. He finds practically the whole of life one big, excruciatingly funny joke! He has a wonderful sense of freedom and well-being and usually feels incredibly pleased with himself.

He may have just ended a longstanding, tiresome relationship and is busy congratulating himself; perhaps he's achieved some astounding exam results or been given promotion at work, or maybe some other equally marvellous and fantastic thing has happened to him.

It could be though, that he's just looking pleased with himself because you make him feel good. In this mood, he's marvellous company and a terrific friend to have around.

If he usually sits like this, he's a real character, full of fun and frivolity and never giving himself time to be serious over anything.

His sense of humour dominates his every action, thought and word. He'll never brood for long over problems and difficulties, but will float happily along always seeing the funny side when things go wrong. He does tend to be a bit reckless, though, and is inclined to be over-impulsive in some things. But he doesn't demand a great deal — just so long as you laugh at his jokes and keep cheerful, life will be wildly hilarious for both of you!

DO YOU MEAN WHAT YOU SAY?

Are you one of those nice girls whose every word rings sincere and true? If you are then you shouldn't be reading this! But probably, like most of us, you quite often say one thing and mean another. It's the kind of technique that comes in very handy for settling old scores, as you are able to be downright rude with a sugary smile on your face!

So here's our Jackie Guide to What People Actually Say and *What They Really Mean . . .* and if they come out with any of these little gems — beware!

YOUR HOME

What a cosy house.
Boy, what a poky place you live in.

How nice! Everyone has matching specs.
Eye trouble must run in the family.

Your kid brother/sister's a real bundle of fun.
Spoiled brat!

You must come back to my house for tea sometime.
I'll put it off as long as I can.

See you.
Not if I see you first though.

You know, it's funny, I've never had liver and bacon for tea before.
Liver brings me out in spots! And I can't stand bacon—specially the way your mum cooks it.

Gosh, isn't your room bright?
Wow! She must be colour blind!

It's really nice and quiet round here, isn't it?
How can you stand it?

Your mum/dad/brother's not at all like I expected.
Whatever happened to the Paul Newman, Debbie Reynolds and David Essex I was led to expect?

YOUR BOYFRIEND

You seem to be crazy about him.
You must be mad!

He seems a really nice boy.
But . . .

Don't you ever wonder what John does on Wednesday nights?
He's seeing Stephanie.

You're always so trusting.
He's playing around with every girl in town.

He's got a really unusual face.
Must have modelled as the original gargoyle.

He's crazy about you.
He always is – for the first week.

You're meant for each other.
Nobody else would have you.

I don't think Simon's as shy as you say he is.
You should have seen him under the table with Susie at Belinda's party!

Has he got a skin problem?
It's lucky nobody dies of acne.

I bet your mum likes him.
He's REALLY boring.

But nobody trains five nights a week.
He's trying to tell you something!

We were surprised to see you without Steve the other night.
So the rumours about you breaking up are true!

Didn't your boyfriend and Lesley get on well at the party?
How embarrassing for you – he was all over her!

It must be nice to have such a popular boyfriend.
What a flirt – I'd kill him!

I wouldn't tell you this if I weren't so fond of you.
So I will, 'cos I'm not!

Anyone can see you're mad about each other.
Which is just as well for everyone else!

It's funny you're still just friends.
He wouldn't fancy you in a million years!

You've done really well for yourself.
I fancied him!

YOUR FUTURE

You're sure to get a good, steady job.
You're so predictable and boring.

Don't suppose we'll be seeing you around for a while.
Thank goodness.

Why don't you travel?
They tell me the Gobi Desert is quite nice!

You should be a model or in films.
She'll believe anything.

I wonder what you'll make of your life?
Not much.

You'll always do OK for yourself.
You're so selfish.

Oh, you'll do OK, you've got a fantastic personality.
Pity you missed out on the brains, though.

Well anyway, good luck and see you around.
Around the year 2000, I hope.

YOUR APPEARANCE

Are you feeling O K? You look tired.
You look terrible! Like death warmed up.

Bet you're looking forward to your holiday.
You look ghastly.

I wish I was always neat and tidy like you.
You're so boring it's not true.

Those jeans are a really good fit.
But not when you've got 40 inch hips!

I've always liked you in that dress.
You're not going to wear it for yet another year, are you?

You've had your coat cleaned!
At last!

That dress is really sexy.
So long as you like looking like a barmaid.

Freckles can be very attractive.
Not in your case, though.

You look very sophisticated in that dress.
Must be a relic from the Boer War.

What an unusual hairstyle, it's really different.
Different, yes – like a haystack set with spray starch.

You must have been a beautiful baby.
Pity you didn't stay that way!

I remember you as the prettiest girl at primary school.
What happened?

You really take a lot of care with your appearance.
You've got to!

YOUR PERSONALITY

You're so sensitive.
Oh no, she's off again! Where are the tissues?

We must seem right nutters to you.
You're so creepy and boring. What are you doing hanging around with us?

It must have taken you ages.
What a waste of time.

You do have a very serious outlook on life.
No sense of humour, that's your trouble!

I wonder what you're dreaming about now?
Dope, you've never got the faintest idea of what's going on!

You're so much more responsible and mature than I am.
But all the boys fancy me!

Your mum must be proud of you.
She's the only one!

Good for you!
But only average for anyone else.

You really know a lot about make up/cooking/parrots.
And you really go on about it too!

You're bound to be successful!
At scrubbing floors.

You always seem to be meeting boys.
So how come no-one ever sees them?

You're too deep for me.
I can never understand a word you're saying.

When did you last read a book?
Thickie!

It wouldn't be a party without you there!
Loud-mouthed exhibitionist, wonder what you'll get up to this time?

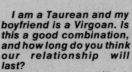

Star Quest

Could you tell me how romance is starred between a Scorpio girl and a Taurus boy?

A relationship between a Scorpio girl and a Taurus boy should have a lot going for it. There are two factors you'll have to watch — your jealousy and his stubborness.

The Taurus boy is very loving and easy going-on the surface, that is! Don't make the mistake many girls do and think you can treat him just as you please, because you're in for a terrible shock. If he gets *really* upset he'll make mincemeat of you.

Many Scorpio girls treat their boyfriends with about as much respect as a bundle of last week's washing — and they get away with it! But not with a Taurus boy.

Apart from that you are both people who enjoy a steady relationshop and you are both very loyal. If you treat your Taurus boy well, you've got it made.

My friend is a Virgo girl and I'm a Sagittarian. The problem is, we both like an Aries boy. Could you tell us which one of us would get on with him better – or doesn't he like either of us?

It's unfortunate that you and your Virgo mate both fancy the same Aries boy, but it often happens that way. Being born under Sagittarius, you are far more compatible with Aries than your Virgo friend could ever be.

Both Aries and Sagittarius are fire signs — made for each other, you might say! This is a case where two sensible girls should get together and talk the situation out. I don't think you'll have much trouble, as your Virgo friend is too much of a realist to want this boy for herself when she realises that he can be very selfish and unreliable.

But don't let that put you off him, as Sagittarians are very adaptable. You know what they say: "People in glass houses shouldn't throw stones!" If you don't expect too much, you two could have a great time together.

I am a Taurean and my boyfriend is a Virgoan. Is this a good combination, and how long do you think our relationship will last?

It's always very difficult to predict how long a relationship will last, because there are always so many unknown quantities which should be taken into account.

Certainly a Taurus girl and Virgo boy should have a lot in common, as you are both earth signs. It's basic to both your natures to want a steady relationship — nothing spectacular, just nice and comfortable, going out together, doing things together. I think you'll find that you share lots of interests, and very often these are the things which make for a happy and lasting relationship.

I'm a Pisces girl, and I wonder if you could explain something to me. Why is it that an Aries boy brings out a devilish side of my nature, while a Capricorn boy makes me act and feel like a saint?

It's no puzzle to me that an Aries boys bring out the devil in you, and a Capricorn boy makes you act and feel like a saint. It's exactly what I would expect of a Pisces girl like you.

You see, you are so sensitively attuned to what is going on around you that you naturally adapt to any situation. Your Aries boy is probably a wild and likeable boy who is game to have a go at anything, and sensing this, you immediately play the same role.

Your Capricorn boy, on the other hand, is quiet, serious, possibly even a bit of a stick in the mud, and almost without realising what is happening you put on your saint-like image.

UN JOUR AVEC DAVID À PARIS!

DAVID ESSEX is a Cockney, born and brought up in the heart of London. And although he's now an international star, travelling all over the world, he hasn't forgotten his origins. As far as he's concerned, England's the greatest!

But his love for his own country doesn't stop David enjoying the other places he visits. France for instance, is a great favourite of his — and Paris in particular.

"I love Paris," he told me. "It's a beautiful city. I've been there about ten times now, and the more I see of it, the more I like it!

"The funny thing was that the first time I went there, one or two things went wrong, and it wasn't a very nice trip. I came home feeling a bit disappointed, because I didn't like it as much as I'd expected.

"But the second time I went, it was completely different. Everything went really well for me, and I just fell in love with the city!"

When it comes to the music world, the French people tend to stick to their own stars. Very few British or American singers are successful over there — which means it's all the nicer for the few, like David, who are!

David's single "America" was one of the most popular foreign records ever released over there, selling over 400,000 copies, and he's appeared several times on French television shows with stars like Mireille Matthieu and Sacha Distel.

"I really enjoy doing French TV," he told me, "but it's quite strange for me, since I can only speak about a dozen words of French! I can never understand what everyone around me's talking about!

"But luckily, the French people don't seem to mind. In fact they tease me and make jokes about it! One time I was on television they kept asking me long complicated questions that they knew I wouldn't understand! So, to get my own back, I answered every one with one of the only French words I know — 'L'amour'!"

The only thing that David regrets about his popularity in France is that it means most of his visits to Paris are working ones, so he doesn't often get the chance to be a tourist and go sightseeing.

"I get recognised in the streets," he said, "so it's not all that easy to walk about. I've never been on the Metro either because I usually travel by car.

"But, when I have the chance, I like wandering up and down the quieter boulevards, and maybe stopping at a pavement cafe for a cup of coffee. I find that really relaxing."

David also likes wandering round the shops of Paris — but he admits he prefers window-shopping to actually buying anything!

"Most of my clothes are British," he said, "but I do buy the occasional thing in Paris. I've bought quite a few French jackets, for instance. I like them because they're always so beautifully cut.

"But most of the clothes over there are very expensive. In fact everything in Paris is expensive."

ALTHOUGH David hasn't had much time for sightseeing in Paris, he has managed to visit most of the famous tourist attractions.

"The Champs Elyseés is one of my favourite places," he told me. "I always try to spend some time there when I'm in Paris. I haven't managed to visit the Louvre, and I haven't been to the top of the Eiffel Tower, but I hope to do both some day.

"I have been up the Arc de Triomphe, though of course that's not so big! I went to Versailles the last time I was there, and I thought that was really impressive. I also went up to Montmartre, and that was lovely.

"But my favourite part of all is the Latin quarter, where all the students live. I've spent a lot of time down there, and I love it."

Apart from its beautiful buildings, there's another thing Paris is famed for — its beautiful food! David admits he's a big fan of French cooking.

"Paris has some really good restaurants," he said. "I must admit I don't eat snails, but I'll try anything else! I adore French onion soup — that's one of the nicest things you can get. But really, I just like French cooking in general.

"So if I have an evening off, I'll spend it at a restaurant having a nice meal — or maybe I'll go to a nightclub.

"I've discovered a fantastic night-club called the Alcazar. It has a clever show, which has a bit of everything in it — comedy, singing, impersonations — all sorts of things. I found it entrancing.

"And the nice thing about it was that when I went there, they spotted me in the audience, and so they kept mentioning me in the show!

"That was a super night out. I'm definitely looking forward to going back there. In fact I'm definitely looking forward to going back to Paris again!"

FACE UP TO HIM

DID you know that just looking at the boy you fancy gives you the power to discover his hidden characteristics? No? Well, it's perfectly possible with the help of the ancient art of face-reading! Face-reading helps you to find out if he really is as nice as he looks — and it can also tell you exactly how to act with him . . .

The first sign to look for is the shape of his face. So take a long, hard look at the boy you think is for you and decide whether his face is:

BROAD: He's confident, very sure of himself and likes to be the boss. By nature he thinks big and seldom "chickens out" of awkward or difficult situations. He's a very strong character and has a high opinion of his own abilities!

HOW TO ACT WITH HIM: Don't start something with this self-confident boy that you can't finish. He's a very determined type so don't let him browbeat you too much either, as you'll soon find that he's a really determined character!

ROUND: This boy makes the most of life as he's very friendly and out-going. He loves entertaining and keeping everybody around him happy and comfortable, including you! He's always organised but he does love his home comforts and expects you to provide them.

HOW TO ACT WITH HIM: Make him feel at home, cook like his mum and volunteer to darn his socks. Don't let him get too cosy and comfy though, as he does tend to be a bit lazy at times.

NARROW: This boy needs a boost to his ego. He's just as talented as anyone else, and often more gifted, but his own opinion of himself is low. He's continually surprised to find he can do really well if he puts his mind to something.

HOW TO ACT WITH HIM: Encourage him all the way and don't be over-critical. He won't believe you love him unless you make it pretty obvious, so reassure him that he's the most marvellous person in the world, then he will be!

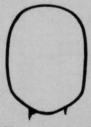

SQUARE: He's determined to change the face of the earth! This boy is born to build and dig and fight. He's always on the move, but inclined to get so wrapped-up in his latest project that he could forget all about you.

HOW TO ACT WITH HIM: Keep him interested, spring new ideas, new aspects of your personality on him — all the time. Otherwise he'll soon get bored, and to him there's nothing worse!

Now take a look at his *EYES* a decide whether they're:

SMALL: Don't expect a great sho of affection from this boy. He's go feelings all right but he finds it ve hard to express them. In fac he's extremely wary of letting hi emotions show through at all.

HOW TO ACT WITH HIM: He needs a lot of patience an understanding to help him tell yo exactly how he feels about you. Sho him *you* care and he'll return you feelings.

UPPER EYELID PLAIN TO SEE: This boy likes to take dire action, he likes to get straight to th heart of the matter — whatever it i Everything is in black and white to hi and he can't be bothered with girls wh play around.

HOW TO ACT WITH HIM: Always answer his questions with direct yes or no, don't drive hi mad by saying "maybe," or "I don know." Be as decisive as he is b be careful not to get too aggressive.

SMALL IRIS: These are know as melancholy eyes, so don't expect th boy to be light-hearted and cheerf He always seems a bit miserable, though he has a lot of unsolve problems weighing on his mind.

HOW TO ACT WITH HIM: If you get this boy to one side and he him out as someone who's genuine interested in him, he'll open u and pour out his worries to yo Wait for the right moment and he soon start feeling happier when realises that somebody cares about hi

EYES THAT SLANT DOWNWARDS: This boy highly critical, he's never satisfi unless everything is perfect. To live up these high standards you need to very special kind of girl.

HOW TO ACT WITH HIM: Don't let him trample all over yo Try to show him that this critical tr in his nature, if not controlled, could g in the way of love — of which definitely has a lot to give. He'll loyal and passionate — with the rig girl.

Now to move on to his **EYEBROWS**. Are they:

HIGH: He's the kind of boy who's rather hard to get to know. He seems detached and aloof at first but once he gets to know you he could be your warmest and truest friend. Most people will think he's a show-off and a know-all but underneath that cool exterior he has a very warm heart.

HOW TO ACT WITH HIM:
It'll be up to you to open the conversation and show, in a friendly way, that you've noticed him. Take the lead in a subtle way but be careful not to be too pushy.

LOW: A boy with eyebrows that sit down on the eyes is easy to get on with and enjoys a good laugh. Nobody's a stranger to him. When he first meets you, he'll act as if you're an old friend he's just met up with again.

HOW TO ACT WITH HIM:
Respond by being just as friendly, even if you are a little taken aback by his openness. Otherwise he could well get the idea that you're rather cool and reserved and not relaxed enough for him!

EYEBROWS WHICH FLARE UP AT THE ENDS: This boy is a dramatic exhibitionist who loves being the life and soul of the party. He's a great mimic and shifts easily from one role to another, so don't take all he says and does as being completely true to nature.

HOW TO ACT WITH HIM:
Try to calm him down a little if he seems to be getting too carried away, but show that you appreciate all his carefully managed exits and entrances. If you're a good audience and laugh at all his jokes and listen attentively to his stories — he'll love you (madly!).

STRAIGHT: This boy is sensitive and very artistic with a strong romantic streak in his make-up. He loves beauty and harmony so don't let him catch you cutting your toe-nails or, Heaven forbid, squeezing a spot!

HOW TO ACT WITH HIM:
Give him the elegant atmosphere he craves — be serene, romantic and beautiful, light your perfumed candles and play soft, soothing music.

Now, are his **LIPS**:

THIN: "Nice day" is a long sentence for him so expect this boy to be brief and to the point. Unless he's talking about his favourite subject, he won't have much to say for himself. He's also very efficient and hates waste in any form.

HOW TO ACT WITH HIM:
Don't be hurt by his abrupt manner. He just has a short way of doing and saying things. Find out about his favourite subject, (apart from you!), and show a real interest in it. Try to bring a bit of humour into his life but be careful not to overdo it!

FULL: In contrast, the full-lipped boy is generous with time, words and love. He's lavish with money but has no idea about time. He's almost bound to be late everytime you meet him but he'll make up for it when he does arrive!

HOW TO ACT WITH HIM:
Be spontaneous, don't analyse your relationship too much. One thing's for sure, if he's on time for your dates, he's really interested in you!

TURNED DOWN AT THE CORNERS: Just as you'd expect, this boy is a bit of a pessimist and generally not much fun to have around. The muscles which are supposed to lift the corners of his mouth in a smile have become weak because he doesn't use them enough!

HOW TO ACT WITH HIM:
Fortunately this condition needn't be permanent. Make him laugh and smile by talking about good times and places. He'll lose that "sour-puss" look eventually, but be patient as it could take some time.

UPTURNED CORNERS:
This shows the opposite type of boy, he's a true optimist. He likes to look on the bright side and is easy-going with a great sense of humour. He's always smiling or laughing, and looks like he's having a good time and usually he is!

HOW TO ACT WITH HIM:
Enjoy yourself!

What's his NOSE like? Is it:

ROMAN: This boy is business-like and likes to get a job done. He has a strong sense of duty and his tendency to always put business before pleasure can be a bit irritating.

HOW TO ACT WITH HIM:
Don't let him get too serious, make him see that there's more to life than work. Try to broaden his outlook and his interests and bring out the light-hearted side of his nature more.

UPTURNED: This boy is really kind and helpful, he has a great desire to be of service to other people. Human beings are all that matter to him, but he may be so busy worrying about other people and the state of the world, that it'll take him a while to get round to you!

HOW TO ACT WITH HIM:
Always ask him for his advice and assistance, make him feel that *you* need him just as much as the rest of humanity does.

STRAIGHT: Very romantic, this boy, but he's also impractical, idealistic, sensitive and poetic. He's usually up on Cloud 9 and can be annoyingly vague.

HOW TO ACT WITH HIM:
Don't try to force him to be someone he's not, but appreciate his gentle, loving qualities. If you nag him too much, he'll gently float out of your life.

SNUB: This boy is an optimist. He's easy going but he also has a strong practical streak in his nature. He's a bit of an extrovert, a joker and you'll always know when he's around!

HOW TO ACT WITH HIM:
He can't bear miseries, life's too short, so if you want to attract this boy, show him you can be as fun-loving as he is!

So there you are, now you know how to read your boy's face like a book! But remember, exactly the same is true for you. So take a piece of paper and make a list of your facial features, then you, too, can discover what you're really like.

Now, from your list, you'll be able to find out the qualities that draw other people to you, such as magnetism, generosity, optimism, humour, helpfulness and affection. If you find that from your facial features you tend to be critical, unemotional or a bit miserable, then decide to do something positive about it! Face up to yourself, and you can't go wrong!

Do you believe in ghosts? Do you shiver with fear every time an owl hoots or something goes bump in the night? Or are you the fearless type who isn't worried by anything — least of all a few strange noises in the dark?
To find out how you really feel about the supernatural, just follow our eerie ghost story.
Choose the alternatives you think fit in best, and we'll reveal your innermost fears, and some secrets of your personality which may surprise even you!

ARE YOU SCARED TO D[

1. It was my summer hols. I was bored and needed money, so I applied for a job as a maid at Black Crag Mansion. It seemed like a good idea at the time, but I began to feel very uneasy as I sat in the train looking out at —
(b) dense eerie woodlands,
(c) open moorland, grey and empty,
(d) soulless suburbs, seeming to stretch into infinity,
(a) jagged cliffs and turbulent seas.

2. Suddenly the train stopped at a tiny country station. "All passengers for Black Crag change here," announced the guard, and I shivered as I realised I was the only passenger for Black Crag. It was dusk, and the place had a dead feel to it with strange noises of —

(c) wind whistling and echoing across the platform,
(a) the persistent hooting of owls, like a strange cry of warning,
(b) bats, swooping under the eaves of the platform shelter, like a premonition of evil,
(d) the rain splattering down on my coat collar.

3. At last a small old-fashioned steam train appeared, and I cautiously stepped into a deserted compartment. The doors of the train shut instantly, and I suddenly felt horribly, inexplicably trapped.
(c) I told myself I was being silly, and tried to dismiss my fears.
(d) Interesting! I began to suspect that there was more to this job than met the eye.
(a) My stomach turned to jelly, and I wished with all my heart that I could turn round and go home.
(b) I knew I had to cope with strange forces I couldn't begin to understand.

4. Eventually I got out at Black Crag, and my suspicions that something peculiar was happening were confirmed when the station master said —
(b) "You're the first person I've seen off that train in the past twelve years."
(a) "Sorry, Miss, you startled me — I thought you were a ghost for a minute."
(d) "Well you won't need your return ticket, Miss — there's no return from Black Crag."
(c) "I don't mean to pry, Miss, but are you sure you really wanted to come to Black Crag?"

5. Mystified by what he had said, I steeled myself and walked away from the station. After walking down a wide track past a few cottages, I suddenly realised I was lost, so I knocked on a cottage door and asked an old lady for directions.
(c) She said she had never heard of Black Crag Mansion.
(d) She gave me directions with a sly smile on her face.
(b) She looked at me with large frightened eyes, and begged me not to go near it.
(a) She fainted on the doorstep!

6. At last, Black Crag Mansion came into view. It was —
(d) an old style villa surrounded by barbed wire.
(b) a stark stone building like a prison with tiny windows.
(a) an elaborate castle with turrets against a black sky.
(c) a crumbling Georgian mansion.

7. At the gate I saw —
(a) a sinister-looking guard in a black cloak.
(d) an electric alarm system.
(c) a huge Alsatian dog.
(b) two enormous stone dragons.

8. I walked fearfully up the driveway, and rang the bell. There was the sound of clanking chains and creaking wood, and the butler opened the door. He was —
(c) young and handsome but with a steely look in his eyes.
(d) a deaf mute who looked more like a bodyguard than a butler.
(b) a tall thin man who looked as though he'd been carved out of wax.
(a) an old, bald cripple with shuffling feet.

9. He got a footman to show me to my room, up winding stone staircases, through a maze of rooms and corridors to the east wing. My room was like a prison cell, and sitting alone I could hear —
- (b) loud breathing behind me wherever I turned.
- (c) tapping on my window.
- (a) strange high-pitched moaning and wailing through the wall.
- (d) the scuffling of rats in the dark corners of the room.

10. I tried the door and realised with horror that I was locked in.
- (c) I banged at the door, yelling and screaming to be let out.
- (a) I sat and waited and prayed.
- (b) I looked frantically for a way of escape.
- (d) I sat and played ''I Spy'' with myself out of the window while I waited.

11. After terrible hours of waiting in the cold, damp room, the footman led me downstairs, and told me I was going to meet the master of the house. I told him I'd changed my mind about taking the job, but he grasped my arm and pushed me into a room —
- (a) like a graveyard with weird stone statues, lit by a ghostly green light,
- (d) like a weird space laboratory, with machines and strange mobiles hanging from the ceiling,
- (c) like a room in a stately home, but everything was faded and covered in dust,
- (b) like a jungle with weird flowering cacti, and huge rubber plants.

12. ''Come here, young lady,'' echoed a voice all around the room, but I could see no-one.
- (c) My mind was in total confusion, and I was too stunned even to feel frightened.
- (b) I took a deep breath to brace myself for what was to happen next.
- (a) My heart thumped like a steam engine, and I thought I'd faint on the spot.
- (d) I suddenly became intrigued with the situation, and determined to get to the bottom of it.

13. ''Who is it? What are you playing at?'' I called out, trembling in every limb. There was silence, and then —
- (b) a black cat leapt from nowhere on to my shoulder, digging its claws into my flesh,
- (c) a blinding light suddenly beamed on to my face,
- (d) the sound of ghoulish laugher rang in my ears,
- (a) a current of cold air froze me to the spot.

14. Suddenly, to my horror, a panel in the wall opened out, and the master

of the house appeared before me, wearing a mask so I couldn't see his face.
- (c) ''Congratulations,'' he said, ''You have passed the first test — now I will tell you the reason you are here.''
- (b) ''You have come at my command as I knew you would,'' he said. ''Now you are in my power.''
- (a) ''I have searched the earth for you for a hundred years,'' he said. ''Now at last I have found you!''
- (d) ''Ha, ha,'' he said. ''You fell for my trick hook, line and sinker, and walked right into my trap!''

15. For a moment I was too shocked to fathom out the meaning of all this, but as the master of the house went on talking, it gradually dawned on me that —
- (a) he was a ghost,
- (c) the whole thing might be a clever cover for an organisation dealing in top secret government work,
- (d) the whole thing must be an elaborate practical joke,
- (b) the master of the house was an exponent of Black Magic, with a warped, evil mind.

Now count your scores, mainly (a), (b), (c) or (d) and turn to the conclusions on page 91.

WANTED— SUPERCOPS

ONE thing's for sure, some of the most popular TV series in the past year have been those with detectives in them. These cool, handsome hunks have kept us gripped to the edges of our seats as they sort out the baddies, and had us heaving sighs of relief as they made everything work out right in the end!

What is it that makes detectives so appealing? Well, it could be something to do with that combination of mystery, courage, insight and super-calm that makes them so riveting! Here are some favourites who've definitely got it all!

Kevin Dobson's got everyone's dream job — as Crocker, he's Kojak's assistant in one of the most popular television 'tec series of all time! And we think he's lovely!

Peter Sellers is his usual hilarious self — but even more so, as Inspector Clouseau.

Lovely Ben Murphy stars in "Griff" with Lorne Green, whom you may remember from "Bonanza." Ben himself, of course, was also a star of that memorable series, "Alias Smith and Jones."

Mike Douglas is Steve, the good-looking assistant to top 'tec Karl Malden in "The Streets of San Francisco." Wouldn't you guess he's the son of that famous and distinctive-looking actor, Kirk Douglas?

Dustin Hoffman and Robert Redford aren't really detectives, but they are investigators in the exciting film, "All The President's Men." And even though they're not cops, we think they're lovely anyway!

Peter Falk plays Columbo — he looks slow and shabby, but don't be fooled — he's one of the sharpest detectives around!

You'll probably remember Robert Wagner from the exciting TV series "Colditz." Detective fans will also have lapped up "Switch," in which he starred with Eddie Albert.

One of the first-ever detectives to be shown on the screen, film star Humphrey Bogart who appeared in lots of exciting films. His ever-popular pictures are now being re-made and up-dated!

The rough, tough 'tec in Thames Television's "The Sweeney" is played by lean, blond Denis Waterman.

James Garner's already a famous film star — now he's a star of the television series, "The Rockford Files."

Handsome heart-throb George Peppard, star of many films in the past, now stars in the title-role of the television detective series, "Banacek."

Everybody's favourite — he doesn't even need introducing! Telly Savalas, as big, calm, soft-hearted Theo Kojak!

David Soul (left) and Paul Michael Glaser are "Starsky and Hutch" — Dave Starsky and Ken Hutchinson, the young, tough and dedicated undercover police officers.

QUIZ CONCLUSIONS
Continued from page 77

Mostly (a)

You're a great believer in ghosts, ghouls and things that go bump in the night, and you enjoy being terrified. You feel a pull towards the unknown, towards the occult, and spend a lot of time thinking about the meaning of life. You're an extra-sensitive person. Earthly things are only superficial to you and you're very curious about the world beyond. However, your fear stops you from delving too deeply.

You are sincere and easily hurt as a person, and rather prone to the influence of others. You take yourself very seriously, and love and romance are important and serious, too. You have sound intuition about friendship and romance, and you often manage to sum people up quite accurately by instinct. However, very often your rich imagination gets mixed up with your intuition and you can make mistakes.

Guard against depression, and against your tendency to brood on morbid thoughts. Ghosts are OK for a laugh, but try not to take them too seriously.

Mostly (b)

You can certainly cope with ghostly apparitions and sinister situations. You're drawn towards the unusual and the bizarre, and have an excellent awareness of the unknown. This highly developed sense of awareness makes you very alert and helps you to see through situations in general.

You're very curious about the occult, but deep in your heart you have to admit you're not a serious believer. Ghosts and ghouls give you a thrill, but they're not for real. You have great faith in the power of the human mind, and perhaps even feel you're rather psychic or telepathic. However, you don't altogether agree that these are evidence of a world beyond.

You are a thinking person, living very much in your mind, and for this reason you're good at analysing people and situations. Although you tend to dramatise yourself and life around you, and are prone to emotional ups and downs — underneath you're far more level-headed than you might think. You have a great deal of faith in yourself, and although you're often influenced by people and circumstances, you have basic good sense which will keep you out of danger.

Mostly (c)

You have mixed feelings about ghosts, ghouls and the occult in general. Your common sense tells you it's nonsense, yet your emotions seem to contradict you. Perhaps you're more psychic than you realise, and only a fear of the world beyond has stopped you from believing in it.

Basically you live in *this* world, and enjoy all the good things it has to offer. You're a sophisticated and ambitious person who enjoys comfort, and likes to make a good impression on others.

Your head tends to rule your instincts and although you cope with life very well in general, you are thrown by the unusual or the bizarre.

You demand a lot from life and relationships and in general you get on well with people and tend to be rather a leader. There is a tough, cool side to your nature which doesn't often appear, but which is very useful indeed in many situations. Carry on avoiding the lure of the occult — you are far too vital and busy in this world to have time for the world beyond.

Mostly (d)

You can stand up to ghosts and ghouls and occult happenings any day, because you have the knack of dismissing them entirely and overcoming any difficulty by sheer force of personality.

You are a brave, active, adventurous person. Being basically practical, you can cope with situations and people without getting into emotional tangles. You cut your way through life in such a decisive manner that you usually end up getting your own way. You are determined and single-minded, and your mind is usually occupied with what is in front of you. You haven't much time for wondering and soul-searching and, as far as you're concerned the world beyond can go back where it came from!

You are a strong person with strong feelings and opinions, and you're never likely to be worried by ghouls and phantoms — in fact, the poor, innocent spirits don't stand a ghost of a chance with you around!

I WAS SO SURE I'D LANDED A DREAM JOB

LOOKING back now on the time I spent working for Louise, I can hardly believe it happened. It's like a nightmare, strange and unreal.

When I first got the job, though, it was more like a dream. Companion/help to a 22-year-old disabled girl, living right in the centre of London in a luxury flat.

Since I was a kid I've had this dream of being independent, getting away from our quiet little town to somewhere alive and exciting. When I read the newspaper ad and then actually landed the job, I was walking on air.

I knew my mother was a bit worried. I'd never been anywhere without the family before. But she knew how much I wanted to go, and she never tried to stop me. She and Gran insisted on coming down to London with me to see me settled; and though they didn't say as much, to meet the girl I was going to work for and see if she was OK.

I hadn't met Louise either till that day. Her mother, who was very posh and lived in a big house with a heated-swimming pool and servants all over the place, had taken me on. Louise seemed nice. She was very quiet, and I thought that, like me, she probably felt a bit shy with strangers.

Four years before, her car had been in a head-on collision with a lorry, and she had spent a year in hospital. Now she was confined to a wheelchair and would never walk. But she insisted on living her own life away from her wealthy family, and she had just taken this flat. She even did a part-time job as a telephonist, driving to work in an invalid car.

She didn't tell me all this, her mother did. I thought she must be very brave, and my mother did too. If a crippled girl could leave home and manage alone, I ought to be ashamed of myself for being nervous at leaving the nest.

When Mum left, she hugged me and said something about promising to come home if I wasn't happy. I laughed it off, I was determined to make a go of the job, and being unhappy didn't seem likely.

HOW wrong can you be? In the first week, any illusions I'd had about having time off to see the sights and enjoy myself, went up in smoke. Louise had to be helped with everything, including having a bath every day, and I found I was working seventeen hours a day. I was on duty seven days one week, and five the next — but by the time my weekend off came round, I was too exhausted to do anything except sleep.

Maybe the work wouldn't have mattered if Louise had turned out to be nice as I'd thought, or even bearable. Her quietness certainly wasn't shyness, more a feeling that she was my employer and I was her servant, and talking to me was beneath her.

She acted like a queen, shouting for me every few minutes, to put a book back on the shelf or take a speck of dust off the carpet. Even being in the bath was no excuse for me not rushing immediately.

I had to eat my breakfast standing up in the kitchen, washing tea-towels, and if she had friends in, I was banished to the kitchen and not allowed to come out till they had gone.

At night, when she got back from work, she would check the cutlery and crockery and the contents of the fridge. In case I was stealing the silver or eating more than I should, I suppose.

I tried to make excuses for her. She'd been brought up with servants. She was used to being waited on. Things would change when we got to know each other. You have to make allowances for how frustrated and unhappy she must be, being in a wheelchair. I was much more fortunate than her really — even if I was poor and miserable and homesick, and she'd inherited a fortune from her grandparents.

But all the brainwashing I could manage didn't help when the workmen came in to do a few jobs, and she made me hide the towels in case they used them, and instructed me to charge them 2p for coffee. At night I'd lie awake, thinking of my nice family who hadn't any money to spare but would give anyone anything.

I thought of Mum, worrying maybe that I was out too late, living it up. I never told them the true story when I wrote. A few times I almost did, but I ripped up the letters. Once I even packed my suitcase, but I couldn't crawl home and admit I'd failed,

especially when my family had told everyone back home what a great job I had.

ONE day, pushing her round the supermarket, I thought the breakthrough had finally happened, she wanted to be friends. She asked me if I liked cheesecake, and when I said yes, she bought two pieces. Back home she had me cut one piece in half and handed me half, while she ate all the rest herself. She watched me all the time to see how I took it, and I almost threw my piece in her smug face.

Shortly after that came the night I had my "funny turn." I got violent pains in my stomach and had to be taken to hospital, where I was examined and questioned by a doctor for two hours. It was my nerves, he told me. I needed to do less work, or I was heading for a nervous breakdown.

I didn't even mention the diagnosis to Louise, who didn't look worried anyway. Things just carried on where they left off, and I suppose I might have had a breakdown if it hadn't been for Dave, who came to mend the phone, and succeeded in making me see sense.

He was so nice and friendly and it had been so long since I had talked, really talked, to anyone, that I poured out the whole story. I even made him a cup of coffee.

"You must be mad," he said. "Why don't you just walk out?" Then, without waiting for an answer, "I suppose you're ashamed to go home and admit the streets of London weren't paved with gold after all. Everyone fails sometimes, love. It's not your fault. Nobody will love you less."

I laughed. I'd almost forgotton how. "There's something else, though," I said seriously. "I don't like Louise, but I feel responsible for her. She depends on me. What would she do without me?"

"Find someone else, maybe someone who suits her better. Having a girl your age around must be a constant reminder of what her life was like before the accident. I expect she's jealous of you."

IT seemed incredible that Louise could envy me. But then I hadn't really thought much about her feelings. I'd been too busy hating her and trying to hang on to my sanity. I'd never got through to her. Maybe some of it was my fault. I hadn't that much patience and understanding. Someone older might have. Just telling someone about it made it a bit better. I wished I'd done that before.

My next weekend off, I left for good, the coward's way, I'm afraid. I knew Louise's mother was coming for her, so I left a note saying I wouldn't be back and slipped away.

I'm in my new job now, looking after a lovely little girl, still in London, and I love it. I'm relaxed and not neurotic about making a "success" of it. I know now I don't have to prove anything to anyone. Dave was right. People don't love you less just because you can't work miracles.

But I often think about Louise and I hope she is happier. I wish I could have helped her. I only hope someone else can.

THE MOST BEAUTIFUL MAN IN THE WORLD (see page 18)

Well . . . maybe we'll just settle for them the way they are!

RUSSELL MAEL

DAVID ESSEX

DAVID BOWIE

DAVID CASSIDY

DONNY OSMOND

Are You A HUMAN DUSTBIN ?

✗ AVOID . . .

Butter or margarine: 266 calories per oz.

½ pint white sauce: 527 calories

Salad cream: approx. 100 calories per tablespoon

Large slice of bread: 105 calories

Cream of tomato soup, 1 portion: 111 calories

Egg Mayonnaise: 280 calories
Cheddar cheese: 120 calories per oz.
Cream cheese: 180 calories per oz.
Cod, fried in breadcrumbs, 1 portion: 583 calories
Mackerel, 3 oz can: 240 calories
Roast beef, 3 oz portion: 327 calories

Chips, average portion: 250 calories

Carton of coleslaw: 320 calories

Large banana: 80 calories
Tinned fruit salad, 1 portion: 140 calories
Strawberry fruit fool, carton: 213 calories
Apple pie, average portion: 300 calories
Chocolate pudding and sauce, 4 oz portion: 661 calories
Danish pastry: 473 calories
Scone with butter, jam and cream: 515 calories

Chocolates, toffees, fudge: 160 calories per oz.

Glass of milk (½ pint): 190 calories

Coca Cola, 1 glass: 80 calories

✓ INSTEAD . . .

Outline: 110 calories per oz.

Sauce made with Outline, low fat milk: 255 calories

Waistline: 40 calories per tablespoon. Or dressing made from vinegar (no calories) or lemon juice (no calories) with dried herbs (experiment yourself!)

Crispbread: approx. 26 calories per slice

Kidney soup, 1 portion: 67 calories

Boiled egg: 80 calories
Edam cheese: 88 calories per oz.
Cottage cheese: 33 calories per oz.
Cod, grilled, 1 portion: 188 calories

Sardines in tomato, 3: 120 calories
Roast chicken, 3 oz portion: 162 calories

Potatoes, boiled, average portion: 115 calories. (If you can substitute green vegetables, so much the better. Average portion of cabbage — only 12 calories!)

Own salad made from grated carrots, shredded cabbage and onions with vinegar dressing: 24 calories

Medium apple: 40 calories
1 orange: 60 calories

Plain low fat yoghurt, carton: 60-90 calories (depending on make)
Baked apple: 150 calories
Chocolate swiss roll, 1 slice: 82 calories
Piece of sponge cake: 150 calories
Cream meringue: 150 calories

Boiled sweets and pastilles: 100 calories per oz. Liquorice: 84 calories per oz.

Glass of skimmed milk, or made up dried low-fat milk powder (½ pint): 100 calories

Low calorie drink, per glass: 8 calories

EVERYBODY knows the only way to get slim is to cut down on what you eat. That means consuming less calories — a calorie being a unit by which the "fattening" value of food is measured.

So you probably know a cheese salad is far less fattening than a Wimpy and chips (because it contains a lot less calories), and you'd be better off munching an apple for your mid afternoon break than a bar of chocolate.

But that's often about as far as it goes. Unless you go around with a complete calorie list in your hand and swot it up before every morsel goes into your mouth, you'll probably find it pretty hard to remember what's good and what's not so good, out of the hundreds of things you consume every day.

And that's where would-be slimmers meet their doom! It's easy enough to stick to ideas like "cakes and biscuits are fattening" and "cheese and meat are good for you," but you *could* be kidding yourself along all the while. You see, if you cut out those couple of plain biscuits you usually eat when you get home but fill up with Cheddar cheese, you might well be a few hundred calories worse off!

There are dozens of things you just get used to eating, without imagining what they're doing to your calorie intake. That all-milk bedtime drink for instance; a couple of buttery scrambled eggs on toast, a toffee or two . . .

So, what we're going to do is tell you how to be your own calorie counter — *without* re-membering loads of figures,

without having to follow a rigid, boring diet.

First, then, here's your own magic no-diet diet! Once you've got the basic rules in your head, you'll be able to eat sensibly and slimly for as long as you like! All you've got to remember is: **IT'S BAD IF**

There's a lot of oil in it.
It's very buttery.
It's a combination of sugar, fat and flour (e.g. pastry!)
It's heavy and solid rather than watery or airy (e.g. fruit cakes are much higher in calories than light sponges.)
It's anything in or on pastry.
It's processed and tinned (most of these foods have added sugar or fat) — unless specially for slimmers!

And IT'S GOOD IF
It's grilled or boiled.
It's in its natural state.
It's specifically labelled "low fat."
It's a vegetable cooked without any fat.

Remember, these are general rules; but to put you right about the foods you're most likely to eat, read on! We're *not* telling you the obvious and the boring, like "Have a stick of celery instead of a cream bun." Of course that's the ideal, but if you've *got* to have something sweet, and nothing else will do, you'll see you *can* indulge yourself. So we're suggesting realistic alternatives, not torture-yourself ones!

You'll find lots of surprises here — a few things you never thought of as fattening, but which can be disastrous; and some that are allowable, rather than a far worse alternative!

And these are all things that may give you a big surprise, so — watch out!

Cheese and biscuits (average portion): 306
Cheesecake (one slice): 606
Milky bedtime drink: 322
Scrambled eggs on toast: 527

Nuts: 170 per oz.
Chocolate brazil, 1: 65
1 square of chocolate: 40
1 crisp: 5 calories
1 chip: 31 calories
Pastry, shortcrust: 157 calories per oz.
1 peanut: 6 calories
1 walnut: 18 calories

Remember, if you're planning to lose weight, 1,200-1,500 calories a day — and no more! — are what you should aim for.

Real dangers to diets, then, are things that are: FRIED, FATTY, SUGARY, HEAVY or PRO-CESSED.

◉ Dieting's difficult, but it's going to be a lot easier now you know the basics!

WATCH OUT

Here's an "annual" look at our TV favourites! It's a very special selection of people whom we think made really good TV viewing! We'd like to give them all a Watch Out award — and here are a few reasons why . . .

Good old **NOEL EDMONDS** must be one of the busiest men around, but in his role of host on "Swapshop" he never let the action flag, and he keeps us laughing!

ow could we miss the ost famous frog of them ll! **KERMIT** has a ough job keeping those uppets in order. He efinitely has something o be able to emerge nscathed from Miss iggy's attacks!

Here's someone who's come from down under to up top — lovely Australian, **JEFF PHILLIPS.** We'd like to give him a special award for always looking as if he's really enjoying himself!

Someone with a real talent for comedy — **PAULINE QUIRKE.** In her TV appearances, she shows that she's a born comedienne and deserves to go far.

ROBIN ELLIS as the dashing Captain Ross Poldark captured all our hearts. It must be the way he copes with major disasters without batting an eyelid. Added to the fact that he's very handsome, of course, and looks marvellous in his 18th century costumes!

Whatever show he's in, **RICHARD O'SULLIVAN** always seems to be cooking up something good!

CHARLIE'S ANGELS brought a great deal of glamour and fun to our screens, and we thought it was great the way they solved all those crimes so effortlessly. Of course, Farrah has left the series now but with her looks we think she'll be a successful "fallen angel."

ROBERT POWELL must ave one of the most eautiful pairs of eyes ver, and those, coupled ith his superb acting, made "Jesus of Nazareth" compelling viewing.

For sheer smoothness we couldn't ignore lovely **GARETH HUNT** and his smooth acting in "The New Avengers"!

Here's someone frightfully smart — it's **ANTHONY VALENTINE** in his role of "Raffles." Whatever happened to him, he always remained cool and calm, showing that a successful jewel thief and safecracker can be a perfect gentleman, too!

Blimey, guv, we couldn't forget this geezer! **DENNIS WATERMAN** isn't just a talented actor, though, he's turning his attentions to singing and songwriting — quite a change from Detective-Sergeant Carter's hobbies!

IAN OGILVY is the lucky actor who landed himself the starring role of "The Saint." But if you take a look at him, it's not very difficult to see how he managed it!

We all *had* to stay in to watch "Rich Man, Poor Man" and we hold **JAMES CARROLL JORDAN** in his role of Billy Abbott personally responsible for completely changing our Saturday night routines!

ARE YOU A SPACE-AGE STAR?

COULD you be a fearless space explorer, travelling through time and space to uncharted planets and unknown dangers? Find out if you really fit into the Space Age by whizzing through our special quiz journey. Travel round the Universe with us, and when your trip's over there'll be some home truths waiting for you!

1. You need a bit of a break, and rush to the Galaxy Travel Bureau to book a trip round the Universe — well, it's a change from Bognor Regis, anyway. You hire a space-craft called —
   - (d) Eagle-Ray,
   - (a) Endeavour,
   - (b) Bertie,
   - (c) Queen of the Skies.

2. The friendly old moon is your first stop, where you're booked into —
   - (a) The Sea of Tranquillity Retreat,
   - (c) The Man-in-the-Moon Motel,
   - (d) The Lunar Hilton,
   - (b) Habitation 23rd Crater West Central.

3. You bounce about happily on the moon for a few days, but it's rather crowded and you keep bumping into people, so you shoot on to Mars. A young Martian falls madly in love with you and follows you around everywhere. The only trouble is —
   - (d) these holiday romances never seem to work out,
   - (b) you don't really fancy kissing someone with an emerald green face and a TV aerial sticking out of the top of their head,
   - (a) you haven't really got a great deal in common with each other,
   - (c) you don't want to be disloyal to your boyfriend back home?

4. So you decide to breeze off along the planetary tourist trail, but something seems to have gone wrong. Jupiter and Saturn go whizzing by and you seem to be hurtling through —
   - (b) a remote, unmapped cluster of bright young stars,
   - (a) a weird echoing black void into infinity,
   - (c) a star-spangled fairyland swathed in a floating gaseous blue mist,
   - (d) a fiery furnace of angry sky, with glowing burnt-out suns, and black smoke clouds.

5. Well, you wanted to get away from it all but this is ridiculous! You fight with the controls as you're carried further and further off course. Suddenly a strange object comes towards you. You can't quite make it out, but —
   - (c) it seems to be a flock of giant golden birds, their wings shimmering and their beaks bared,
   - (b) it's only a common or garden exploding meteor, that's all!
   - (d) it's a hostile space-ship with menacing arrow-heads and huge ungodly black metal claws,
   - (a) it's like some kind of ectoplasm, a ghost cloud changing shape, now a human form, now a monster . . .

6. You plunge on —
   - (d) through magnetic storms and hurtling comets,
   - (a) beyond the hideous, wailing caverns of darkest Pluto,
   - (b) through solar systems and galaxies,
   - (c) into the timeless heavens of no return.

You realise you are hopelessly lost. What's your reaction when the awful thought strikes you that you may never see the dear old planet Earth again?
(a) I'll just have to find a new kind of spiritual existence, and develop a new character to cope with a solitary life in space.
(c) Oh no, please God, it's too terrible! Never to see my family and friends again. I'm lonely and homesick. I can't even send Mum a postcard!
(d) Never see planet Earth again? Don't be silly, of course I will. I'll fight with everything in my power to get back again.
(b) Oh well, at least I'll get out of the end of term exams, won't I?

. Suddenly you are pulled by a magnetic force onto an unknown planet. You peer hesitantly out of the window to see —
(d) a time-switched scene of ancient Greek palaces, golden harps and magnificent warriors on horseback,
(c) a snow-covered wilderness with the strange sound of the wind across the ice, a silver palace in the distance.
(b) a civilisation so advanced it makes your mind boggle.
(a) a network of rumbling caves with unearthly reptiles and weird music echoing from within.

. Terrified, you step out of the spacecraft to be greeted by a handsome boy, who says his name is Damian Jones and he's —
(c) a flying doctor on a mercy mission,
(a) a space artist and photographer on a magazine assignment,
(b) Dr Who's trainee assistant, out to get the Time Lords,
(d) on a secret mission for the Foreign Office.

10. You think Damian is the most amazing person you've ever met because —
(d) he's wearing a black velvet cape and is carrying a weird-looking briefcase,
(b) he obviously knew how to get here - so surely he can get you back home,
(a) he has the most fascinating eyes you've ever gazed into,
(c) he looks just like Robert Redford.

11. It's love at first sight and as you stand hand in hand gazing out over the starry skies, he tells you —
(b) he'd love you madly even if you weren't the only girl around for fifty billion light years,
(c) he wants to do something incredibly old-fashioned like taking you back to Earth and marrying you,

(d) he's been around in Space for a long time with a girlfriend on every planet, but he's never met anyone like you!
(a) it can't just be coincidence, it must be fate meeting him in this desolate place.

12. Clever Damian gets you both back to earth simply by —
(d) swallowing a time capsule,
(c) borrowing a magic carpet,
(a) using his psychic powers of auto-suggestion,
(b) phoning the inter-space rocket taxi service.

13. So there you are safe in your lovely earth-bound home, with your cosy bed, your Starsky and Hutch pin-ups and your hot cocoa. What's your verdict as you think back over your "holiday?"
(c) It was a long way to go to meet a new boyfriend, but it was worth it!
(a) It was a wonderful, enriching spiritual experience.

(d) Never mind spiritual enrichment, I'll sell my story to the highest bidder.
(b) I think I'll stick to Bognor Regis next year!

Count your score, mainly (a), (b), (c) or (d) and turn to the conclusions below.

Conclusions

Mostly (a)

Your planet is Uranus, that mysterious far away planet shrouded in the secrecy of the unknown. This is because your questing mind is always fascinated by the strange and mysterious. You are also rather a private sort of person, with your own thoughts and feelings and your own individual way of looking at life.

You're introverted and thoughtful, good at sensing atmospheres and using your instincts. You're also self-sufficient, with a quiet, inner confidence in yourself, and this makes you very adaptable. Therefore you could cope feeling lonely and isolated. You need a few really good close friends around you, that's all, and a super boy who is as aware and sensitive as you are.

As for life on the planet Earth, you tend to find some people shallow, and daily routine a bit boring. You're rather an idealist and would like to create your own beautiful world around you. You're good at that — but remember to come down to earth occasionally, won't you?

Mostly (b)

Your planet is Mars, the planet of action, sometimes warlike, sometimes friendly, but always strong and practical. You have a great deal of confidence in yourself, and although you're generally easy-going, you also have a hot temper and a will of your own. You can cope with life and look after yourself and you're nobody's fool. You're also sociable and extrovert, with a great sense of humour. You have faith in yourself, and courage, and this means that you could cope with life on Earth. You have a lot of energy and drive, a sense of adventure and a hard-headed attitude to life. You're seldom worried by doubt and your positive approach usually guarantees you success in whatever you set out to achieve.

You seem to be doing very well on Earth, so you might as well explore this world to the full before you go blasting off to Mars!

Mostly (c)

Your planet is Venus, the planet of love, beauty and sensitivity. You're a sensitive sort of person, living on your emotions, and your relationships are the most important part of your life. You tend to romanticise people and situations, sometimes reading too much into people's actions and motives.

You're a very imaginative person with a genuine appreciation of nature and beautiful things. You're not very practical, but your feminine intuition usually leads you to the right judgments and decisions.

You are honest and sympathetic, a loyal friend who respects confidences and can be trusted with secrets. You're nostalgic and sentimental by nature, so you're not a very good candidate for becoming an astronaut of the future.

You love the world you live in, so why waste time whizzing about in Space? You want to find beautiful places and beautiful relationships as near to home as possible.

Mostly (d)

Your planet is Jupiter, most powerful and magnificent of all the planets! You're a dramatic person, with change-able moods. You love the limelight and hate being second best. You want to be a special person, with special powers and talents so that others admire you and look up to you.

People perhaps think you're a bit conceited sometimes, and that you sulk if you don't get your own way. It's simply that you have a very strong personality and perhaps haven't learnt to cope with yourself yet. But the sky's the limit as far as you're concerned; you're ambitious and dynamic with a magnetic charm.

Although you're not afraid of Space, you're a worldly sort of person who wants all the best things the planet Earth can provide.

But you'd be happy wherever you could carve out some space for yourself — and where you weren't alone.

97

WILL HE BE YOUR PRINCE CHARMING?

— or will he be your Toad of Toad Hall? Find out with our fun panto guide to boys!

WINTER'S the time for pantomimes, when all the Principal Boys take the stage. And could some of those Principal Boys be appearing in your life this winter? Some of them are super enough to be top of the bill, but others deserve to be booed out of sight. So read on and see how to get (and get rid of!) your Principal Boys!

PETER PAN

You remember, he's the one with the secret of eternal youth. You *must* know some boys like this. They just can't grow up.

COSTUME: Jeans, sneakers, and horrible sweaters with Donald Duck motifs knitted by their adoring grans.

ACT: To prove he has the secret of eternal youth, Peter Pan will be full of boyish pranks. When it snows, you'll get hit in the face by a snowball. When it's frosty, you'll be pushed over on the ice. All this is just to show his affection, of course!

If he's *really* beginning to grow up, he might ask you out . . . fishing! Which means sitting on a freezing riverbank for hours while he boasts about his maggots. Don't let him see how disgusted you are, or he might shove a few down your back!

HOW TO GET RID OF HIM Talk non- stop at the top of your voice so you frighten the fish away.

KING RAT

The leader of the pack. The evil one. His very presence casts a chill and yet some girls (yes, even you) might be attracted by his air of sinister mystery.

COSTUME: Could be leathers, could be football supporter's gear; depends on whether he's into deafening people or flattening them!

ACT: King Rat doesn't believe in charm. With him it's the strong-arm approach. He'll expect you to fetch his crisps at break, let him copy your homework, and buy his fags for him — and to show his contempt for pain, he'll stub out the fags on the palm of your hand. To King Rat a girl is there just to be impressed.

So your job's to sit around and look enthusiastic as he bullies people, revs his motorbike, and punches walls to show how hard he is. If this sort of life appeals to you . . . keep quiet about it, for goodness' sake! And if not . . .

HOW TO GET RID OF HIM Get a cat (try Dick Whittington) or call in the Rodent Exterminating Officer.

BUTTONS

The boy-next-door, the brotherly ty~~pe~~ who's always there to put his arm rou~~nd~~ you (and that's all!) when things are go~~ing~~ badly. When things are going well, ~~of~~ course, you're off like a shot (nea~~rly~~ breaking his arm as you go!).

COSTUME: The ordinary boy-next-do~~or~~ gear of jeans, sweater and anorak. ~~But~~ don't forget the BUTTONS; usually la~~pel~~ buttons saying things like, *IF YOU CA~~N~~ READ THIS YOU ARE STANDIN~~G~~ TOO CLOSE* or, *WATCH OUT, I BIT~~E~~* (Actually, of course he doesn't bite; h~~e's~~ totally harmless, but you can't go rou~~nd~~ wearing a lapel-badge saying, *I~~'M~~ TOTALLY HARMLESS,* can you?)

ACT: Being a Nice Guy to everybo~~dy.~~ He's even nice to your little broth~~er,~~ which takes a bit of doing. Buttons ~~will~~ do your nasty jobs for you (such as pum~~p-~~ ing up your bicycle tyres on freez~~ing~~ mornings). If an old lady slips up on ~~the~~ icy pavement, he'll be out there in a fla~~sh~~ with bandages, blankets, and kind wor~~ds.~~

If there's any trouble at school, h~~e'll~~ own up right away — even if he has~~n't~~ done it! And he always remembers eve~~ry-~~ body's birthday, even the maths teache~~r's.~~ Of course, he *adores* you, and has do~~ne~~ for years. Which is why he's just ~~the~~ slightest bit of a bore.

HOW TO GET RID OF HIM Give h~~im~~ a lapel-button which says, *PRE~~SS~~ BUTTON TO RELEASE . . .*

DANDINI (Master of the Revels)

Winter brings out all Dandini's love of finery and entertainment. It's the season for parties, and Dandini knows where they all are — and if there aren't any, he'll throw one himself.

COSTUME: Velvet trousers, three-piece suits, cashmere sweaters, posh fur coats, leather boots . . . etc.

ACT: Prepare to play second fiddle, because as far as Dandini is concerned, you're just a fancy accessory and not *quite* as attractive as his Indian silk scarf!

He'll want to parade up and down the High Street on Saturday mornings, and he'll always be eager to show his clothes off at the disco that night, so if you like window-shopping and bopping, he's great. But if not . . .

HOW TO GET RID OF HIM Greet him one day with, "Hello, you look scruffy!" Or borrow his best coat and fall down in the mud.

TOAD OF TOAD HALL

The main thing about Toad is that he's always boasting about his gadgets. And they're always new and expensive. You know the type of thing.

COSTUME: He may have goggly eyes and be covered in warts, but we all have our problems, don't we?

ACT: You can hear Toad coming: "I'm getting this Honda 125 with chrome crash bars and . . ." He'll try to impress you with details of his calculator (hyper-bionic and technicolour with a built-in cassette deck), his fountain pen (centrally-heated for comfort during November exams), and his pushbike (with new hovercraft attachments).

If you're technologically inclined, Toad can be fun, but if you're not, it can get quite a lot like a Consumer's Report from the 21st century!

HOW TO GET RID OF HIM Borrow one of his gadgets and flush it down the lavatory.

PRINCE CHARMING

He doesn't have to be a real prince — there aren't enough of them to go round, nowadays! But there are a few Prince Charmings lurking in even the most ordinary streets.

COSTUME: Prince Charming has good taste and whatever he wears looks good on him — even if it's a grey wig, white tights and high-heeled shoes!

ACT: Prince Charming is aptly named. If it's freezing cold, he'll insist on putting his coat around your shoulders. If it's pouring with rain, he'll put down his coat for you to walk over puddles. (In fact, he seems to want to get rid of that coat!)

He's a real old-fashioned gentleman. If anyone tells a rude joke, he'll raise his eyebrows and look disgusted. (Maybe he laughs about it alone, afterwards.) He's totally enchanting to all ladies — even your mum. In fact, it's when you realise that Mum likes him that you begin to think something might be wrong . . .

HOW TO GET RID OF HIM Say, "Cor coo o mi GAWD BLIMEY***" and wipe your nose on the back of your hand.

ALADDIN

Remember him? The boy from the laundry who loved exploring? And got rich with the help of his genie?

COSTUME: This is a rags-to-riches story, so he wears rags or at least, raggy jeans. (Still, everybody wears raggy jeans nowadays, so he may be difficult to recognise.)

ACT: Aladdin likes exploring, so prepare yourself to be taken up hills (draughty), down dales (boggy), and across moors (bare, boggy and draughty). Snow and ice will not deter him. In fact, it'll spur him on, so make sure you have at least three jerseys (get him to lend you some from the laundry).

As for his other interest — doing magic tricks and giving people expensive presents . . . well, it's a bit suspect nowadays. So if he gives you a brand-new transistor radio and says it's from his genie, be suspicious! It might well have fallen off the back of a lorry — and what judge is going to believe that story about a genie?

HOW TO GET RID OF HIM Have a word with his genie. He might be able to arrange something.

Write for the present!

Did you know that just by looking at your boyfriend's signature, you can tell an awful lot about him? And, at Christmas you might wonder what he's like when it comes to the present stakes — will he give you one for a start, and if he does, how will he give it? Will he press it into your hands and run away blushing or organise a presentation in front of all your friends? Well, take a good look at our special guide and it'll tell you a lot about the boy in your life at the "present" time!

If his signature is large and flamboyant with lots of flourishes and twirls to it, then he's friendly and extrovert. He'll buy you the biggest bunch of flowers, the largest box of chocolates — yes, he's a bit showy! — and he'll shower you with kisses when he hands them over, too.

If his signature is the same size as the rest of his script he doesn't put on any act, he's just what he seems to be — reliable and sincere. He's loyal and you'll know where you are with him. His present will be practical and something you want. He'll make no bones about handing it over and expect a friendly kiss in return.

The small signature writer will demonstrate his slight secretiveness and wrap his present carefully. He's very cautious and if he does put a message with his present, it could be a very brief one. It's because he's shy and thoughtful, but he does mean what he says.

If his signature is tall and narrow — watch it! — he could be quite mean when it comes to gifts. He's not really keen on going out and when he does he might even expect you to pay for yourself. He's likely to be mean about presents because privately he thinks they're a waste of money.

If his signature is small and has a left slant you could be in for a nice surprise. He isn't going to reveal his affections for all the world to see, but he'll have good taste and go searching for something that's just you. If he genuinely likes you — you're in luck!

If his signature is threadlike — tapering off with thin strokes at the end, or like Steven's with a straight line in the middle of his name, then he knows how to handle people. He will know exactly what to buy to please you. The only thing is, he might not remember to get the present, since he's not always very reliable.

Watch the writer who underlines his name — he's full of himself and a bit of a show-off. He'll want to make an impression in his own style. He's determined, ambitious and sure of himself and he could be pushy. He might give you something that looks impressive, but isn't very useful!

A large rounded signature denotes a fun-loving personality, even if he's a bit lazy — he's not very dishy, but that's just the way he is! His present could be useless or a piece of nonsense, but one that will give you a laugh anyway!

With a long starting stroke to his name, he's not going to be impulsive or spontaneous in his present-giving or his affection. He's a ditherer and very, very cautious about money. So don't look for anything too exciting from him, he's not good at being generous!

If you find yourself looking at a signature that's ringed round, this is a danger sign. It means, "keep off." This writer is afraid of too much involvement with people and isn't really interested in friendships. He's a loner and you'll be lucky to get a present at all!

The writer who races across the page with a very pronounced right slant is emotional and changeable in his behaviour. He could drag you along with him to buy a present or he could forget about it altogether — it depends on his mood, but whatever he does he'll do it with a great show of emotion!

This type of signature reveals a very unemotional boy who doesn't like fuss or flattery, so he won't bother to give it himself. His approach to giving presents will be strictly down-to-earth but if he has a right slant to his signature a little bit of the romantic could lurk behind that calm, collected surface. So he could come up with a nice surprise!

SURVIVAL GUIDE TO PARTIES

It's the season of parties — well, what else is there to do when the weather turns nasty? But if the thought of parties makes you feel quite weak, here's a few tips to help you through — and to make sure it really *is* the season of goodwill!

Here's how to cope with:

THE OFFICE PARTY

Do make sure you get there on time.
Don't take your coat off until there are at least six other people between you and the office Romeo!
Do wish your boss a Happy Christmas.
Don't go and meet him in the Post Room at midnight as he suggested!
Do offer to serve the drinks round.
Don't let the Office Manager mix you a special Gin Fizz!
Do wear your new dress.
Don't experiment with low necklines — unless you intend to keep your cardigan on!
Do try and look as though you're having a great time, even when everyone around you is doing the Hokey-Cokey for the fifth time.
Don't imagine it's a good time to ask for a rise — even if the cleaner does earn more than you.
Do have a go at dancing, just once, even if it's only with the pimply creep in the corner.
Don't ask the DJ to play the Stranglers' new record when everyone else is waltzing.
Do keep a clear head — it doesn't look good to fall on the floor after only two shandies.
Don't bother about causing a scene when the dumb blonde secretary on the dance floor makes eyes at your fella — go out there and quietly tread on those twinkling toes of hers.
Do avoid the smoothie young executive when he comes round with the mistletoe for the sixth time — he's got no plans for getting you home on time!
Don't believe that kiss and cuddle with the advertising clerk goes unnoticed — it doesn't!
Do get to work on time the next morning — otherwise tongues will wag!

THE FAMILY PARTY

Do help get things ready — even though you can't stand Uncle Bert and Auntie Ivy.
Don't tell your mum you refuse to go — though the thought of hearing Uncle Jack's dirty jokes for the third year running makes you cringe.
Do some of the food preparations — if they're good, perhaps everyone will eat too much and go home early.
Don't be spiteful and sprinkle salt over the Christmas pudding.
Do put all the presents round the Christmas tree.
Don't let Grandad get hold of your brother's Sex Maniac's Diary, a special present from you.
Do set place-names on the dining-table.
Don't put Granny too near the brandy butter.
Do offer everyone a festive drink.
Don't let Uncle Arthur near Dad's whisky — he drank the lot last year!

Do pull the crackers — but not too near the cat.
Don't encourage your younger brother to practise his party tricks on Auntie Ethel — he lost her false teeth last Christmas!
Do remember to hang up the mistletoe.
Don't get caught by Uncle George like last year — he counted the number of berries then insisted on the same number of kisses!
Do play party games like Charades and Chinese Whispers.
Don't encourage cousin Bertha's request for a game of Monopoly using real money.
Do invite your friends over to join in the fun.
Don't ask the boy you fancy — if you want to see him again!
Do wish everyone goodnight — if you can stay awake long enough.
Don't stop to think what fun it'll be next year, when the party starts all over again!

A FRIEND'S PARTY

Do take your coat upstairs to her room.
Don't get pinned against the wall by the first eager beaver you meet on the stairs.
Do circulate — it keeps the eager beavers on their toes!
Don't get trapped in a corner with the guy who reckons he's the life and soul of the party.
Do look like you're enjoying yourself.
Don't spend too much time in the kitchen if the strip-lighting makes you look like a puffy peach.
Do remember to eat some food — you don't want to keel over after a glass of fizzy orange.
Don't get carried away and pile your plate with too much — it'll only end up in someone's lap.
Do make sure you've got a glass in your hand — you never know who'll come along and fill it up!
Don't go to the wrong cupboard and take one of their best cut-glass goblets by mistake.
Do experiment with some new make-up.
Don't go mad and risk the sparkly sort if there's any chance it'll bring you out in boils.
Do go along to the hairdresser and have your hair done.
Don't listen when they say everyone's having their hair sprayed silver for Yuletide.
Do flirt a little — it's Christmas after all!
Don't let your boyfriend catch you.
Do stand near the mistletoe — just in case.
Don't go and get off with your best friend's bloke because *he* was standing near the mistletoe!
Do go home with the guy who brought you.
Don't expect an invitation next year if you were the belle of the ball!

And since (hopefully) you're going to be spending eight hours a day, five days a week of your life in some sort of job, it's only natural that you want an interesting, worthwhile one that's suited to your own, unique talents.

So whether you're still at school and don't have much idea of what you want to do, or are still looking for a job, or maybe already have a job but don't like it much, we're going to help you take a fresh look at your problems and show you the first practical steps to take to put things right. After all, it's *your* life — and you don't want to waste a minute of it in work that's pointless, boring or just plain hateful!

I just haven't any idea what I want to do when I leave school. My parents tell me I should try for one thing, my Careers teacher says I should try something else — and I'm just stuck, very undecided and confused, in the middle.

If this is your problem, the first thing you should do is — *leave as many options open as you can.*

This means that if, for instance, you're trying to choose a course to follow at school, university, polytechnic, training college or whatever, but have no very definite career in mind, don't choose a narrow course, but get the widest one you can, which leads to the most career possibilities later.

If you're job-hunting and can't find exactly what you have in mind, don't throw the whole thing up in despair. Try, instead, to get into some job that has links with the career you've got in mind.

For instance, if you have ambitions towards writing, in journalism or advertising or anything similar, but prospects are dim, don't throw away your dreams and head for the nearest factory — take secretarial work in a firm with strong connections with advertising, public relations, magazines or publishing.

There may be ways of edging your way towards that dream career, and in any case secretarial work is always helpful to a would-be writer!

I've just started a course to help me towards my future career — but I've been in it two months now, and I hate it!

If this is your problem, we'd say that you really should try never to leave a course unfinished.

Dropping out halfway through or (worse still!) at the very beginning, is going to damage your self-confidence and it won't look good on your record. So you have absolutely nothing to gain by dropping out. On the other hand, if you finish the course, you have a very great deal to gain.

If you put your mind to it and pass the course, you don't *have* to use it in a follow-up career, but the very fact that you have qualifications of ANY kind shows prospective employers that you have intelligence and perseverance, all good points to have on your side in these days of high unemployment.

Also, you may be able to use the qualification in a way you haven't realised — specialist training like nursing, or O levels in maths and science subjects, have wide application in many jobs.

And even if you do fail to obtain a pass or other qualification at the end of your

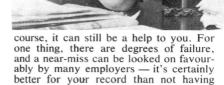

course, it can still be a help to you. For one thing, there are degrees of failure, and a near-miss can be looked on favourably by many employers — it's certainly better for your record than not having taken the subject at all!

Of course, if you've embarked on a course and you really have given it every chance, but realise that you'll never, ever, make a nurse, hairdresser, dental assistant or whatever, you really ought to have a word with your parents and your teachers at college. They may be able to reassure you that you're not doing quite as badly as you thought you were — or they may advise you to change courses.

A change of course, like this, though, should never be embarked on without a lot of thought and without a lot of discussion with parents and teachers alike. If you start to make a habit of chopping and changing from one course to another, you may end up with no qualifications at all — *and* a record of indecision which won't look good to *any* prospective employer!

I don't have enough O or A levels to get any sort of decent job. But, since I've already left school, I can't see me taking them now.

If this is your problem, remember, it's *never* too late to re-take an exam if you want to.

If you have left school and have since realised that you could be in a better job, with more interesting work and brighter prospects if only you had one or more O or A levels, you can still take them and improve your career.

Get advice from your Careers Officer at the local Education Authority, or by asking at your nearest Careers Service office, or by consulting the Adult

Education Department in your area. Y can take evening classes to get these and A levels, or study with the Op University, or possibly get your employ to put you on a Day Release course.

If, though, you're worried about t year's exams and regret time wasted, still not too late to make sure you get th vital passes. Speak to your teachers even if you've been a lazy or bad stude if you're willing to work even at this l date, something can be done.

You might not be able to make missed work in a few weeks, but ye teachers can advise you which are most likely areas to be covered by ex questions, and you can concentrate those.

And in your local paper, you can f people willing to give additional, priv tuition for particular O and A leve especially maths and english.

You can also contact the university bo setting the O and A levels for your scho and buy copies of old exam papers. The are usually two years old by the ti they're issued, but are good practice a show how the examiners' minds work.

They normally cost around 50p one subject. Your staff at school c tell you where to write or telephone, a may even have papers you can borrow

I already have a job — and hate it! I thought I'd like doing thi type of work, but it hasn't turned ou at all as I expected. What am I supposed to do now?

If this is your problem, there just may be all that much you *can* do about Especially if things are tough at home.

Your family may quite likely discoura you from job-hunting if they really ne

...e money your wage-packet brings, ...nd you may feel guilty if you know your ...ather is out of work, or his job is on short-...me or hanging in the balance.

If you are miserable in the work you're ...oing, though, there are still steps you ...an take to make life more enjoyable, ...ithout putting anything at risk. The ...olden rule these days, though, is NOT to ...row up the job you have until you are ...eally quite certain you have a better job to ...o to!

When job-hunting it is best, sometimes, ... keep it absolutely quiet, and don't let ...e fact get whispered round the offices of ...ur present employers, or you might find ...u get the boot before you're ready!

Also, if your employers learn you are ...ssatisfied, you're not likely to be offered ...ances of promotion or improvement.

So, look around for something ...itable — but do it tactfully. Secondly, ... it with common sense.

There's not much point yearning to be a ...ain-surgeon or film star if you don't have ...e qualifications, whatever they may be! ...nd if your main complaint about your ...esent job is that it's boring, you ...ould be practical and realise that most ...ork is fairly routine.

...You get your enjoyment from liking ...e people you work with, the satisfaction ... doing the work well, and the fun of ...ending your money at the end of the ...eek! So don't set your aims too high.

...In fact, the change you need might be ...lot closer to hand than you realise. ...y to discover why you feel so dissatis-...d.

...It may be because you don't have ...ough to do, or feel you could cope ...th more challenging work, or don't get ... with the people you work with. In any ... these situations, it is possible there's a ... you'll like a lot better inside the ...ganisation you're currently working for. ...Don't be afraid, in this case, to ask ...und. Take the line, "I like this firm, ... I think I'm ready for more challenging ...rk" — and then nobody will take ...nce. Even if there isn't a vacancy ...t away, you could be ear-marked for ...mething better quite soon.

...Most organisations much prefer to ...ve staff up from the inside, rather than ... on new people, so by looking around

inside your present firm, you stand a better chance of a change of job, than by approaching outsiders.

If you really feel you simply *must* change your job before you go totally mad, though, go back to your local Careers Service or Job Centre, explain your problem to them and you'll find them very sympathetic and helpful.

> **6** *I left school ages ago, and I still haven't found a job. What's wrong with me? Why don't people want to employ me? I'm beginning to think I must be a failure at everything.* **9**

If this is your problem, don't, for goodness sake, think that not being able to find a job is some sort of judgment on you and your abilities.

Thousands of good men and women are unable to find work, and it's mainly due to the economic situation. So don't write yourself off as a failure.

Instead, be positive about your predicament. First, check that you really are doing everything possible to find work. Don't expect Careers staff to do it all!

You should be regularly checking employment vacancies in local papers, at agencies and employment bureaux, at your nearest Job Centre and on notice-boards at large local organisations. If you have a definite career in mind, don't wait for notices of vacancies to appear — try writing to the Personnel Officer of the organisation concerned, stating your qualifications and asking about possible future vacancies.

Quite often the large organisations have lists of possible candidates for future employment, and you could be put on a short list for inverview in a few months' time.

Also, use the free time you have now — it's an advantage, and you should make full use of it. You may be able to improve your qualifications by home study.

You can make yourself a more useful person, too, simply by widening the scope of your local knowledge — get to know your home town, find out all that the local libraries have to offer, discover how many different types of work are carried on locally, take an interest in your local paper, town hall, community centre, etc.

If you keep an alert and lively mind, life becomes more interesting, you have more chance of noticing an opportunity for a job, and you develop the kind of personality that makes employers want to give you a job when you do go for an interview!

You can also use the time to practise things like writing letters for jobs, shorthand (try taking down the between-record comments of disc jockeys) and typewriting (you can buy a second-hand machine very cheaply). You can also make life more interesting and save money by learning to make your own clothes, teaching yourself a language (ask at the library for books and records), or by learning to type or cook.

And don't despise part-time employment! Naturally, if you are hoping to get a job some day as a teacher, a dental receptionist, a laboratory technician or whatever, you don't want to have to admit defeat by working full-time as a loo cleaner!

But a variety of part-time jobs adds enjoyment to life, gives you the independence of a little earned income, and can also be surprisingly useful in giving valuable experience of what a working life is really like. Look for part-time work like jobs in canteens, pubs, shops, offices — you'll find them in local papers, on cards at newsagents and stationers, and on notice-boards of large organisations.

Also, be prepared to do a full-time job for a few weeks only now and then, working at something you maybe wouldn't care to do for the rest of your life. You'll be surprised how much even the most boring-sounding job can teach you about work, life and people — and all this will come in useful later.

But don't fall into the trap of being sidetracked. Keep looking all the time for the *real* career you want. Your ideas may change as you go along, but you should gradually find out more about what you're looking for.

Keep that ideal in mind, keep looking — and keep trying to improve your qualifications or abilities, so that when a chance comes along, you're the ideal person and *must* get chosen for the job!

If you have career problems don't forget that you can get a lot of information about training, qualifications, pay and prospects by reading one of the excellent Career Guides put out by the Employment Service Agency. They cost from 8p to 45p each.

You can get a catalogue of all the careers booklets, with an order form, from H.M.S.O., 49 High Holborn, London WC1V 6HB (enclose an s.a.e.) and you can often read any of the leaflets free, at your public library. There are over 40 leaflets available and, to give some idea of the variety, new titles added to the list include Forestry, Road and Rail, Home Economics, Remedial Professions, Advertising and Speech Therapy!

So go to it – and good luck!

TREE OF LOVE

Like to try your arm in the love stakes? Well, our tree of love game is ready and waiting for you to climb it, from the tricky lower branches of meeting and having that extra special first date with your dream boy, up through the dangerous boughs where you meet his mum and dad, to the dizzy height at the very top of the tree where you find true love! Happy climbing!

Branch 7
HE SAYS HE LOVES YOU. Would you —
a) simply say, "I love you, too",
b) go all red and pretend you hadn't heard,
c) wish your friends could hear him say it,
d) reply, "Oh, you're just saying that"?

Branch 6
YOUR FIRST QUARREL. This could be the beginning of the end unless you —
a) drive him back into your arms by having a great time with other boys . . .
b) "accidentally" bump into him and act as if you've never fallen out,
c) beg him to take you back,
d) get a friend to tell him how much you miss him.

Branch 5
YOU MEET HIS FRIENDS and want to convince them you're the greatest thing since Farrah Fawcett-Majors. Would you —
a) give every one of them a great big kiss,
b) wear your sexiest dress,
c) laugh like a drain at all their jokes,
d) try to be one of the boys?

Branch 4
YOU MEET HIS PARENTS FOR TEA. Alone with his mum, do you —
a) ask if she thinks apricot is a pretty colour for bridesmaids,
b) ask for her plum cake recipe,
c) leave her to get on with the washing

You can play the love game on your own, with friends, or — if you really want to live dangerously — with your boyfriend!
All you need is a dice. Throw a six to start and climb on to the first branch. Answer the question you'll find there and then look at the base
of the tree to see if you're romantically correct! If you're wrong, you'll be given a penalty before you can start climbing again. So think carefully — and good luck!

Branch 1
YOUR FIRST GLIMPSE: You see him at a party. You fancy him like mad! Would you —

a) flirt with someone else to make him jealous and desperate to get to know you,
b) talk to him, saying you don't know a soul at the party,
c) give him a big smile,
d) offer him a crisp?

Branch 2
IT'S YOUR FIRST DATE, and he seems nervous and shy. Would you —

a) chatter on about this and that,
b) suggest going to see a film,
c) gently ask him about himself,
d) tell a long joke?

you —
a) gaze deeply into his eyes,
b) ask where you can park your chewing gum,
c) throw your arms around him,
d) hope he doesn't smudge your lipstick?

Branch 1
SCORE. If you chose a, you can't move on until you've thrown a six, because he'll think you're not interested in him! If you chose c or d, miss a turn, because although either move would do for starters, they're not as direct or half as effective as b. So, if you chose b, move on to the second branch without delay!

Branch 2
SCORE. If you answered a, b or d, don't move till you've thrown a five, because all these moves would only make him feel even more self-conscious and inadequate. But if you chose c, you'd be right, because this would encourage him and give him more confidence! So move on to branch 3 . . .

Branch 3
SCORE. If you chose b, c or d, you can't move on until you've thrown a six, because you were either too cool or too keen! If you chose a, move on to branch 4!

Branch 4
SCORE. If you score a or b, don't move on until you've thrown a six. You see, your boy's mum would regard these questions as potential threats. If you chose c, throw six twice before moving on. This is a cardinal sin.
If you chose d, you've realised that the corny moves are often the best. Every Mum loves drooling over her little treasure (if only she knew!). So now move on to branch 5.

Branch 5
SCORE. If you chose a, b or d, don't move until you've thrown a three. If you chose c, then you've found the easiest way of flattering your boy's friends, without annoying him! So now move on to branch 6.

Branch 6
SCORE. If you chose a, c or d, don't move until you've thrown a four. These moves are all present too many dangers, he might: a — believe you really are having a great time without him, c — treat you like dirt because you're so obviously vulnerable, d — go off with your best friend! If you chose b, though, you've allowed both of you to save face (sensible girl!). So now you can move on to branch 7.

Branch 7
SCORE. If you chose b, c or d, then you're not ready yet for the love of your life! So go straight back to branch 1 immediately and start climbing the tree of love all over again (but full marks for being honest!).
If, though, you chose a, then lucky you, you've reached the top of the tree and can now pluck the fruit of true love!

I KNEW HE WAS MARRIED~BUT I DIDN'T CARE!

THE Newberrys are fairly new to our small country town. They came down from London about six years ago, when their daughter Kerry was two years old.

She was a pretty kid with little bunches of hair behind each ear and great big blue eyes. She and I took to each other straight away.

Her mum was very young — only about four years older than me, in fact, and her dad wasn't much more. They lived a couple of streets away from us, so I used to see her out walking with Kerry quite a lot.

One day she asked if I could look after the little girl for an hour or two while she and Brian — her husband — went out for a drink. It was their wedding anniversary. Of course, I said yes.

I liked going to their house, so I was quite happy to go a second time, and a third. Brian was one of those really funny guys — you know the type — that keep egging you on and teasing you and well, a bit sort of flirty, I suppose.

We all used to have a good laugh — Brian, Kit and me. Of course, I knew everything didn't always go well for them. They had rows.

You could often, well, *sense* an atmosphere although they'd put on a front when anyone came, like me. I suspected that most of their arguments were over money.

The only thing that bothered me slightly was that whenever they had had a fight, Brian used to be extra nice to me. It was as if he was trying to make Kit even madder by sitting chatting to me for ages, both before they went out and after they got back and Kit had gone to bed.

One evening he even said, "You know, Elaine, I'm really glad you're baby~sitting for us. We get along so well. You ought to drop round more often, just for a chat."

I can't remember what I replied then, but I do remember that, when I told Mum about it later, she made some stupid comment like, "You seem to be pretty friendly with Brian Newberry. Doesn't Kit mind?"

Why *should* she mind? I kept telling myself that there was absolutely nothing suspicious about Brian. He was probably nice to everyone.

Things went on like that for a few weeks more, although I noticed Kit was looking quite upset whenever I went round. She never said anything so I tried to ignore it. It was none of my business, anyway.

Until the Saturday when Brian came over to my house and asked if I could sit with Kerry that night. He seemed in such a good mood that I couldn't help asking him what he was so pleased about.

And he showed me the two tickets he'd got for the Bryan Ferry concert.

Well, they were like gold-dust in our town.

"Kit must be really excited about going!" I told him.

"Well, actually, I haven't said anything to her yet," he said. "It's to be a surprise.

"They were a bit expensive," he said. His face clouded just for a minute. "Tell you the truth, I had to borrow the cash off a bloke at work.

"Still," he said cheerfully, "we don't go out all that much. What's money, after all? Can you be at our place at six?"

JUST as I reached their back door that evening, I heard the shouting. A real humdinger of a row. I couldn't make out the words, and after a few seconds there was the awful sound of sobbing, and then a slam.

I waited a few seconds, then rang the bell. The door opened almost straight away. Brian stood there, a bit red in the face but obviously ready for the concert because he looked really good.

He stared at me for a minute as if he didn't know me, then pulled himself together and said:

"Oh, Elaine, hello."

"I've come to baby-sit," I reminded him.

"Yes. Well." He shrugged his shoulders. Then he put out a hand and touched my arm. It felt — well — nice. Sort of friendly.

"Kit doesn't want to go. She — er — she isn't feeling well. Look, Elaine, I suppose you don't want to?"

"Want to what?" I asked, bewildered.

"Go to see Bryan Ferry. It seems a pity to waste the other ticket. Actually, Kit sort of suggested it."

"*Kit* did?" I found that surprising, and deep inside me, although I pushed the thought away, I knew it wasn't true.

"Oh, OK," I added, suddenly making up my mind and feeling as if I really was doing something — well — exciting. "OK, I'll come."

"Great!" The old Brian broke through his smile lighting up his face. He grabbed me round the waist, and pulled the door to behind him. "That's my girl! Let's go!"

I had a great time. Really super. Bryan Ferry was fantastic. So was the whole evening.

"We must do this again, Elaine," Brian said, holding my arm and helping me into the car. "I haven't enjoyed myself so much for ages.

"Tell you what. Let's just have one drink to celebrate before I take you home."

We called in at the Nag's Head, which is only a few yards from my house. Brian had told me some sort of silly joke just before we went in, and we were clutching each other and giggling like crazy.

I didn't notice straight away who was at the bar, not until they spoke.

It was Mum and Dad.

"I thought you were baby-sitting," Mum said. She looked at me so accusingly that I felt like a criminal. She didn't speak to Brian at all, and neither did Dad.

"I was," I said, feeling stupid.

"It looks like it," Mum went on, drily. "I don't think you've even *seen* Kerry tonight at all. Have you?"

shook my head.

"Look here, Mrs Minster, I can [exp]lain," Brian began. He looked a bit [she]epish, like you do when you've been [cau]ght doing something you shouldn't.

"You've no need to explain to me, lad," [Mu]m told him. "Save it for your wife. She [ran]g earlier to speak to me."

"Oh." Brian sounded deflated. He [did]n't seem to know what to do, and then [he] suddenly seemed to decide. "'Bye, [Ela]ine," he said to me. "See you around." [And] he went off, whistling as if he didn't [car]e, as if we hardly knew each other and [had]n't shared such a great evening [tog]ether.

[D]AD bought me a Coke, and then we all went home. Mum was kind of [qui]et, and thoughtful. When we got in, she [ask]ed me to go into the sitting room because [sh]e wanted a word with me.

"No lectures, Mum, please!" I [ple]aded. "I haven't done anything wrong."

"No, maybe not yet," she said. "But [wit]hout meaning to, you just *might* be [ma]king a mistake you're going to regret. [Yo]u like Brian Newberry, don't you?"

I nodded. "Of course. He's fun."

"He's also married." Mum sounded [gri]m. "And it's time he grew up and faced [his] responsibilities.

"Kit rang me tonight in an awful state. [Sh]e said you'd gone out with Brian. Oh, [sh]e guessed where you were going all [rig]ht."

"He said she wanted me to go with [hi]m," I muttered.

"You knew that wasn't true," Mum [sai]d. She looked at me so hard that I had to [tur]n away to avoid meeting her eyes.

"You knew what he was like really. You [ju]st sort of — fancied the idea, didn't [yo]u?"

I could feel myself blushing right up to [th]e tips of my ears.

"He's *married*, Elaine," Mum repeated. "[H]e should have stopped playing around [ag]es ago. Think of it from Kit's point of [vie]w.

"For a start, she won't ask you to sit [wi]th Kerry again because she'll feel she [ca]n't trust you where Brian's concerned. [Br]ian's the sort of person who's never [re]ally accepted he's married.

"He's been seen around with quite a [fe]w girls, you know. Kit's got quite a lot of [wo]rk on her hands trying to keep the [fa]mily together. There's Kerry to consider [to]o, remember."

"Well, that's Kit's problem," I [gr]umbled. "It's nothing to do with me."

"But Elaine, can't you see? You're part [of] that problem and you're adding to the [tro]uble between Kit and Brian. Don't you [ca]re about upsetting other people's [liv]es?"

"It's just a silly fuss about nothing. It's [ne]ver meant anything." I muttered. But I [kn]ew I didn't really believe that.

"No, it isn't," Mum persisted. "And [yo]u know it."

Oh yes, I knew it all right. Deep inside. [An]d Mum was right.

Kit hasn't asked me to baby-sit for her [ag]ain. She sees me as a threat, and you [ca]n't really blame her. If I think about it, [I] suppose I did encourage Brian. It [se]emed fun flirting with him, knowing it [wa]sn't serious.

I knew it was wrong, of course. And I [k]now Mum's right about him. I won't see [hi]m again.

But — I can't help wondering — if she [an]d Dad hadn't happened to be in the pub [th]at night, well, who knows what might [ha]ve happened . . . ?

TEST YOUR EYE·Q!

If you think you've got an eye on the pop people of today, see how you get on with our eye-Q test. We're sure you'll get them all — no matter how far away you are. But if your eyesight's poor, the answers are on page 108. . .

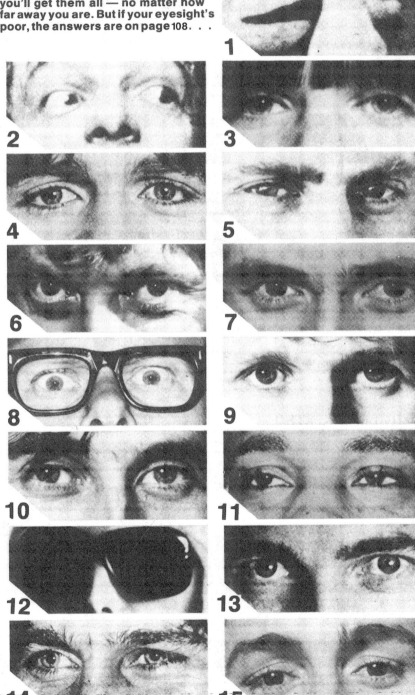

1

2

3

4

5

6

7

8

9

10

11

12

13

14

15

Getting Him Into Shape..

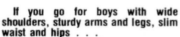

WHAT type of boy do you go for? The strong well-built guy who looks as if he's the King Kong of the building trade, or the tall skinny boy who looks as if a good gust of wind would have you helping him to his feet?

Well, whichever male shape turns you on — or off — reveals an awful lot about you.

Recent research carried out by a team of American psychologists revealed that quite apart from being inspired by a boy's personality, conversation and brains, different girls are attracted to different physical types. (If only they'd asked, we could have told them that a long time ago!)

So now, just for fun, test yourself according to their findings. Choose from the boys below, the one that is closest to your ideal — or nearest to the boy(s) you've been dating recently. Then read on to find out something about the shape you're in!

If you go for boys with thin arms, chest, shoulders, waist, hips and legs . . .

You're sensitive and emotional. You're concerned about your appearance and how your friends rate you. On the other hand, you tend to be rebellious, refusing to accept other people's opinions and determined to try out everything for yourself.

You've got a lot of nervous energy and can't stand being bored. You value your freedom and tend to be very independent, so you refuse to tolerate boys who act as if they own you.

On the whole, you're ambitious and able to stand on your own two feet.

If you're attracted to a boy with medium-weight shoulders, waist and hips with solid arms and legs . . .

According to the psychologists you're a conventional, indoor-type girl who comes from a traditional home. You're steady and reliable, so you go for a boy who looks comfortable and relaxing — rather than madly exciting. He'll be readily accepted by your parents as he obviously poses no threat. In fact, your mum might feel driven to give him the highest praise and say, "He looks exactly like your dad did when he was young!"

On the whole, people trust you and like you and you probably have lots of friends.

If you go for boys with wide shoulders, sturdy arms and legs, slim waist and hips . . .

Extrovert girls like this shape. You're probably cheerful and outgoing with few emotional problems or hang-ups.

You tend to be unsophisticated, athletic and country-loving. You probably enjoy tennis and swimming and dislike smoking. You and your boyfriend would definitely enjoy keeping-fit together! You're also very feminine and like the idea of your boyfriend being strong enough to protect you and to keep you safe from harm!

On the whole, you're fun to be with — people think you're a good sport.

If you go for a boy with hefty arms, legs, shoulders, waist and hips . . .

You're the maternal type. You like to ''baby'' your boyfriend and run after him.

You prefer to stick with things you know and sometimes it takes you ages to accept a new fashion, usually just as everyone else drops it!

You like to read a lot — usually romances — and aren't too keen on sport or anything energetic. It could well be that you're a little overweight yourself.

Generally, though, you're very sympathetic and soft-hearted — the kind of girl others lean on!

So there you are! Of course, it's not as simple and straightforward as that. For instance, the psychologists discovered that the girls they interviewed were rather unscientific and claimed that their favourite boy of the moment had their favourite body shape, even if this wasn't strictly true!

In fact, nowadays the V-shaped boy with wide shoulders and slim hips and thighs is considered the most fanciable. So if this is the type that you go for, it doesn't really reveal much about you, just that you go for the ideal shape that's fashionable at the moment.

The psychologists summed it up this way . . .

Girls who are feminine and rather conservative, like strong, tough, musclemen to protect them from the nasty old world.

More liberated, independent girls who think they can take car themselves, tend to go for the slim-line look.

Big girls like big boys!

In fact, on the whole, girls tend to fancy boys who have sim physical characteristics to their own.

The one shape, though, that really handicaps the poten Romeo is a small chest with big hips. Sadly, most girls the pear-shaped boy the ultimate turn-off!

So next time you see a boy and size him up, it could j be that he'll reveal the psychological shape you're in!

HOW TO HAVE THE LAST LAUGH...

Nobody likes being laughed at. Well, not unless you're attempting to be a second Morecambe and Wise, you don't! For most of us, though, there's nothing worse than suddenly finding everyone laughing themselves stupid only to discover that it's *you* they're laughing at. Being made a joke of is one of the things we dread most, along with having a spider run up our leg and eating spinach, that is!

So here's our special Jackie guide to help you through those awful times. There are lots of useful phrases for various occasions — just to make sure it's *you* who has the last laugh!

LAUGHTER is a lovely emotion and having a good laugh *with* other people is one of the best ways of making you feel good. The trouble is that laughing *at* other people is one of the most common of human failings.

There's a very basic bit of sneakiness in all of us that quite likes to see other people embarrassed and uncomfortable. And the strongest feeling you get when you're laughing at others is, "Thank goodness it isn't me!"

Everyone gets laughed at once in a while and often it's because of something silly they've done. Other people's clumsiness makes people laugh.

Some people make a living out of it, like Charlie Chaplin did. But one thing he always managed to do was turn the tables and get the last laugh. And that's the hardest thing of all.

But if you know you're quite likely to do something silly, then build up a few useful phrases so that people end up laughing *with* you and not at you.

Having a sense of humour and using it can bring you out on top so that people don't remember so much the daft thing you did, as the funny way you got out of it.

If you storm off in a sulky huff you'll end up the loser all round. So if you find yourself in any of the fairly common situations below, make sure you get the last laugh:

1. Hurtling home from school on your bike, you wave to your friends, wobble a lot and end up in a heap under the handlebars.
Try saying: "I think it's about time I went in for a service."
Or: "How come the Queen manages to wave to the crowd — and she's on a horse!"
Or: "Throw me a lifebelt, I'm sinking!"

2. You've knocked your own, or somebody else's, lunch into your lap.
Try saying: "I've heard of quick snacks but this is ridiculous!"
Or: "What's for pudding?"
Or: "I've always liked tossed salad."

3. You've leapt for the vaulting horse in the gym with gay abandon — and got stuck in the middle.
Try saying: "Is there a doctor in the house?"
Or: "I think I'll take a smaller size."
Or: "I never could stand heights."

4. You've tripped up. That happens all the time, but usually when it matters.
Try saying: "What a silly place to put a pavement."
Or: "I knew I shouldn't have had that last glass of cherryade."
Or: "That ant must be at least nine stone!"

THERE'S another reason why you might get laughed at, at some time, and that's due not so much to something you've done, as to a much more unpleasant need some people have to put others down.

It usually means that they pick on others because they haven't got much confidence themselves.

Fortunately, it doesn't happen too often but again, humour is the best way out of it or, if you can manage it, in some cases, a snooty "put down" phrase which puts you in control of the situation and makes them look very silly, childish and spiteful.

It's not the easiest thing to cope with, but now and then it happens to everyone in a crowd and if you can, try very hard to cope with it so that you're not picked on again.

If you blush and stammer and look uncomfortable, the jokers in your crowd will soon get to know you're an easy target. But it's not hard, with a bit of preparation, to find a quick answer for some of the situations that might arise!

1. You're at the swimming pool and somehow last year's bikini doesn't seem too roomy. Someone in your crowd calls you "fattie."
Try saying in a confidential whisper: "Well, you know what they say about thin people, don't you?" (It doesn't matter if they know or not — they're not going to ask!)
Or: "Yes, I really must ask my mum not to give me strawberries and cream *every* night."
Or: "Yes, I've tried counting calories but I haven't seen any yet."

2. You've told a joke which you know is funny but everyone is standing around looking deadpan.
Try saying: "Oh, well, I thought you wouldn't be able to understand it."
Or: "My brother warned me I should only tell that joke to an intellectual audience."
Or: "Now don't applaud, just throw money."

3. Someone's played a practical joke on you. They've left some pretty strong cheese in your desk at school or work.
Try saying: "Dr Watson, come here quickly, I've found a clue!"
Or: "If I'd cleared my desk out more often this would never have happened."
Or: Sniff and say, "Funny, I could have sworn Angela Drummond (or whoever) was walking past."

4. You've appeared at the youth club with a new hairstyle or a new dress. A few people start to giggle.
Try saying: "It's the newest style for winter but I don't expect your barber would know about it, Sharon."
Or: "There are a few fellas I want to shake off, so I thought I'd change my image."
Or: "The lady in the shop said you had to have the right face and figure for it, so at least no-one will copy me."

Don't be surprised if after you've managed to get yourself out of a difficult situation a few times, you actually begin to enjoy it and start playing for laughs most of the time.

"He who laughs last has only just seen the joke" might be true if you're a comedian but "He who laughs last, laughs longest" could become *your* motto — even if the joke started out being on you!

WILL YOU LIVE HAPPILY EVER AFTER?

Well, what are your chances of living happily ever after? Find out by answering our very special fairytale quiz, designed to reveal your secret hopes and fears, and what you can expect from life.

Are you sitting comfortably? Then we'll begin!

1. When you were very young, which of the four following fairytale heroines was your favourite?
(a) Goldilocks.
(b) Rapunzel.

(c) Cinderella.
(d) Red Riding Hood.

2. Which of these fairytale heroes did you most admire?
(a) Aladdin.
(b) Prince Charming.
(c) Jack and the Beanstalk.
(d) The Frog Prince.

3. Which of the four following girls did you like best?
(a) The Little Match Girl.
(b) Alice in Wonderland.
(c) Snow White.
(d) The Little Mermaid.

4. And which of the following male characters, from this mixed bunch?
(a) Pinnochio.
(b) Robinson Crusoe.

(c) Dick Whittington.
(d) The Little Tin Soldier.

5. Which "Magic Roundabout" character was — and probably still is — your favourite from the following four?
(a) Zebedee.
(b) Dougal.
(c) Florence.
(d) Brian.

6. When you were a little older, which of these four was your choice for a bedtime book?
(a) Grimm's Fairytales.
(b) Alice in Wonderland.
(c) The Arabian Nights.

(d) Hans Andersen's Fairytales.

7. Lots of nursery rhymes had "baddies". Which one of the following did you *hate* most?
(a) Wee Willie Winkie.
(b) Humpty Dumpty.

(c) Tom, Tom the Piper's Son.
(d) Little Jack Horner.

8. Which nursery rhyme character wou *you* most like to have been?
(a) The lady who went riding to Banbu Cross.
(b) Goldilocks.
(c) The girl who had a little nut tree.
(d) Mary (the one who had a little lamb

9. Even in nursery rhymes, people ha problems! Which of these four did you hav most sympathy for?
(a) Polly Flinders.
(b) The Old Woman Who Lived in a Shoe
(c) Simple Simon.
(d) Bo Peep.

10. Which do you consider the perfe friendship from among the following tw somes?
(a) Jack and Jill.
(b) Tweedledum and Tweedledee.
(c) Jack Spratt and his wife.
(d) The Owl and the Pussycat.

CONCLUSIONS

Mostly (a) answers

YOU definitely have star quality, and, although you may appear to be quiet on the surface, you secretly long for admiration and fame.

Almost certainly, your career will be full of interesting ups and downs — but the blazes of glory, however brief, will more than make up for any hard knocks you have to take — and there may be quite a lot of these, because you love to dice with danger! Your eagerness for excitement may lead you into situations you can't handle. Then you'll have to run for safety, like Goldilocks did! Probably you've already escaped from some tight corners, but don't push your luck! The day may come when you can't make a getaway fast enough, and trouble catches up with you.

The thing you hate and fear most is authority. In a job where you can do things your way, you will work hard and shoot to the top surprisingly quickly, but a fusspot boss who is a stickler for punctuality, will really bring out the rebel in you. You would probably be happiest as a journalist, actress, or working for the sort of charitable organisation where you are expected to turn your hand to anything, and live on a few pounds a week pocket money. For starters, you could always get a temporary job at a holiday camp, or looking after children in a nursery.

Only three things could sour your non-stop love affair with life. One is working for a big organisation, where the bosses are faceless, and the workers are simply numbers on a time sheet. However, there's little chance of this quenching your bright spirit, because nothing, not even a wage of £100 a week, would induce you to stay here for long.

The second thing you must guard against is rebelling against *all* authority, that of parents included. They are only doing their job, which is to protect you to the best of their ability, and see you don't come to harm.

Thirdly, it would be very easy for you to get into bad company. You are the kind who will always spring to the defence of her friends, but be careful that you don't follow them into folly!

Your adventurous nature, courage, and ability to live for today instead of worrying about what tomorrow may bring will ensure that you live happily, especially if you cultivate your talents in every way possible. You should also keep some emergency money on hand and always tell some really responsible person where you are going before setting out to seek your fortune!

Mostly (b) answers

You're the type who never, ever loses her cool, which must put you well on the way to living happily ever after!

The thing you hate and despise is weakness. You respect people who are trying to cope with a difficult situation, like the Old Woman who lived in a shoe and found it hard to handle her big family and housing problem! But you have no sympathy at all for hopeless, helpless, Humpty Dumpty types.

Being caught in an embarrassing situation is something which happens to other people; never to you. Of course you have your secret doubts and fears like everyone else, but you've learned already that nothing succeeds like success, and if you *look* confident people will be prepared to give you the opportunities you need to show you can do lots of things very well!

Probably you've already been given responsibilities, perhaps as a school prefect or sports team leader, and in the job market what you look for is a situation which offers lots of "oportunities for advancement." You seem ideally suited to become a nurse, or a secretary, but really, whatever career you decide on you are almost certain to receive speedy promotion!

As you make definite goals in life for yourself, and work hard to reach them, you *ought* to live happily ever after, but if you don't seem to be getting as far as you would like as fast as you should, this is probably because there are people whose sole ambition seems to be trying — usually unsuccessfully — to take you down a peg. You are not so self-sufficient as you seem, and it hurts to be called "Miss Know-All," and "Granny" by people you are only trying to help.

You must resist the temptation to outsmart everyone; they won't like you being always right; or at least acting as if you are. Many of your friendships are sure to be love-hate affairs, like that of Tweedledum and Tweedledee, but the important thing is that you're always loyal to your friends when they are in trouble, or anyone else dares to criticise them — and usually they show the same loyalty to you, because they respect you.

You are one of life's winners, but can only live happily ever after when there are others to share your triumphs. They'll be glad to share your troubles too, if you give them the chance to advise *you*; just for a change!

Mostly (c) answers

You tend to gain your own ends by fair means, which includes soft, flattering words and playing the role of damsel in distress; something you can do very well! You like to live in harmony with everyone, and this makes you quick to stop quarrels springing up amongst your friends.

Extravagance is likely to be a problem with you, because you love luxury. Money burns a hole in your pocket, and you can't resist fast-talking door to door salesmen, and the like! Your wardrobe is full of clothes you hardly ever wear! In fact, you are what's known as a "soft sell."

If you can't beat the sales staff, you can always join them! Working in a shop selling luxury goods would suit you ideally, and most store managers welcome you with open arms, because of your even temper, patience, winning smile, and genuine enthusiasm for the beautiful things surrounding you. You'd be a good demonstrator too, or maybe even a model. Other work possibilities are as a receptionist, or working with children, old people or animals.

As you find it easy to observe rules and regulations, realising that they usually help things run more smoothly and benefit everyone, you have no sympathy for rebels.

Despite your gentle, easy-going nature you admire success very much, and the kind of boy who is industrious and hard-working as well as capable of taking risks, would be just right for you. However, you get along well with practically everybody, because you believe in compromise, so your friendships are as trouble-free as the partnership of Jack Spratt and his wife who agreed so happily to differ!

Unless one of those friends lets you loose with a mail order catalogue that is! Just tell yourself firmly that people are much more important than possessions, and don't even *look* at it!

Mostly (d) answers

You really don't expect to live happily ever after, and you're certainly not one to wail "Why did this happen to me?" when things go wrong. Yet, because you are never short of the three essentials — trust, hope and a cheerful smile, life is bound to hold a lot of joy for you.

Like the princess who was so kind to a humble frog that it was able to shake off an evil spell and become a handsome prince again, you bring out the best in people. Of course, some of your friends take you for granted, and treat you carelessly, but how they value your loyalty. In fact, it may be because they feel so safe in your friendship, and know you would never wittingly hurt anyone, that they don't try to conceal their moods and are occasionally rather off-hand with you.

However, there are several things which could make life more bitter than sweet, unless you can bring yourself to be firm with people. You're far too ready to accept every hard luck story, not necessarily because you believe it (you're no fool), but because you are sorry for people who find it necessary to tell lies!

Also, you allow people to take advantage of you. So don't always be the one to volunteer for the background jobs which aren't much fun, like spending parties seeing that everyone gets plenty to eat, or listening to the non-stop nattering of some self-centred bore.

You do tend to wallow a bit in feelings of unrequited love. You could become a martyr if you set your sights on someone who couldn't care less about you!

Social work appeals to you, and jobs such as that of speech-therapist, assistant in a childrens' home, teacher of handicapped children. Your career possibilities are endless, but you must feel you are helping people, otherwise you'd practically pine away. Although you set high standards for yourself, you can sympathise with inadequate people like dozy Bo Peep!

Most of us get what we work for and deserve but do remember that people are only human, yourself included. Instead of trying hard to behave like an angel *all* the time, see what a dash of devilment can do for you, now and again!

TAKE TWO GUYS

Two of the most exciting — and successful — groups to have made a stand in the charts this year are Generation X and the Boomtown Rats — and we talked to their two lovely lead singers, Billy Idol and Bob Geldof . . .

Beat Rat!

BOB GELDOF can't believe what a tremendous year he's h
"This time last year the Boomtown Rats were celebrating th
first hit, 'Looking After Number One,' and since then we have
looked back!" he said.

Not only has every single they've put out been a massive hit,
this year Bob and the rest of the group have recorded their sec
album in Holland and completed a successful British tour, too.
can't beat this bunch for working hard!

The Boomtown Rats deserve every single ounce of success
achieve — never before have we met a more genuine bunch of re
nice guys. They work hard, they produce some amazing music, ar
doesn't matter how tired they are — they've always time to talk to

"It's about two and a half years since we formed," Bob told
"and the reason we did was because we were so bored of hea
country-rock, funk-rock, jazz-rock — anything but *real* re
We knew that we could make it if we tried, and, as we were unemplo
at the time, there was nothing to stop us trying!

"I always wanted to be a star, and there's no point denying th
enjoy all the fame we have gained. When I was eleven I wanted t
like Mick Jagger of the Rolling Stones; at twelve I wanted to be J
Lennon of the Beatles and after that I wanted to be Pete Townsh
of the Who. Now I'm glad to be me!

"We played the music we wanted to play and now it's paid
Bob went on. "We have a great time when we're touring and so do
audiences.

"At one concert we did in Scotland everybody was on their
clapping and dancing and generally having a fantastic time. Aft
had finished the manager of the hall came backstage and told us
he'd never seen anything like it in his life.

"He'd never seen so many people enjoying themselves and
managing to behave. Apparently not one seat had been broken, w
was pretty unusual.

"But that's what the Boomtown Rats are all about," Bob explai
"Having fun. We certainly enjoy ourselves — and we like to think
audiences do, too!"

Billy's Our Idol!

WHEN we talked to him, Christmas was very much to the fore
in the thoughts of Billy Idol of Generation X!

"I don't see my mum and dad very often because I live in London,
but they always invite me over for Christmas Day and to be honest,
I'd be surprised and upset if they didn't bother to ask me!" Billy told us.

"Although I wouldn't feel guilty about not spending Christmas Day
at home with them, I know it would upset my mum if I didn't join
in," Billy went on. "I know the family will be there with the tree and
the presents, so just to show I care about them, I take part, too. But I
don't get totally caught up in the Christmas spirit because I think a
lot of it's silly.

"Christmas only means something to people who have to work
from nine till five, five days a week, because they really look forward
to having a holiday. I don't have holidays.

"Just as every day's a holiday, every day's a work day," he explained.
"I don't know what they mean by celebrating each New Year either as
I'm never aware of a new year or seasons — I don't even know what
month it is! I don't know today's date. I'm not aware of things like that.

"But when people want to create fun, I suppose Christmas provides
the perfect excuse!

"To me, the actual occasion of Christmas is just going home for a
day, like any other normal day, except all the shops are closed," Billy
explained. "But to my parents it's **Christmas** and much more, so I
enjoy being with them.

"I like seeing my sister, and my cousin, too. My family try to make it
like a traditional Christmas and we all have to wear hats round the
table when we eat our Christmas dinner," Billy went on. "Once I upset
everyone by taking mine off!

"Apart from my cousin, we don't have relatives coming over to see
us on Christmas Day, thank goodness! We're not like that and I'm glad
because I can't stand all that family business.

"I think it's a shame when relatives meet and no-one's got anything
to say to each other, and they come to family gatherings because it's
more like an obligation.

"I've always felt like that. Relatives just pretend to each other all the
time and say it's wonderful to see you when they don't mean it, and
you know it!

"I know I play a sort of game at Christmas time," Billy admitted.
"I mean, I like Christmas but it's not all that special to me, but if I
told my parents I didn't think Christmas was important, just
imagine how they would react to that!"

Now turn to page 128 to find out all about two of our favourite
stars!

L. to R. – back: Simon, Bob, Gerry
front: Johnny, Pete, Garry.

L. to R. – Billy, Mark, Bob, Tony.

A JACKIE QUIZ

Which Is The Season For You?

ARE you a sunny summertime girl, or a winter wonder girl? Each season has its own very special character — autumn's changeable and unpredictable, while summer's full of fun and carefree! But which one are you? Which season of the year reflects your personality? Answer our fun quiz truthfully and find out! You might be in for a few surprises!

1. If you could change your name to something which suits your character more, which of the following would you choose?
(c) Charity.
(a) Felicity.
(d) Faith.
(b) Verity.

2. Which do you think would make you look most interesting?
(a) A long, sweeping black velvet cloak.
(d) A misty lace veil, which hints at your beauty underneath.
(b) A sparkling diamond and pearl tiara.
(c) A zany, shocking pink paper party hat.

3. If you were to take up a thrilling new hobby, would it be —
(a) athletics,
(b) fortune-telling,
(d) horse-riding,
(c) writing poetry?

4. Is your favourite colour —
(d) lively red,
(a) sizzling yellow,
(c) romantic pink,
(b) glowing orange?

5. Where would you most like to go for a swim?
(a) In warm, sky blue seas, tinged with the pink of coral, and filled with rainbow-coloured tropical fish.
(d) In sparkling crystal clear water, ruffled by tiny lacy waves as it hits golden sands.
(b) In a rocky, craggy cove where you can dive into the murky green depths of the sea.
(c) In brilliant turquoise sea at the edge of miles and miles of white sand glittering in the sunlight.

6. If you suddenly won a fortune, would you invest in —
(c) a 16th century cottage in deepest rural Somerset,
(b) a mansion on the Yorkshire moors,
(a) a villa on the coast of Cornwall,
(d) a castle in the Highlands?

7. Would you rather be the proud owner of —
(c) your very own strawberry garden,
(d) a thoroughbred racing stable,
(a) your own disco,
(b) a boutique?

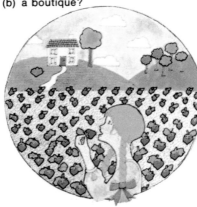

8. Which of these strange pets wouldn't give you the creeps?
(b) A vampire bat.
(d) A poisonous lizard.
(a) A tropical bird-eating spider.
(c) A bright green bullfrog.

9. What would your recipe for warding off bad luck be?
(d) Will-power and foresight.
(a) Two frog's legs on a bed of garlic.
(c) Your zodiac sign on a silver chain.
(b) A thread of silk from the robe of a Tibetan monk.

10. If you could live in any house you wanted, which would you prefer?
(c) A tiny stone cottage with roses round the door, nestling in green country-side.
(b) A magnificent mansion with miles and miles of desolate, craggy moorland all around.
(a) A super-modern white villa on top of a cliff, with a terrific view of the rocky coastline and the sea.
(d) An ancient castle, complete with towers, turrets and secret passages, hidden deep in the Highlands.

11. Which musical sound sets your heart beating faster, and makes you feel romantic?
(a) A brass band playing in a busy street.
(d) Mournful bagpipes carrying over the hills.
(b) A lilting lone flute echoing through the green woodlands.
(c) Beautiful, mellow violins, floating through your window, by the light of the moon.

Which sight gladdens your heart
st?
An outstretched cat basking
on the lawn.
Wild geese flying over the marsh-
land.
Baby lambs frolicking in the wild
flowers.
An eagle hovering over snowcapped
mountains.

If you had lived in olden times, which
these gorgeous boys would you
ve chosen to go on a date with?
The poet-minstrel.
The brave young gladiator.
The knight on his fast white
horse.
The handsome young court jester.

. Which of the following hotels
ould you choose as being most
omising for a fabulous holiday
mance?
) A wayside lodge, with miles of
beautiful garden stretching behind
it.
) An enormous hotel with all mod
cons and a disco, on the coast of
Spain.
) A country hotel, where you can
enjoy lovely home cooking and
long walks in the countryside.
) A pretty little inn, on the outskirts
of a seaside town.

5. Where would you prefer to acquire
our beautiful golden suntan?
a) In a deck-chair on the French
Riviera.
1) On a chair-lift over the
Swiss Alps.
c) On a yacht off the Greek Islands.
) On a pony through the forests of
Bavaria.

*Now count your score, mainly (a), (b),
:) or (d) and turn to the conclusions
elow.*

CONCLUSIONS

Mostly (a)

You're a Summer Girl, living for the moment, enjoying the sunshine, sailing happily without a care in the world. Life for you should be perpetual summertime, with a holiday atmosphere and lazy, hazy heatwave days.

Virtues — Your main virtue is your naturally warm personality to match the summer months. With your charm and great sense of humour you have an infectious personality, so that others around you catch your zest for pleasure and enjoyment. You're extremely generous, both with your money and your friend-ship.

Faults — One of the unfortunate side-effects of your easy-going nature is that you tend to dismiss problems and ignore danger signals, so that you sometimes think before you act. Curb that impulsive nature a bit and you could find life a lot easier.

Relationships — You tend to fall in love often and quickly with good-looking boys. At the moment, you don't want to get involved with anyone — you're only interested in having a good time. Though you think you fall in love easily, you're usually completely in command of your feelings. Really, it takes time (and a very special person) for you to get into a really deep involvement. But, right now, the fun and good times are all you need because you're an incurable flirt! True love can wait till you've settled down a bit and allowed yourself to be a bit more serious!

The Future — Although you might some-times *appear* to be lazy, you have hidden strength and boundless energy when you want to use it. You're not afraid of life, and once you put your mind to a career or course of action, you have the guts, confidence and vitality to achieve sucess!

Mostly (b)

You are an Autumn Girl, changeable and unpredictable, sometimes stormy, sometimes sweet and gentle. You can be secretive and difficult to under-stand yet at other times full of wit, conversation and enthusiasm!

Virtues — Your main virtue is your lively, questing mind. You want to get at the truth, to understand people and situations and to formulate your own ideas about the world around you. You're an interest-ing person to talk to, for you're aware and sensitive with a great deal of creative talent. You're emotionally honest with strong convictions and emotions. You're an original person with the courage to be different from the herd.

Faults — Patches of depression and moodi-ness are your main problem, coupled sometimes with an unrealistic view of yourself and the world. You expect a great deal out of life and tend to be dis-appointed when things don't work out right. Your inner life sometimes causes you to appear distracted and aloof and you make no effort to be nice to people you're not interested in. We're not suggesting you should put on an insincere act, but a bit of polite consider-ation wouldn't come amiss!

Relationships — You have the ability to become extremely emotionally involved and it's all-important that your friends should be on your wavelength. When you fall for a boy it's the real thing and you become totally involved (dare we say obsessed?) with that one person. Love is extremely serious to you, and your relationships might tend to be difficult and stormy at times, full of dramas and com-plications. But it's worth going through the bad times, because you get so much joy and pleasure from the good times!

The Future — Like your personality, the future is unpredictable because there are so many ways you could go, so many abilities and talents you could develop. So, by trusting your instincts and being an individual, you can look forward to a future full of rich experience, variety and interest.

Mostly (c)

You're a Spring Girl, romantic and dreamy, exciting and feminine, with all the good qualities anyone could wish for. You have a creative spirit, you appreciate beauty and you bring hope, encouragement and love into the world!

Virtues — Your main virtue is your kindness and affectionate nature. People seem to sense that they can trust you and confide in you, for you have endless sympathy and understanding. Although you appear to be shy and modest, you have a lot of inner strength and an instinctive faith in yourself.

Faults — Your only faults stem from your over-emotional character, which makes you easily led and extra-sensitive to criticism. On an emotional see-saw, you can cry one moment and laugh the next, and for your own self-preservation it would be wise to try to toughen up a tiny bit. You tend to be impatient for perfection, and you're bound to be dis-illusioned occasionally if you set yourself such high ideals.

Relationships — Love and affection are second nature to you and you fall in love easily and deeply without ever thinking whether you might get hurt. Other people might make do with friendship or surface romance and flirtation, but for you it has to be a grand emotion. In all your close relationships you're loyal, loving, and are prepared to give a lot. As well as being romantically loving, you care for those people you love, and make them feel secure and happy. You of all people know how powerful love is, and your life would be meaningless without it.

The Future — You look for beauty, peace, true love and affection and an atmos-phere that radiates quiet, inner happiness. This, needless to say, is sometimes hard to find, but you won't give up and your spirit refuses to be dampened. So you have every chance of making your dreams a reality!

Mostly (d) —

You're a Winter Girl, strong-willed, quick-witted and independent. You can use your head as well as your heart, and reflecting the power and influence of the winter season, you're a courageous person and a natural leader.

Virtues — You have high standards and ambitions and you want to make your mark on the world; but at the same time you're without vanity or conceit, and you have the determination and the practical ability to achieve your goals. Although you can be quite tough and calculating when you need to be, you have a great sense of justice and others know that you are reliable with a genuinely kind heart.

Faults — Impatience is one of your faults, together with a hot temper and a very obstinate streak. It would be worth your while at least to *listen* to others some-times — even if you decide to reject their advice in the end! Although you give the impression of not needing people, this is far from the truth and perhaps you need friendship and reassurance more than you're prepared to admit.

Relationships — You're so cool and capable, people tend to be scared of you sometimes, and, being a very strong personality, you often dominate others without even realising you're doing it. Your taste in boys is high-powered, and a boy has to be a really clever, strong character to keep you interested. You look for equal partnerships of mutual love and respect, and although love is essential in your life you can't bear to be caged and you need space to be free and independent.

The Future — You're good at planning and organising and you like to have goals and objectives to work towards. You should make the most of your clear-sighted mind and studying ability. You're one of life's natural survivors and whatever you decide to do, we can't see you going far wrong!

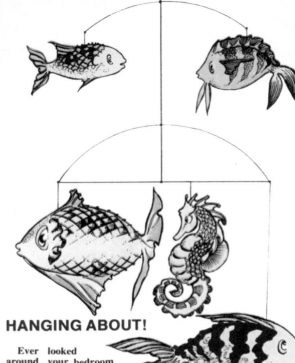

CHRISTMAS FARE!

Christmas time nearly always means party time, so if you're having people round it would be even nicer if you could say that you'd made some of the food yourself. These recipes are really simple, but very tasty, so go ahead, try them!

TOMATO FIZZ

You need several large bottles or cans of tomato juice and bitter lemon for this recipe, depending on the number of people invited.

Simply pour the tomato juice onto ice cubes in tall glasses, and top up with bitter lemon.

MUSHROOM AND HAM DIP

2 oz. lean boiled ham; ¼ pt. fresh double cream; 1 carton yoghurt; 1 medium can condensed mushroom soup; cayenne pepper to garnish.

Chop the ham. Lightly whip cream and stir in the yoghurt and soup. Add the ham to this mixture. Now place the mixture in a serving dish, garnish with a sprinkling of cayenne pepper, and arrange small biscuits, bread and crisps around it.

SPICY WHIP

Makes a lovely ending to any party, especially when it's cold outside!

You'll need: 1½ pints milk; 2 oz. syrup; grated nutmeg.

Bring the milk almost to the boil, stir in the syrup, and pour the mixture into mugs. Sprinkle with a pinch of nutmeg.

WHOLEMEAL BREAD

You don't have to use yeast, so this bread recipe is much simpler and quicker to make than most.

Mix together — 4 oz. plain white flour; 4 oz. plain brown flour; 1 teaspoonful salt; 1 teaspoonful baking soda; 1 teaspoonful cream of tartar.

Rub in 2 oz. margarine, until the mixture is the consistency of breadcrumbs. Add 2 table-spoonfuls syrup and a little milk until the dough is stiff. Place in a greased loaf tin and bake in a moderate oven for 1-1½ hours.

HANGING ABOUT!

Ever looked around your bedroom and thought what a lot of wasted space there was between the top of your head and the ceiling? Well, so have lots of other people — and they came up with mobiles! Mobiles are three-dimensional decorations (usually with some movement) that you can use to brighten up your bedroom, any room, in fact! They're usually suspended from the ceiling, so they don't take up space *and* they brighten your room.

It isn't always easy to find something that's cheap, easy *and* original to make your room more interesting and more your own, but mobiles fit the bill! You can use almost anything for the actual decoration once you have the wire for the framework. It can be any size or shape, too.

So, if you're sitting comfortably, this is how you begin . . . Wire is usually used for the framework so a couple of wire coathangers are ideal for this. Use them in a cross-shape, binding them together with thread — or have them hanging at different levels to give an interesting effect. Then you need some fine string or strong thread to use for

hanging the shapes from the frame.

Leave the hook on the hanger so that you can Sellotape it to the ceiling above a window, or hang it from a picture-hanger on the wall. This means that you can move it around and have it in different positions in your bedroom, too.

All you need to do now is choose what you'd like as the subject of your mobile, and this depends a lot on where you're going to hang it. If it's in your own room, you might like to stick pictures of your favourite pop star — or boy! — on to some card (covering both sides). If so, cut the card into heart-shapes and attach the thread neatly to the top of the card then to the long bottom section of the hanger. To make them all hang at various levels, just use different lengths of thread. If you place the mobile near a window, air movement will make the pictures turn, so that you're always getting a new view of that gorgeous fella!

Basically, that's all there is to it!

GOLDEN OLDIES!

So you're lying slumped in a chair absolutely stuffed after ploughing your way through Christmas dinner. You're occasionally craning your neck a couple of inches to the right to gaze at all the lovely pressies you got from Santa, and you're making a really big effort to ignore your father who *always* gets a bit carried away at this time of the year and tries to get the whole family to do really energetic things, like pulling Christmas crackers!

Never mind, it could be worse, you know, you could have been celebrating Christmasses past and they would have taken a lot more out of you than just the effort of lifting the last spoonful of Christmas pud to your mouth!

In ye olden dayes things were a little different!

There were dozens of courses to the Christmas meal — goose, beef, swan, venison, peacocks with their beaks gilded, and their tails spread out, and just to finish things off, boar's head — garlanded with rosemary and bay and with an apple in its mouth!

There was a great deal of ceremony connected with bringing the boar's head into the feast. In the time of Elizabeth the First it was carried in by a young woman of high rank, on a gold or silver platter. Trumpets

were blown and a procession of minstrels and servants followed it. It was considered a great honour to be chosen for the task of carrying in the boar's head, but things could — and did — go wrong!

One young damsel who tripped daintily into the Queen's presence with the dish managed to get herself into really hot water. Her Majesty was entertaining some foreign guests, and the boar's head was carried in on a silver platter instead of a gold one! Horrors! The young lady had hoped to get the Queen's permission to marry but she withheld it for a year as a punishment!

Of course, many of the things you'd be eating then would be quite familiar to you — mari-

golds, primroses, cowslips — yes, we *do* mean the flowers! And pies made from carp's

tongues, which are rather fiddly things to eat, but then you wouldn't have had to bother about getting them to stay on your fork because you wouldn't have been using one — that's why finger-bowls were so necessary!

And on the subject of fingers, one of the games played was Snapdragon. It consisted of snatching raisins from a bowl of burning brandy —*without* burning your hand(!).They still do this in France, on New Year's Eve, to this day!

So, be thankful that all *you* cope with are turkey and Christmas pud!

FLATTERY GETS YOU EVERY-WHERE!

"FLATTERY will get you nowhere" is one of those sayings like, "Life is just a bowl of cherries" — it's hardly ever true! Flattery will get you plenty of places. The question is, will it get you where you want to go — which is out on a date with the boy you fancy. Of course it will — if you know how to go about it . . .

You *can* overdo flattery, just like you can overdo eating, drinking and jumping up and down, but in small doses it can be very useful and, be honest, don't you love someone paying *you* a compliment?

Everyone likes to be told something nice about themselves and they will appreciate you for telling them, but it's no use rushing up to the fella you like and gushing, "You move like Mick Jagger, you look like Andy Gibb and I'm free on Friday night."

The first lesson to learn is BE SUBTLE.

If there's someone you want to get to know better, watch what he enjoys doing, the things he's good at. If it's football and you're standing on the sidelines shivering, don't rush up when the whistle blows, fling your arms round him and burble, "You were terrific!"

Just saunter up quietly, catch him on his own and tell him seriously, "You know, that pass you made across the goal about ten minutes into the second half, that reminded me very much of Kevin Keegan. You have the same ball control."

Smile gently and stroll off. You may not know who Kevin Keegan is. It doesn't matter.

Your victim will feel so tall he'll be able to touch the top of the goal post and you'll have learnt the second lesson about Good Flattery which is — SOUND CONVINCING.

If there's a boy you want to impress, learn about the things that matter to him so that you can appreciate when he's doing well at them. He may be a musician and you're probably tired of making endless cups of coffee while he's ploughing through, "Learn the Guitar in Ten Weeks."

So pick up a few useful words like "riff" or "middle-eight" and instead of walking in with ear-plugs, listen for a while and when he stops, pretend you're lost in thought for a second and then say, "I heard Peter Frampton play a riff like that at Wembley, but I think it sounds better when it's played gently."

If he says, "Actually that part was the middle-eight" then you'll have to go back to studying "Handy Hints for Guitarists' Girlfriends," but don't be discouraged, half the battle is over.

He knows you're trying to compliment him — and that counts for a lot.

MOST boys like to be compared favourably with their idols, whatever they want to shine at, but sometimes flattery is at its best when it's just a direct statement like, "I really like that shirt." You can bet he's taken trouble choosing it and he'll enjoy the fact that someone's noticed.

If you're dancing with someone you like, it does no harm at all to say, "Hey, where did you learn to move like that?" It's a dead cert he'll ask you for another dance, especially if you add, "I've watched a lot of guys here tonight and half of them just don't *feel* the music, do you know what I mean?"

He'll know what you mean all right. And it's highly unlikely he'll sit down for the rest of the disco. He'll be dancing — with you!

It's not difficult to flatter boys when it comes to things mechanical, either. To most girls the inside of a Kawasaki engine is about as easy to understand as "A"-level Chinese, and if you seem to spend most of your Sundays huddled in the garage while he tunes up his bike, there *are* a couple of alternatives.

You *could* study the Works Manual and either end up buying a bike of your own and dismantling it next to his, which won't go down too well (especially if you end up with a faster bike!) or you can accept the fact that what's inside the bike is strictly his territory and concentrate on the outside.

Helping him clean and polish it shouldn't be beyond you — and that's a form of flattery in itself. And when he finally slides out from under the exhaust, don't tell him he's covered in oil and you'll see him when he's washed. Grit your teeth, snuggle up close and say, "Why don't they make an after-shave that smells like engine oil? It's lovely."

Besides, imitation is supposed to be the sincerest form of flattery. So don't try to beat him, join him. Turn up in your oldest jeans and tightest T-shirt with a large spanner, making sure your hair and face look good and ask him how his tappets are.

Either he'll be so touched with your concern that he'll actually *tell* you, or more likely, he'll decide to do other things on Sunday afternoons. Like go out with you.

ONE thing you'll have to learn if you intend to become a tip-top flatterer, though, is to receive compliments graciously yourself. Because once you've said a few nice things to a boyfriend, it's fairly certain you'll get one or two flying your way.

It's easy to get embarrassed when someone's being nice but try being confident. If he says, "Your hair looks terrific," smile and say, "Thank you" rather than muttering, "It's absolutely filthy really, I was going to wash it tonight."

If you do, don't be surprised if he replies, "Oh, I was going to ask you out but I suppose you'll be staying in to wash your hair."

Yes, flattery is a two-way thing. Take it gently and try it out on one or two people you know well first. Tell them their hair or clothes are smashing and you'll be amazed how they blossom and light up.

Lots of people are too quick to criticise and too slow to flatter. Don't be like that.

A good flatterer is nice to have around. She's popular because she makes people feel good and if you get flattery down to a fine art you won't have to worry about what to say to friends — they'll be too busy telling you how terrific *you* are!

BACK TO BASICS

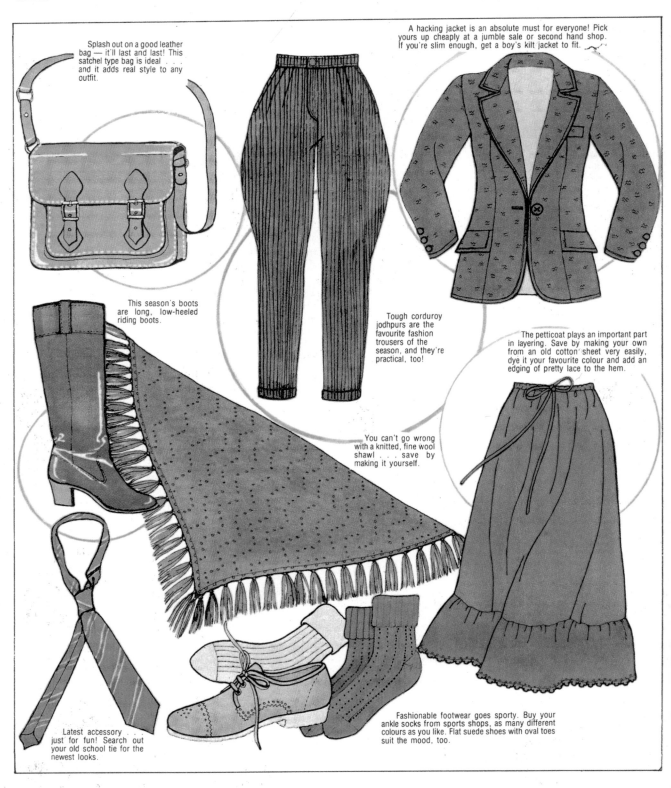

Splash out on a good leather bag — it'll last and last! This satchel type bag is ideal . . . and it adds real style to any outfit.

A hacking jacket is an absolute must for everyone! Pick yours up cheaply at a jumble sale or second hand shop. If you're slim enough, get a boy's kilt jacket to fit.

This season's boots are long, low-heeled riding boots.

Tough corduroy jodhpurs are the favourite fashion trousers of the season, and they're practical, too!

The petticoat plays an important part in layering. Save by making your own from an old cotton sheet very easily, dye it your favourite colour and add an edging of pretty lace to the hem.

You can't go wrong with a knitted, fine wool shawl . . . save by making it yourself.

Latest accessory . . . just for fun! Search out your old school tie for the newest looks.

Fashionable footwear goes sporty. Buy your ankle socks from sports shops, as many different colours as you like. Flat suede shoes with oval toes suit the mood, too.

It's back to basics for winter dressing . . . and here's how to look absolutely stunning on a low budget! The secret lies in sticking to basic colours, unusual mixing and matching, and choosing the right accessories! Start off with the basics, then follow our ideas and you'll have at least a dozen different outfits to see you through the winter — beautifully!

Steal an idea from the French . . . they're all mad about tartan! A plaid skirt in muted colours looks terrific. Knife pleats are in, too.

A man's tweedy cap is the perfect accessory for your winter wardrobe.

Don't splash out on an ultra-fashionable jumper which dates quickly. Instead go for something simple with style, in a colour which goes with everything.

Chunky cream fisherman's polo looks good, keeps you warm and mixes and matches.

Make sure your tights match everything . . . thick, woolly ones look terrific with your ankle socks.

Be prepared for the weather! Get yourself a super, chunky, wooden-handled umbrella, more expensive than usual — but definitely worth the extra.

Wear two belts together — unusual ideas give you special style.

Your pretty cotton summer dress becomes part of your winter wardrobe too! Give it a new lease of life by dyeing it a different colour.

Try A Fry-up!

Fancy a fry-up or see yourself in super stripes? Either way, our fantastic bag and beret pattern designed by knitting des[...]
Alan Dart, is just the thing to brighten up a dull winter's day! So go on . . . we're egging you on to be rasher than ev[...]

WHAT YOU'LL NEED

NEEDLES: A pair of 4 mm (No. 8) needles.

WOOL: Stripes: 3 (25g) balls of Sirdar Superwash wool D.K. in Black (013), 1 ball each of Gorse (124), Emerald (034), and Cyclamen (005).

Fry-up: 3 (40g) balls of Sirdar Wash 'N' Wear Double Crepe in Lemon (252), oddments of double knitting (or 4 ply used double) in beige, brown, pink, white, yellow and green.

PLUS: A 15 cm (6 in.) nylon zip.

TENSION: 22 sts and 28 rows to 10 cm (4 in.) square stocking stitch.

ABBREVIATIONS: K — knit, P — purl, sts — stitches, tog — together, inc and K — increase by knitting into front and back of next stitch, making 2 sts from 1.

WHAT TO DO

FRY-UP
BERET: Cast on 121 sts and work 8 rows K1, P1 rib.
Continue in stocking stitch (1 row knit, 1 row purl).
Work 2 rows.
Next row: (Inc and K, K 13, inc and K), repeat to last 1 st, K1 (137 sts).
Work 3 rows.
Next row: (Inc and K, K 15, inc and K), repeat to last 1 st, K 1 (153 sts)
Work 7 rows.
*1st row: (K2 tog, K15, K2 tog), repeat to last 1 st, K 1.
2nd row: Purl.
3rd row: Knit.
4th row: Purl.
Repeat these last 4 rows, decreasing the amount of sts in brackets by 2 every time round — e.g. next row: (K2 tog, K 13, K2 tog), to last 1 st, K 1.
Continue in this manner until 25 sts remain on the needle and a block of 4 rows has been completed.
Next row: (K3 tog) to last 1 st, K 1 (9 sts).
Next row: Purl.
Break off yarn, thread through sts on needle and pull up. Join seam.
BAG (2 pieces alike): Cast on 153 sts and work 4 rows stocking stitch. Repeat as for beret from * to end.

STRIPES
BERET: With black wool cast on 121 sts and work 8 rows K1, P1 rib. Continue as for 'fry-up' in 2 row stripes of yellow, black, pink, black, green and black.
BAG: As for 'fry-up' starting with 2 rows black and continuing in pattern to end.
FRIED FOOD MENU —
CHIPS, garter stitch (K every

row) used throughout. With beige wool cast on 6 sts and work 20 rows. Cast off.

SAUSAGE, stocking stitch. With brown wool cast on 20 sts, and work 40 rows. Cast off.

BACON, garter stitch. With pink wool, cast on 60 sts and work 8 rows. Work 4 rows beige, 2 pink, 2 beige, 2 pink, 6 beige. Cast off in brown.

EGG, stocking stitch. With white wool cast on 56 sts and work 4 rows.
Next row: (K2 tog, K 3, K2 tog) to end.
Work 3 rows.
Change to yellow wool and work 2 rows.
Next row: (K2 tog, K 1, K2 tog) to end.
Work 3 rows.
Next row: (K3 tog) to end.
Next row: Purl.
Break off yarn, thread through sts on needle and pull up. Join seam.
Repeat for second egg.

PORTION OF PEAS
With green wool cast on 19 sts.
1st row: K 1, make bobble by knitting into front and back of next st twice (4 sts from 1), turn and P 4, turn and K 4, turn and P 4, turn and K 4 tog, (K 3, make bobble) to last 1 st, K 1.
2nd row: Purl.
3rd row: K2 tog, K to last 2 sts, K2 tog.
4th row: P2 tog, P to last 2 sts, P2 tog.
Repeat these last 4 rows 3 more times (3 sts left on needle).
Next row: K 1, make bobble, K 1.
Next row: P 3.
Next row: K3 tog, and cast off.

TO MAKE UP: Sew ends in and press all pieces lightly on the wrong side with a damp cloth. Sew bag pieces together leaving 15 cms open. Sew in zip. Cut a 12 metre length of wool, fold in half and half again (4 strands). Make a loop in open end and slip over a door-knob. Pull yarn taut and twist tightly. Bring ends together and cord will twist. Attach to ends of bag opening. Join long side of chips to make tubes. Gather short ends of sausage and sew along length leaving an opening. Stuff with wadding, kapok or old tights, and sew up. Attach egg to beret by sewing round yolk line, padding yolk lightly with wadding. Sew edges of egg to beret.

Sirdar Superwash DK wool costs 40p for a 25 gram ball and Wash 'N' Wear Double Crepe costs 40p for a 40 grm ball. both come in a large selection of assorted colours, available from most wool shops and many department stores throughout the country. If you have problems with stockists, write to Sirdar Ltd., P.O. Box 31, Alvethorpe, Wakefield WF2 9ND enclosing an s.a.e. for the address of your nearest stockists.

...red with shoulder-length hair but don't ...ally want to have it cut? Try out these ...per styles and you can look different ...ery day — so start now for a ...mpletely new you!

BE RIGHT ON TOP!

YOU'LL need lots of hairgrips and special covered elastic hair bands which are on sale at most chemists and department stores. Ordinary rubber bands are rough and will break the hair shaft as they rub along the hair, so don't use them. Now you're ready for:

A Beauty Box Special

MODEL-GIRL CHIGNON

Pull all the hair up on the top ...your head and secure it with ...band, then tuck all the ends ...der and secure them with ...ips. This will make a tight ...tle bun that looks really good ...d will stay for hours, if you ...n it up properly.

SEVENTIES' PONYTAIL

Great . . . just pull the hair together to a point off centre and close to the front of your head and secure with a covered band. If your ponytail flops over and you'd rather have it straight, try back-combing the ends a little to make it stiff.

THE PINEAPPLE

Gather all your hair together and secure on top with a covered band. Leave the ends to bounce loose as shown. This is a bubbly style that looks great for parties . . . try a simple pair of earrings to finish off the look.

FIFTIES' PONYTAIL

This is really simple! Just draw all your hair into a band high up at the back of your head, then tie a really bright ribbon into a super bow for a really lively rock 'n' roll fifties' look!

BALLERINA CHIGNON

This is a little bun at the back ...f the neck. Just pull all the hair ...o the back into a ponytail held ...ith a band, then turn the ends ...nder and secure them with grips ...o make a small, neat bun. Let a ...w wisps of hair escape to ...ften the hairline!

PRE-RAPHAELITE BUNCHES

Nice for shoulder-length or longer hair. All you do is wash your hair and plait it into lots of tiny plaits while it's still wet! Let it dry naturally, then undo the plaits and you'll find you've got lovely, crinkly hair. Make two bunches high on the sides of your head, secured with covered bands.

SWISS PLAITS

Part your hair in the middle and make a plait each side starting at ear level. Pull the plaits up across your head and secure them with grips. This style will show off your ears, so earrings will look really good.

TWENTIES' HEADPHONES

Try this one just for fun! Part your hair in the middle and plait each side, starting at ear level. Coil each plait carefully into a wheel, over your ears, and pin securely so the coils sit over your ears!

All these styles will look best if your hair's clean and shining, so make it a rule to wash regularly with a shampoo that's made for your hair-type . . . greasy, normal or dry, or use a mild, medicated shampoo if you have dandruff. Visit a good hairdresser every six weeks for a trim and don't be afraid to experiment with different styles. Your hair tells people a lot about you, so don't neglect it!

WHO WANTS THEM?

There are some boys we'd all give anything to go out with — like David Soul, Barry Gibb, etc., etc.! Everyone knows the most-wanted boys around and no-one in their right mind would want to avoid them. But — what about the boys you *do* want to avoid? The ones you'd pay your little brother 50p to take on a toad-hunting expedition; the ones you tell lies to about not being able to go out because you've got to visit your granny/ look after the hamster/finish off your macramé. In short, the ones you'd rather be seen *without*! These are the unwanted men — the ones for whom there's positively no reward for capturing! The trouble is, though, they're out to capture *you*! So, to help you avoid them, here's our fun list of unwanted men. Memorise them so you can recognise the bad lads at a glance!

STEVE SLOB

UNWANTED FOR SMUGGLING GERMS INTO THE COUNTRY

Appearance

5 ft. 5 ins., heavily built, thick dark hair with dandruff and spiders in it, black fingernails, and toadstools growing out of his ears.

Haunts

Filthy old caffs, slagheaps, rubbish tips and waste-paper baskets.

Crime

Germ Smuggling. Slob follows girls around. He never has a steady girlfriend but will sit down next to girls on buses and envelop them in his appalling pong as he chats them up, flashing his mossy green teeth at them. He's a great threat to the environment and girls have had to be rescued from his clutches by firemen.

WARNING: Slob's fumes can cause unconsciousness and make paint blister off buses. So if you see him . . . call the Fire Brigade.

WILLIE WEEDY

UNWANTED FOR WHEEDLING AND CLINGING

Appearance

5 ft. 5 ins., pale, thin, knock-kneed, wearing thick vests knitted by his mum and a weenie beanie crocheted by his Auntie Jeanie.

Haunts

In his mum's kitchen, or watching TV, curled up on her knee. That was OK once, but now he's sixteen!

Crime

Wheedling and Clinging. Weedy is spoilt, a definite Mummy's boy. So he expects his girlfriend to wait on him hand and foot, massage his brow when he's feeling weary, and embroider his initials on his teeny hankies. Whatever **he** wants to do is law. The girl is never consulted. After all, she's a mere female, and if his mum never taught him anything else, she sure taught him this — girls aren't fit to kiss the soles of his Hush Puppies. He'll wheedle and cling till he gets his way, so watch out!

WARNING: Weedy really needs a stiff blast of pesticide. It's the only thing that'll solve his problem. So if you see him, inform the Ministry of Agriculture, and they'll send a weed-killing aeroplane over.

JERRY JEALOUS

UNWANTED FOR EMOTIONAL BLACKMAIL

Appearance

5 ft. 10 ins., red hair, green darting eyes, usually carries a pair of binoculars, a telescope and a magnifying glass.

Haunts

Anywhere! Cafés, cl cinemas, parties . . . so w out!

Crime

Emotional Blackmail, Petty Jealousy. Jealous ge know a girl, and at first he c extremely attractive. Grad though, she finds herself cross-examined. "Where you been?" "You're late." " have you been with?" "Who i bloke across the road o you?" "What do you mean don't know him?" If she to other boys at par Jealous can turn nasty, sho sly looks at her, looking da at everybody else, and ge poisoning the atmosphere.

WARNING: Jealous ca extremely poisonous, so i see him, jump into a paper and call the Health Inspecto

HARD HARRY

UNWANTED FOR BREAKING AND TAMPERING

Appearance

6 ft. 3 ins., burly build, broken nose, huge fists, a Pumping Iron T-shirt and a tattoo on each arm which says ROCK HARD.

Haunts

Gymnasiums, backstr sleazy alleyways, outside aways, leaning up against machines, etc.

Crime

Breaking and Tampe Basically Harry goes ar proving how hard he is by b ing windows, furniture, t walls, and bones. And he tam with locks, slot-machines, doors and anything else he lay his big hairy mitts on approach to girls is crude, and more like a rugby than anything else. His emb crack girls' ribs, his kisses k their teeth out, and whe grabs them by the hand, a crackling noise.

WARNING: This guy' monster. If you see him, your local safari patrol wh shoot tranquillising darts him and remove him to the

How to disguise that you love him

So you love him . . . but does he love you? He talks to you, he says hello, but he hasn't actually asked you out yet. Is he going to? Does he feel about you the way you feel about him? You don't know, and you've got to cover up the fact that you think he's the greatest thing on two legs until *he* gets round to thinking that about *you*! So here are the reasons why you *shouldn't* let him know you love him and some tips for disguising the fact that you do . . .

OK. You've seen him once or twice and thought, "He's nice." Then you've noticed how good he looks. Then suddenly you find you're looking out for him and you're disappointed when he's not there. The whole evening seems pointless if he doesn't show up. You find you're thinking about him all the time — at the bus-stop, at school, watching television. That's love.

And falling in love is a bit like falling off a log. It doesn't really hurt until you've done it.

You might have been prancing along the tree trunk thinking, "This is fun" when suddenly, "Wallop!" Every bone in your body aches or more exactly your heart aches. And the trouble with aching hearts is that it's hard to hide the fact that you're in agony.

If the same thing happens to him and he asks you out in a couple of days, terrific. But it doesn't usually happen as easily as that.

More often than not, one person falls in love first and if it's you, then it's important to disguise the fact that you're crazy about him — for a number of reasons.

The first is that girls are naturally more romantic than boys.

The second reason is linked to the first. How many boys do you know who listen to the words of love songs? Mostly they like heavy rock.

Well, so do girls, of course, but girls will still spend far more time listening to slow dreamy records and, unlike boys, almost *expect* to fall in love every time they meet someone new.

So, although he may like you, he won't necessarily go home and dream about you — the first time!

And, another reason to disguise that you love him, of course, is that you might, just might, be making a mistake. After a few more meetings you may feel he's not that terrific after all.

Putting on a disguise gives you — and him — time to find out if it really is love or just a five-minute wonder.

SO now that you've decided to hide your love from him, how do you go about it? There are a few things which *will* give you away, so you've got to watch out for them . . .

Blushing

This is a dead give-away! If you're inclined to blush whenever he speaks to you, you've got two alternatives.

Either wear a light tan foundation when you know he's going to be around or, if you feel a blush coming on just say, "I've spent all day in the garden, don't you think I've caught the sun?" But do remember that blushing makes just about everyone look prettier — he might even be flattered!

Eyes

Another problem area because they bare your soul to the world!

Most people are afraid to look someone they really like in the eyes. They want to, but they're afraid of giving too much away if they do!

So try, if you can, to look straight into his eyes when he's talking to you. Firstly, he'll look at you, which means you'll have sweet dreams and secondly, it's a lot easier to have a normal conversation once your knees have stopped turning to jelly!

Excitement

Talking of jellied knees, you'll find it very difficult to behave normally when he's around.

Even if no-one tells you, it's a fair bet that you'll know the minute he walks through the door and you'll want to turn round. **Don't.** Count to ten and take a deep breath. It **does** work.

Awkwardness

You'll find it hard to manage simple things if he's near. Holding a pen can become a severe case of the shakes. Walk out of the door and you're bound to trip up!

Just try to do everything twice as slowly and force your mind to concentrate on what you're doing. You'll feel far less self-conscious if you concentrate on something else — besides him!

Shut up!

In other words, don't, if you can possibly help it, tell anyone else about your feelings, especially not another girl.

Word **does** get around, however good a friend is at keeping a secret. And even if she just raises her eyebrows and looks at you when he appears, it will be enough to send you into a flat spin and him straight out of the door.

Try not to giggle, too. There **are** times when a good giggle is a great idea but keep it to yourselves when there are boys around. Especially **the** boy!!

Be sociable

Talk to other boys within your crowd, but don't keep glancing over to see if he's listening. If he likes you, he will be!

Talk slowly and calmly and don't butt into conversations he's having unless you've **really** got something to say. Think before you speak, and don't rush your words!

And remember it'll all be worthwhile when he finally says, "I've wanted to ask you out for ages but I wasn't sure if you liked me." When that happens, don't give yourself away at the last minute by falling into a dead faint. Just smile and say, "Oh really?"

Continental Sports

Russia

Have you ever dreamed about being a top class international gymnastic star like Nadia Comaneci or Olga Korbut? Have you ever wondered what it's like to be a member of the top Russian gymnast team? When the U.S.S.R. Gymnastics and Sports Acrobatics display teams were at Wembley Empire Pool in London for four nights of sell-out performances, we went along to watch — and to find out exactly what it means to be a world-class gymnast . . .

THE vast "Pool" was alive with colour and excitement, as the huge crowd filed their way into their seats to the cheerful sounds of the band of the Grenadier Guards.

Then, as silence and expectation fell over the hall, the Guards performed the Soviet National Anthem, the lights fell, and spotlights picked out the Russian gymnasts, led by flag bearers, marching smartly into the arena.

There followed a dazzling display of dynamic modern gymnastics. The crowd held their breath as tiny 15-year-old Elena Davidova somersaulted *on* to the beam to start her exercise; they laughed at the antics of World Champion tumblers Yuri Zikumov and Alexander Russolin; they were enchanted by World Champion Galina Shugurova, who used ropes, hoops, balls and ribbons to create a beautiful pattern of rhythmic movement.

They were amazed by the sheer skill of the leading Soviet girl gymnast — Nelli Kim — who, whether on the vault, asymmetric bars, the beam or the floor, was in a class all of her own!

AFTER this amazing display, in which 50 Soviet gymnasts took part, I was lucky enough to go backstage and ask Nelli Kim just what it was like to reach the very top in World Gymnastics.

"It's marvellous," she said, smiling radiantly. "Really a dream come true. But don't imagine that it has all happened overnight.

"I've been working day and night at gymnastics for eleven years and it was only at the Montreal Olympics in 1976 that I really got international recognition!"

Nelli, of course, won the Olympic gold medals in the individual floor exercise and the vault, and the silver medal in the overall competition. She also managed to score two "perfect" ten out of ten marks, once for her vault and once for her floor exercise!

Backstage in her dressing room, while Nelli continued to take off the stage make-up which she wears for displays, I asked her what it was like to be "perfect" in gymnastics. After all, that's something

that very few of us ever achieve in any field!

Nelli laughed and then said seriously, "I may have scored ten out of ten, but there can never really be perfection in this sport, because you *always* feel you can do better. It is very annoying, but it is true!

"There are always new movements, new difficulties, so you can never learn enough. For instance, Olga (Korbut) was the first girl to do a back somersault on the beam, and now Russian girls are doing forward beam somersaults!"

THE Soviet team are always pushing the frontiers of gymnastics forward and everyone's really looking forward to the 1980 Moscow Olympics. But surely none more so than Nelli.

"I cannot wait for the Olympics to begin," she told me enthusiastically. "I've been working on my programme for two and a half years already, and it will take another year to perfect. Sometimes when I have been working terribly hard, the Olympics seem a very long way away!"

So when you watch the Olympics on TV and gasp at Nelli's ability, remember

SPORT FO

that she'll have been practising
particular programme for three and a
years!

When I asked Nelli about the com
tition expected from the Rumanians, an
particular Nadia Comaneci, she answe
confidently:

"I don't think they will be as m
of a problem as during the Mont
Olympics.

"After all," she went on, "you hav
keep cheerful and I'm always optimi
But at the same time, don't think
underestimating the competiti
because that would be fatal . . ."

Nelli is obviously dedicated to
sport and not ashamed of being compet
or admitting she's determined to
to win. But when she isn't perform
Nelli likes doing the same kinds
things as most of us.

"I love listening to records.
favourites are western stars like C
Richard, as well as our Soviet group

"I also enjoy making my own clot
I think the London shops are amaz
so many beautiful fashions which h
given me lots of ideas for when I
home!

"Yes, London is lovely, I just w
we had more time to see the rest
the country.

"But that is one of the penalties of be
a gymnast," Nelli admitted. "We tra
the world — we're touring the Un
States next — but we get very little
time.

"We are always either practising
performing. Still, to be honest, I lov
and wouldn't have it any other way!"

NELLI then had to leave to speak
her coach, so I had a word with
year-old Irena Derjugika — the We
Overall Champion of Modern Rhyth
Gymnastics. This incorporates bal
dance, skips and jumps. You don't n
conventional apparatus, but instead
hoops, flowing ribbons, clubs and ball

There are accepted patterns, cer
moves, skips and jumps which m
feature in the gymnast's programme,
there's also great scope for improvisa
and a wide choice of accompanying mu

Earlier I had seen Irena twirling a 17-f
long ribbon effortlessly around her
tracing beautiful patterns, and weavin
and out of the loops it formed with the m
graceful movement I've ever seen!

Irena Derjugika

Nelli Kim — *British gymnast Denise Jones*

Now she was happy to stop and speak for a little while and tell me about her career so far, in perfect English!

"I started by training for the ballet," she said, "but my mother was a famous gymnast. She's now a coach in Kiev, in Russia, and so I decided to try to follow her.

"My father also won an Olympic Gold Medal at Melbourne in 1956 for the Modern Pentathlon, so you could say sport was in the family!

"Of course," Irena went on, "when people come to see our displays very few of them realise just how many years of hard work have gone into making it appear effortless!

"Gymnastics is a hard life, and you have to be devoted to it. Also it's sad, because by the age of, say, 22, you're considered to be old and past it!"

That was hard to imagine, looking at Irena's perfectly enviable figure, lovely hair and deep blue eyes, so I wasn't surprised when she said, "I'm hoping to become an actress when my career as a gymnast is over. And, luckily, I've already been offered a couple of parts in Soviet films!"

MOST of the top Soviet gymnasts turn to coaching when their careers as performers are over. Ludmila Tourischeva and Olga Korbut, for instance, are now both coaching the Soviet hopefuls for the 1980 Olympics.

And as the Russian gymnasts left Olympia behind for another year, and returned to their West End hotel, I'm sure they'd encouraged lots of girls to start thinking seriously about taking up gymnastics!

If you were one of them, or just think that you'd like to know more about

this fascinating sport (where you can start training for instance), then write to —
Mr Tony Murdock,
Development Officer,
British Amateur Gymnastics Association,
23a High Street,
Slough, Berks SL1 1DY,
enclosing an S.A.E.

And get in training for the 1984 Olympics! After all, we can't let the Russians have it *all* their own way!

Everyone who's ever lived has had parent trouble — it can happen at any age but you probably notice it fi[rst] around the age of twelve. It's a hard time for you because you've got all the problems of your rapidly changing body a[nd] mixed-up emotions to cope with, and it's a tough time for your parents because they're learning to cope with [the] almost entirely new person you're turning into. So it's not too surprising if your life at home sometimes resemb[les] a battlefield rather than "home sweet home"!

Well, here's how to cope with most of the problems you'll come across and how to make this difficult stage bo[th] you *and* your parents are going through right now a lot more bearable!

DO YOU HAVE PROBLEM PARENTS

YOU'VE got your whole life ahead of you — and you just can't wait to live it! You think about all the discos you'll be going to, the places you'll see, the friends you'll have, the boys you'll meet. You're beginning to want to stay out a little later, to try all the latest clothes and make-up — in short, do all sorts of things that didn't interest you at all before . . .

You'd be one in a million if you could actually go on and do *all* of these things, though, as and when you want, because most of us have parents whose idea of what's good for us, and what definitely *isn't*, is the exact opposite of ours!

So what happens? Well, you probably argue all the time, which makes your life and theirs a complete misery. Because they won't let you stay out as late as you'd like, because they might not approve of your friends, your make-up, your boyfriend, clothes, almost everything you care about most, in fact . . .

I HATE THEM!

THIS is a terrible thing to say, I know, but it's true that sometimes I actually hate my mum and dad. And I really mean *hate*. All we ever do is argue. Mum nags me to death about the mess my room's in, the way I leave my clothes lying about, even about the way I *walk*, for goodness' sake, and a million and one other things.

"Dad makes these awful scenes if I ask to stay out a little bit late one night, complains about my make-up and clothes, my friends . . . And, of course, I'm much too young for boyfriends. You name it, we argue about it. They're making my whole life a misery and I don't think I can stand it any longer." — Jill, 13.

To put it mildly, Jill's having a very tough time at home right now. Her parents don't seem to want her to have any fun out of life at all. The way she sees it, they're going to say no to anything she asks. They treat her like a child and refuse to face the fact that she's growing up.

Her parents are going through a pretty tough time too, though. All of a sudden, she's moody, she's wearing make-up, wants to choose her own clothes and even have boyfriends. It seems like only yesterday she was the sweet little girl they'd always known and loved. Now, suddenly, she's almost like a stranger. They can't understand her. She doesn't tell them things the way she used to, and she's taken to locking herself in her room. And all that, you must admit, is an awful lot to get used to!

If you're in a pretty similar situation to Jill, there's an awful lot *you* can do to improve your relationship with your parents. You'll have to do quite a bit of positive thinking. And you'll probably have to change your *attitude* — which in turn will change theirs — and make your life a whole lot easier in the process.

How Do You Behave At Home?

Do you throw tantrums to get your own way, or sulk for days on end in your room, or just slouch around looking miserable when you can't get to go out with that

boy, stay out a little later one night, or get that dress you really, really want?

If so . . . try to stop all that and act responsibly from now on. It's no use throwing tantrums if you can't get your own way — that sort of behaviour's really childish anyway, and you're not a child any more . . . are you? The simple fact is, they won't allow you a lot of freedom if you don't let them see you can cope with it. If you throw tantrums, they're bound to ignore your demands and be unable to take you seriously. So keep your cool.

Is your room a complete and utter pigsty? Do you chuck your clothes any old place once you've finished with them? And is it your mum who's got the charming job of cleaning up after you?

If that's the case, then you're certainly not the grown-up, sophisticated person

you're trying to make yourself out to [be?] Clean up your own room yourse[lf] you shouldn't even need to be asked t[o do] this, you should know it's your job [and] nobody else's. Even better, you c[ould] also help your mum out around the ho[use] make the tea sometimes, go for [the] shopping. Do things for your parents [and] they'll be only too happy to return [the] compliment. You'll soon notice [the] difference in their attitude to you the[n.]

Do your parents object to make-up?

If it is make-up they object to, remem[ber] that nothing's more guaranteed to [give] parents heart attacks than the sigh[t of] their previously well-scrubbed, ultra cl[ean] faced daughter emerging from her bedr[oom] flashing bright blue eye shadow like it [was] going out of fashion, plastered with [?] and generally covered in blusher [and] lipstick!

So go easy on the make-up, to begin with anyway — give them a chance to get used to the idea. Read up on as many beauty articles as you can (turn to pages 17-21 for a start!) and get a good idea of how to apply it properly. It's often quite difficult at first, when you're not used to make-up, to get the proper balance.

And the same goes for clothes. Don't go all out to persuade Mum to buy you that incredibly sexy, plunging satin lurex dress you fancy. Instead, go for something subtle. And to show how sensible you are, save up for one or two things you really want and buy them yourself. Both your mum and dad are bound to be impressed with that!

Do your parents object to boyfriends?

If it's boyfriends that are the trouble, you'll have to figure out why your parents don't want you to have any.

If they think you're too young, for instance, you'll have to show them that you're *not* a child any longer, by acting as maturely as you can. They can't tell you you're too young forever, remember, and maybe you can speed things along a little by getting your parents to respect you and your wishes *now*, by talking the matter over as coolly and calmly as you can, explaining how you feel. Then, wait until the right moment to bring him home on an ever so casual basis, of course (like his dropping by to borrow a school book!), and then take it from there.

On the other hand, if they think he's totally unsuitable, there's nothing else for it but to arrange for him to meet them so that you can all discuss the problem together. If he's serious enough about you (and deserves you), he ought to prove them wrong! But whatever the outcome, it's best not to deceive your parents about boys — they're bound to find out what you're up to eventually, and if they discover you've been going behind their backs, it's going to take them an awful long time to trust you ever again.

SO YOU WANT TO LEAVE HOME?

SOMETIMES, things can get so bad between you and your parents that the worst comes to the worst and you feel there's nothing else for it but to make the ultimate break for freedom and leave home . . .

It's sad, but it does happen that the situation arises where living together in the same house becomes totally unbearable. So what do you do? Well, leaving home is a pretty drastic solution and running away from a problem very rarely solves anything.

So you've got to be positive about it all and examine *why* things have broken down to such an extent.

Do you expect far too much from your parents, much more than they can possibly give? If you're really feeling mixed up and confused about what you want, it's possible that it could be *because* of the fact that you're growing up that you want to leave home and start afresh. Bide your time and when the growing-up process starts to settle down, and when your emotions have adjusted, you'll find yourself much calmer and more confident and better able to get on with your parents and your present environment.

Remember here, too, that your *body* is going through enormous changes to do with growing up, changes which not only disturb your chemical balance, but psychological changes which can play havoc with your feelings and emotions. So it's normal to

feel on top of the world one minute and then down in the dumps enough to want to leave home the next.

But if it really is your parents that are causing all your problems, you must find someone to talk things over with first, before you do anything drastic. If it's your mum who seems to be making your life a complete misery, then talk things over with your dad first of all, and vice versa. Or a friend or her mum, or even your brother or sister — and find out how they cope.

THEY DON'T CARE ABOUT ME!

BUT what if you feel your parents actually don't like you, never mind love you? Sue, who's 16 now, remembers the time when she thought her mum and dad actually *hated* her.

"Things reached a head when I was 14 and Mum was pregnant. When I first found out I was about to have a little brother or sister I was really shocked, not pleased at all," Sue told us. "I thought it was a bit much. We were a happy enough family already and I thought Mum was mad to have another baby at her age!' (Sue's mum was the grand old age of 36 at the time — not exactly a great granny!)

"Well, Mum had a little girl and I could see she and Dad were over the moon about it. But I certainly wasn't. Before, we could always talk to each other and got on really great. Now, it was the baby this, the baby that — no time for me, and I felt really rotten. Honestly, I could have grown horns and no-one would have noticed!"

Sue felt ignored, and worst of all, unloved. Her mum and dad couldn't see past the new baby, or so she thought. So she started staying out later and later, not telling her parents where she was going or who she was with.

"Actually, I wasn't doing anything much — I just used to go round to my friend's, but Mum started narking at me, saying I was to be in earlier and help with the baby. We fought an awful lot at the time — we were always arguing. But what's really awful is the fact that I actually enjoyed making them so miserable and worried about me . . ."

Sue realises now that she acted a bit selfishly at the time, and that most of her resentment was sparked off by a kind of subconscious jealousy and a feeling of being left out in the cold by her parents' new relationship with the baby. It wasn't that they didn't love *her* any more — just that a new baby is a big event in anyone's life, and her parents were behaving completely naturally.

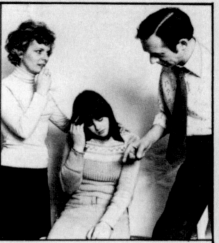

DO you feel a little bit rejected — unloved — like Sue? Well, before you take the same drastic measures she did, try to understand *why* your parents seem to be ignoring you.

It could be they've got money troubles — which most people have nowadays! It could be they've got a lot of worries on their minds about one thing or another— it's up to you to see if you can help them out, even if it's just helping Mum out around the house, doing the garden for your dad — *anything* to show them that you're around and there, if and when they need you. And they'll know you're a responsible person, one they can be really proud of.

The same goes if you're the eldest in the family and feel a little left out — and forgotten at times. It's probably just the case that your mum and dad feel they can trust you to do and cope with a lot more than the younger ones — which is a compliment to you, really!

If you've got any kind of grudge against your parents' attitude towards you it's best to speak up about it. Don't bottle things up — this just leads to even more resentment and, eventually, a hurtful wall of silence.

Remember, always try to air your grievances — don't try to hide them or shut your parents out of your life. It's very rarely hate that causes coldness between you and your parents — just a kind of breakdown in communication, and a failure to understand what makes each other tick. So always try to talk over your problems with them first, or they may not realise there are any!

Finally, act responsibly. Don't shout your head off or lock yourself in your room if you can't get your own way about things.

Remember, too, that if your parents seem really heavy-handed sometimes, it's probably because they're really worried about you . . . that you'll be easily led, get in with a bad crowd, start to take drugs, maybe even get pregnant. They don't mean to be rotten to you, they just want to protect you till you show them that you can look after yourself.

*So if you're going through a bad patch with your parents right now, just try your hardest not to argue or let things get on top of you too much, and be as patient and understanding as you possibly can. And try to **talk** to your parents, too, and let them know how you really feel about things.*

After all, if you really think about it, not only would they feel lost without you, you'd probably feel lost without them, too!

It IS possible to be fifteen years old and a superstar — and here are two fifteen-year-old girls who've proved it! Tatum O'Neal and Jodie Foster are both making big names for themselves, they're both film stars and they're both American. So what do they think of their success? And how far do they resemble each other when it comes to personality? We decided to talk to each of them and find out . . .

TAKE

"My Name's Tatum-NOT Tantrum!"

SOMETIMES, I think newspaper men confuse my name with Tantrum, the stories they print about me!" 15-year-old American film star, Tatum O'Neal, said.

"They make out that I spend my entire life going to parties in low-necked dresses or to discos with a boyfriend on each arm. They say I'm too forward, pushy, a brat, or real nasty!"

Tatum O'Neal is, of course, the daughter of famous actor Ryan O'Neal and an Oscar-winning actress in her own right. In fact, she's a star, the sixth biggest box-office draw in the world.

But life hasn't been a total fairy story for the green-eyed, very attractive Tatum.

"My parents were divorced when I was three," she told me, "and I was brought up by my mother (actress Joanna Moore) on a ranch near Los Angeles. Then my dad won custody of me.

"But he couldn't look after me all the time, so he sent me away to boarding school, which I hated — and I ran away."

Luckily for Tatum, though, round about that time Ryan O'Neal was offered the starring part in the film "Paper Moon" and realised that the part of the little girl was ideally suited for his daughter, Tatum.

"I didn't want to do it at first," Tatum admitted. "I didn't think I could handle it.

"But then I realised I'd be with Dad all the time, and wouldn't have to go back to school — so, of course, I said yes!"

Apart from being able to dodge school for a while, Tatum also managed to upstage her father and win an Oscar for her part in the film — and all at the tender age of nine!

"I love making films," she said, her eyes sparkling, "and, obviously, it's going to be my career. On the bad side, though, there are lots of problems about being an actress at my age.

"For instance, while other kids at school get to do fun things like going to a baseball game, I have to go to work."

STILL, there's one thing Tatum doesn't miss much — and that's school! "As a student, I'm not the best," she admitted ruefully. "And although I have a tutor when I'm filming, I'm still a little behind when I go back to school."

But there's another reason why Tatum doesn't like school much.

Tatum in "International Velvet."

"Because I'm in movies, the other kids don't like it, they're a bit envious I guess, so that makes things awkward.

"Anyway," Tatum went on, sounding just a little bit hurt, "that's why I constantly bug my dad to keep me working, and why I don't bother too much about lessons!"

Not that Tatum would want her life any other way, though.

"Acting in films has given me so much. Things that the average teenager just never gets to experience," she says.

"Take the film 'International Velvet' for instance. That was really fantastic — learning to ride with the best coach in the world — William Steinkraus, the American Olympic Medallist — and with people like Richard Mead (British Gold Medallist in the Three Day Event) on hand to advise me!"

WHEN she isn't acting, Tatum lives at home with her father in a beach house at Malibu, California.

"We look after ourselves, and I'm quite good at cooking," Tatum explained. "A lady comes in to do the cleaning, but apart from that we're very self-sufficient."

She also tends to move round socially with her father, too. Not many girls would fancy going out with their dads all the time, but then Ryan O'Neal isn't exactly an ordinary dad!

"We go to parties together quite often," Tatum said proudly. "And, of course, then I like to dress fashionably — and wear make-up and generally look as good as I can.

"So when people who don't know me see me at parties they think, 'That girl's so forward for her age!'

"In fact, normally I hang around in jeans and T-shirts, don't wear any make-up and look my age!"

It must be said though — Tatum *is* far more mature, poised and graceful than most girls of

her age.

And, of course, she's already going out with boys and thinking seriously about romance.

I NEVER used to be interested in guys," Tatum said, laughing. "I was a real tomboy — my biggest pleasure in life was scrapping with my brothers.

"But I grew up sort of suddenly when I was twelve, and I became much more serious. Now, though, I think I'm at the age to be able to give and receive love, and to have a proper boyfriend."

Tatum doesn't have any one particular type of boy in mind as her ideal, but she's really sure of one thing.

"I wouldn't *ever* want to go out with a man like my dad! Of course, he's the neatest guy in the world with me," she hurriedly explained, "but he runs around with too many girls!"

Most girls would probably find it hard to get used to their father going out with a succession of glamorous women.

But, Tatum says, "I'm very close to my father, and he lets me meet all his girlfriends so I can tell him just what I think of them.

"Actually, I get along with most of them OK. One thing Tatum wouldn't like, though, would be to see her father get married again.

"I should hate that," she said honestly. "We have a nice thing going at home, so why bring someone else in?

"Besides," she added, joking, "I don't think there's anyone in the world in their right mind who would take us both on."

So, for the time being anyway, Tatum is more than happy living with her dad, playing Frisbee on the beach at Malibu, riding her horse and travelling the world making films.

As for the future, she just shrugs her shoulders and says — "I'll think about that when I'm grown up!"

TWO GIRLS!

"I'm Quite A Good Girl, Really"

[KN]OCKED at the door of the flat Jodie Foster [a]nd her mother had rented while Jodie was [maki]ng "Candleshoe" in England. I waited a [mom]ent and then Jodie's clear blue eyes [peep]ed through the letter-box.

["K]ick it," she told me, "it's stuck."

[Fee]ling a bit like a burglar, I heaved the door [and i]t opened.

[Jo]die was standing there grinning. "I'm really [sorry]," she explained. "It's just been painted." [Sh]e ran her fingers through her straight [blond]e hair and led me into the sunny living-[room].

[I] stayed up late watching the midnight [movi]e," Jodie rubbed her eyes, and flopped [onto] a sofa, "and I've just got up."

[Jo]die had hastily pulled on jeans and a T-shirt [when] she heard my knock at the door, but [now] she was wide awake and rushed round the [room] which was stacked with boxes and parcels, [show]ing me all the things she'd bought while [she'd] been in England.

["T]his is great, isn't it?" She plonked a tweed [hat] on her head and peered down her nose, "it [make]s me look like a street kid."

[He]r real name is Elisa, but it's easy to see [why] her mother decided, "she looked more like [Jo]die". It certainly seems to fit her tomboyish [easy]-going attitude to life.

[An]d yet, at 15, Jodie is a very big star. [He]r co-star in "Candleshoe," David Niven, [calle]d her, "the most brilliant, natural actress [I've] ever seen work" — and Jodie thinks he's [abso]lutely terrific as well!

[Bu]t what makes Jodie so unusual is that every[thing] she does something, she does it right.

["It] isn't hard work for me," she told me, [suck]ing a peppermint. "The only hard work is [hang]ing around between shots.

[I] worry more about school plays and things [than] movies. That's why I'd never go on stage. [I'm] so nervous.

[I] love going to the theatre, but I don't want

to be part of it. Films are what I love. I'd like to be an all-round film-maker, maybe a director later."

AND it's quite likely that Jodie will end up as a director because she's been a part of the film and television business since the age of three when she did her first TV commercial in Los Angeles, her home.

Now Jodie travels the world making movies. Her mother is always with her and she also has a tutor on hand to keep her school-work up to date.

"School's OK," Jodie says, "because school's where you meet all your friends and school's where you have your lunch and where you lose weight because you don't eat the lunches!

"And just when you're getting bored, a film comes up and off you go. I remember one time when I was filming ' Taxi Driver '. I went back to school after filming and there were still traces of the make-up I'd had to wear. The other kids really teased me about that!

"Really, though, I don't see why boys go for make-up. It just looks stupid. I suppose it's OK as a cover-up job.

"Maybe I should use it since I've got a big thing about my nose.

"I used to have a perfect nose until I sprained it. Now it goes like this." She drew a hook with her finger.

It doesn't, of course, but it's typical of Jodie that she's very critical of herself. She's equally critical of her screen performances.

She watches her films, often taking friends to see them. "But I keep thinking how I would have done it differently," she says. "I criticise myself all the time."

JODIE has quite a deep voice with a warm Californian accent. Watching her curled up on the sofa, it's hard to believe that she's not just the girl next door. She lives the sort of life most girls just dream about, but she doesn't think it's glamorous.

"Sometimes it's fun and sometimes it's boring, but it's no big deal," Jodie told me.

"We don't live in an enormous film star mansion. In fact, I've always lived in the same house since I was a kid. Maybe we have more money now, but it doesn't seem that different."

Jodie loves watching other actors and actresses like Paul Newman and Shirley Maclaine, but her real hero is rock singer Peter Frampton. When she found out that he was staying at the same hotel in Paris as she was recently, she wanted to sit on the floor by the lift all night, just to say hello, except that her mum decided she needed some sleep!

IN "Candleshoe", Jodie plays a very confident young American orphan, who is believed to be the long-lost heiress of the Candleshoe fortune. In real life, though, Jodie is a very funny girl. "She makes me laugh," as David Niven said.

She leaves all the business side of things to her mother and, unlike Casey in "Candleshoe", she's in no hurry to fly off on her own and be independent.

"I'd like to think of myself as a kid for a long time," she said. "Until I'm eighteen, my mother has to travel with me by law but we get on terrifically and I don't want to grow up too fast.

"I'm not being conceited," she laughed, "but I don't think I do things that need heavy discipline. When I'm away, about all I do when I'm not working is sit and watch TV. I guess I'm quite a good girl, really."

And although she managed a cheeky grin as she said it, she's right. And certainly, as an actress, she's a very "good girl" indeed!

What's The Worst Christma

We all look forward to Christmas — the holly and the ivy, all that kissing under the mistletoe — but admit it, the thing we all really enjoy most is opening all those lovely presents! But what about those beautifully-gift-wrapped boxes that have something absolutely awful inside? What about the presents we'd rather we *hadn't* been given? We asked some of you and lots of your favourite stars about the Christmas presents they wish they *hadn't* found in their stockings!

Jan Williamson, Newcastle.

A friend once gave me a fantastic, very expensive, eye-make up kit that I'd hinted about for ages — and one hour after being given it, and with streaming red eyes, I had to admit I was allergic to it!

Alan Breneton, Edinburgh.

I'd wanted a new Punk album for ages, but what with buying Christmas presents for everyone else, I couldn't afford anything for myself. So when my auntie told me she was getting me something I'd really like for Christmas, and handed me an unmistakable album-shaped package, I was really pleased — but Abba's not really my idea of Punk rock!

RITA RAY of Darts

It's certainly the most ridiculous present I've had as well! When the band first started to succeed, a well-wisher sent us a Christmas present — a shaving kit for every member of the group — not knowing, I suppose, that one of us was female. They must have thought one of the boys had a really high voice! I don't use it, but I didn't throw it away either. I've got it still . . . as a souvenir.

ELTON JOHN

Last Christmas BLUE decided to give me two silly presents. One was a complete gift pack of Brut — everything you can imagine in that line — talc, after shave, pre-shave, soap, lotion — you name it, it was in that pack. They know full well that I don't even like Brut! Also, they bought me a felt mat which — when you unroll — is covered in kiddies' games — ludo, snakes and ladders and the like! I'm sure plenty of kids would've been delighted with it, but it wasn't really me!

ANNA of Abba

Somebody sent me a slimming machine — one of the ones that vibrate and have belts that you put round yourself — for my bottom. It was sent anonymously and I expect it was meant for a joke, but I was very hurt and offended at first because I didn't think I needed it.

Gill Bains, Barnstaple, Devon.

It was when I was twelve, and I knew I was due to get a late present about a week after Christmas. Of course, I started to think about it a lot, and what it might be, and I was really looking forward to it — and it turned out to be a Noddy jigsaw puzzle!

Glenis Beardsley, Yelland, Devon.

A shocking pink cat suit given to me by an aunt who thought, wrongly, that it was really ''trendy''! And the worst thing was, any time this aunt was due to visit, I had to wear the horrible outfit!

Susan Little, Darlington, Yorks.

A relation in Singapore sent me a beautiful, silk, hand-embroidered tunic top. The only thing was, it was two sizes too small — and I had to give it to my younger sister!

ELKIE BROOKS

I don't think I've had one, unless it was be broke. That was the worst Christmas remember, when I was still with Vine Joe before starting my solo career. We w so hard up we had to share one chic between all of us — me, the band, the r crew — for our Christmas dinner. We coul even afford to follow it up with Christr pudding, let alone go out and buy a turke

LEWIS COLLINS (The Professionals)

Every year I get handkerchiefs, and I never, ever, used one. I've got dozens unopened packets of them in my drawers. T other thing I dislike is when someone gives y money, that's always a disappointment. I making the effort of going out and buying sor thing and wrapping it that matters, really. I too far, myself, I'm a bit of a softie and b dozens of things, but it's because the happie times of my life when I was growing up were Christmas and I love it. That being so, of cours I'm usually delighted with whatever I get even at the time, those hankies!

MARTIN SHAW (The Professionals)

A melted Coca-Cola bottle. One of those that's been heated under a blow lamp and then, while it's soft, distorted and pulled out into funny shapes. I thought that was really silly. It was my best friend who gave it to me, too. I suppose it was meant as a joke. We've known each other for about twenty-five years, and practically grew up together, so he'd know exactly how desperately I needed a bent Coca-Cola bottle!

DENIS WATERMAN

When I was young, the first Christmas I was given socks and underpants was when I realised I wasn't a little boy any more, and it meant I wouldn't get sports books, toys, and so on in the future! Those socks meant I was classified as an adult from then on, and I didn't like it!

Present You've Ever Had?

ILLY IDOL (Generation X)

Every year I get the same useless present from my auntie in Canada — a pair of woolly ar muffs!! I wouldn't be seen dead in them! The rst year it was a bit of a laugh, but now it's ot to the stage when I don't even bother to pen up the parcel because I know exactly hat's inside!

OB DAVIES (Mud)

About four or five years ago my parents ught me a really horrible dressing-gown. It as a mauve and black silky thing and when I pened the parcel all I could find to say was gh!' I think they were rather upset by my sponse!

AVID NICHOLSON (Blue)

Several years ago, my older brother Matt ught me two equally stupid presents. One as a kit for making a Chinese Junk, and when pened the box the kit consisted of about five six large pieces which could be put gether within about one minute! The other esent was a tool kit with everything being ade of either plastic or rubber. Something think Matt must have overlooked — the t that I was 16 at the time!

KATE BUSH

The worst of all was a shower set somebody gave me. It had curtains, rails, pipes, the whole bit, and as far as I was concerned, it was useless. You see, I really love lying in the bath for ages and I've practically never used a shower in my entire life! I don't know where it is now, stuck in a drawer and forgotten, I expect — I'll certainly never fit it up.

BOB GELDOF (Boomtown Rats)

About three years ago I received something far worse than a horrible Christmas present — I received no presents at all! It was a pretty miserable day for me.

MIDGE URE (Rich Kids)

Somebody once sent me a huge crate filled with chocolate fudge — and I can't bear the stuff!

PHIL LYNOTT (Thin Lizzy)

The worst Christmas present I've ever had is being ill — and I've had that twice. The first time was when I was ten or eleven and got pneumonia, which meant I had to spend the whole holidays in bed when I wanted to be out with my friends. Then, a couple of years ago, I contracted hepatitis; and this time I was stuck in bed for about four weeks. I hope that never happens again.

NOEL EDMONDS

Three Christmasses ago an uncle sent me a record token! I know it sounds ungrateful, but honestly the last person who needs a record token is a disc jockey! But I felt I had to use it, so I went out and bought an album, but I can't for the life of me remember now which one it was.

OUR FAVOURITE

We could all think of hundreds of gorgeous good guys to choose from if we had to, we know, but how about feasting your beady little eyes on this bunch of beautiful bad guys for a change? We chose some of our favourites, and hope you'll agree that most of them would make you fall for the baddies every time — given the chance!! The worse the better . . . if you see what we mean!

Mick Jagger — We'd take the mick any

Kermit — We've classed him as a Bad Guy because he keeps playing hard to get with poor Miss Piggy!

Jean Jaques Burnel — We'd like to get a stranglehold on him!

Clint Eastwood — The Good, the Bad and the — Oh, he's wonderful!

Ronnie Barker — He may be bad, but, like porridge, he can be soft and slushy, too!

Vincent Price — Fear at any Price!

Darth Vadar — Dark, mysterious a Force is with him!

BAD GUYS OK!

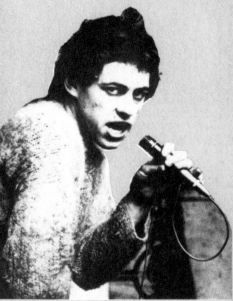

Davison — When he played Tristan in [C]reatures Great and Small,'' we [wou]ldn't have minded giving him the [treatm]ent, anytime!

Bob Geldof — How's about rat!

Animal — He's really wild!

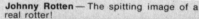

Tom — He's not really bad, 'cos we know he wouldn't do anything nasty to Jerry even if he did manage to catch him!

John Travolta — He's not really bad, either — in fact he's good enough to look at in our photo finish on page 93, too!

Johnny Rotten — The spitting image of a real rotter!

[Ilie] Nastase — We don't care how nasty [he] is, we love him anyway!

Jimmy Connors — He's not quite as nasty as Ilie Nastase, but he's still a smashing bad guy!

THE JUNGLE GAME

How good are your relationships with those around you? Are you beloved by everyone, from your granny to the newspaper boy? Or is the sight of your face enough to scatter everyone to the wind, screaming for mercy?

Well, very few of us fall into those two extreme categories but to discover just how nice a person you are to have around, make your way through the human jungle, with this special game we've devised. You'll have fun and you'll also learn quite a bit about yourself.

Playing the game is also a test of how honest you are. If you give a false answer, the other players have a right to challenge you. And if, horrors of horrors, it's proved that you've been dishonest, the rules of the game decree that you'll have to go right back to the beginning!

The luck of the dice permitting, the person who wins the game is the one who has the best relationship with friends, parents, boyfriends and the whole world in general. Woe betide anyone who can't get away from Rotten relationships though. All we can say for you is that you must be extremely honest!

TO PLAY

You need a dice and different coloured counters, one for each player. (Tiddlywinks, buttons or any small object will do). The first person to throw a six starts the game, and from then on you take it in turns to throw the dice seeing how far you get each time. Follow the Yes and No answers to wherever they lead.

Start at Rotten relationships and (hopefully) you'll be able to battle your way through the jungle up to the treehouse where all is sweetness, joy and Good relationships!

FINISH — Sweetness and joy. Good relationships.

64 Have you or thought anything about today? No

49

All in all, do you think you're a popular person?

50 YES No

Have you made any new enemies in the past couple of months? **48** YES No

47

33

Are you very envious of any of your friends? **34** No YES

Do you often snap at your best friend? **32** No YES

31 Ha pulled face at today? No

17

Have you kicked the dog (or your kid brother) this week? **18** YES No

Have you been rude to/upset/argued with your mum this week? **16** YES No

15 Has any told you nasty yo YES

START — Rotten relationships. **1**

2

GIRLS AT THE TOP!

Gaye Advert wasn't taken very seriously when she first came on the scene as the bass player with the Adverts. But now she's proved to everyone that she plays an equally important part in one of today's best New Wave bands!

1978 has certainly been the best year the music business has se for a long, long time. Not only have we been treated to me super new groups than ever before, but at last girls have finally ma a really firm stand in the charts. And if you think we're exaggerati take a look at the faces below . . . and remember, they're just a fe

Olivia Newton-John has been making a new name for herself — this time as an actress. She must be the envy of every girl because she stars in the film version of "Grease" with none other than dishy John Travolta! Olivia's appeared in films before, but this is the biggest to date. She looks all set to leap into stardom!

Suzi Quatro made a big comeback in 1978 with her hit single "If You Can't Give Me Love." Gone were the leather cat-suits and in their place were silk shirts and a much softer approach. But don't be fooled by it — Suzi's special brand of music hasn't lost one bit of its bounce. In fact, if anything, it's better!

And Suzi's turned to acting as well, with none other than The Fonz himself! She's appeared in several "Happy Days" episodes playing the part of Leather Tuscadero, The Fonz's girl-friend's sister!

1978 must have been the year of the film star, because **Anna** and **Frida** of **Abba** graced the silver screen too, along with Benny and Bjorn in "Abba — The Movie." How many of us dreamed that this Scandinavian quartet who won the Eurovision Song Contest all those years ago would be the huge success they are — and deserve to be!

Rita Ray is the only girl in that group of lovable lunatics, Darts. We often wonder how she manages to survive! She says she really enjoys her life, though, and that she wouldn't swop it for anything.

Lovely **Debbie Harry** is much more than just a beautiful face — she has a great figure, a super voice and she can really dance! Can you blame your boyfriend/brother/father for forgetting everything else when Blondie are on television?

Debbie has brought style and glamour back into the music business but she's quick to point out that it's not all fun and games.

"I sometimes wonder if I could cope with the strain of touring if I were on my own," she says. "I'm lucky that Chris, my boyfriend, is in the group,too,because it's a tremendous help. And I wouldn't want to change what I do for anything in the world!"

Kris Kristofferson isn't the only singing member of his family — his wife, beautiful **Rita Coolidge**, is an established singer herself, with hit singles like "Words".

Linda McCartney is winging her way into films as well. Not very long ago she wrote a little song which provided the inspiration for an animated film called "The Oriental Nightfish", which was a British entry in the Cannes Film Festival. So not only is she lucky enough to be married to Paul McCartney — she's got a lot of talent, as well!

Kate Bush entered the pop world with her very first single, "Wuthering Heights", which flew straight to number one, and since Kate wrote the song herself, it was twice as big an acheivement.

"But I don't want to concentrate on singing entirely," Kate says. "I want to learn more about the art of mime so that I can include it in my stage act!"

So there you are. Eleven lovely ladies who are a very important part of the music business. 1978 has shown that girls expect to be taken seriously when it comes to making hits, and let's hope that 1979 goes the same way, too!

Bonnie Tyler's new image has certainly been doing wonders for her. With her croaky Rod Stewart-type voice she can tackle much gutsier songs, and judging by her chart success they're certainly a lot more popular!

CLEANING AND CARING FOR YOUR ANTIQUE CLOTHES

ONE of the nicest things about old clothes is that the fabrics they're made of *are* so natural — but this can lead to some problems.

Obviously, if you dig up an old garment that's been lying around for years, the first thing you're going to want to do is get it properly cleaned up and looking good. Old garments, though, need a lot of special care and attention — it's not a case of just throwing it into the washing machine and forgetting all about it!

Take care washing your finds — use warm, but not hot, soapy water, using a mild brand of soap flakes — a lot of these old clothes don't have any labels on them, and it's sometimes difficult to tell what fabric they're actually made of.

After you've rinsed the garment thoroughly but carefully in cold water, don't wring or twist or remove excess water — it could damage delicate fabrics. Instead, if the garment is made of heavy material, get rid of any excess water by sandwiching it between two towels laid flat on the floor. To finish drying, hang the garment on a wooden or plastic hanger. For lighter fabrics, drying on a hanger will be fine — you can miss out the first step here.

Finally — ironing and pressing. Always iron old clothes on the *wrong* side, using a low setting, and a pressing cloth.

If you are really in doubt about very delicate clothes, don't attempt any repairs until you've asked your local historical society or museum for their professional opinion — you'll probably find they'll be only too happy to help you!

SHRUG IT OFF!

A shrug is about the most useful thing you could possibly have this winter. It's delicate, fluffy and flattering, neater than a shawl and really easy to wear. It ties at the front so it stays on . . . doesn't keep slipping off your shoulders.

This is a really simple pattern designed for Jackie by Emu wools, using just four balls of Emu Filigree wool which you can buy from most wool shops, price about 54p a ball. This means that you'll be able to knit it up for £2.16. It's in one size only and will fit all shapes and sizes. Emu Filigree comes in loads of delicious colours. The one we chose is Moontide, then there's a gorgeous beigey colour called Silver Beige, Scarlet, Quicksilver, Cranberry, Lavender, Dusky Pink, White, Bluebell, Black, Copper, Turquoise, Mink and Sunset.

You'll need a pair of size 2 needles and a pair of size 6/0 needles—the really thick ones. Make sure you don't make the mistake of using size 6 needles which are much thinner. Remember, for the best results you should use the recommended wool.

Here's what to do:

Amount of wool required – 4 balls of Emu Filigree.

Materials — *Aero Knitting Needles* sizes 2 and 6/0.

Abbreviations — K – knit; p – purl; st(s) – stitch(es); rep – repeat; k.1B – knit into stitch below next stitch on left hand needle; m.1 – make one by picking up the bar that lies between stitch just worked and next stitch on left hand needle and knitting into the back of it; sl – slip; psso – pass slipped stitch over; tog – together.

Using size 2 needles, cast on 49 sts.

1st row (right side) — K 1, *p 1, k 1, rep from * to end.

2nd row — P 1, *k 1, p 1, rep from * to end.

Rep these 2 rows once.
Change to size 6/0 needles and pattern.

1st row — K 2, *k.1B. (see abbreviations), k 1, rep from * to last st., k 1.

2nd row — K 1, *k.1B., k 1, rep from * to end.

Rep these 2 rows 4 times more, then the 1st row once.
Change to size 2 needles.

Next row — Purl.

Next row — K 3, *m.1 (see abbreviations), k 6 rep from * to last 4 sts, m.1., k 4. (57 sts).

Next row — Purl.
Change to size 6/0 needles. Work 1st and 2nd rows of pattern 6 times, then 1st row once. Change to size 2 needles.

Next row — Purl.

Next row — K 6, *m 1, k 5, rep from * to last 6 sts, m 1, k 6. (67 sts).

Next row — Purl.
Change to size 6/0 needles. Work 1st and 2nd rows of pattern 6 times, then the 1st row once. Change to size 2 needles.

Next row — Purl.

Next row — K 6, *m 1, k 5, rep from * to last 6 sts, m 1, k 6. (79 sts).

Next row — Purl.
Change to size 6/0 needles. Work 1st and 2nd rows of pattern 8 times.
Cast off very loosely.

TIE ENDS

With right side of work facing and using size 2 needles, pick up and k 25 sts evenly along one short edge.

Next row — K 3, p to last 3 sts, k 3.

Next row — K 10, sl 1, k 1, psso, k 1, k 2 tog, k 10.

Next row — K 3, p to last 3 sts, k 3.

Next row — K 9, sl 1, k 1, psso, k 1, k 2 tog, k 9.

Next row — K 3, p to last 3 sts, k 3.

Next row — K 8, sl 1, k 1, psso, k 1, k 2 tog, k 8.

Continue to dec in this way until 9 sts remain, ending with a wrong side row.

Next row — K 3, sl 1, k 2 tog, psso, k 3 – 7 sts remain.
Change to size 6/0 needles. Work 1st and 2nd rows of pattern 16 times.
Cast off very loosely.
Work other edge in the same way.

138

21 Ways To Make Him Notice You

YOU'VE got your little eye on this fanciable fella, but as far as he's concerned, you just don't exist! About time the poor lad knew what he was missing, so do him a favour and get yourself noticed. How? Well, work your way through this little lot . . .

THE SUBTLE APPROACH FIRST . . .

1. Get wise to his favourite haunts and just be there, ever so casually.

2. At the club don't strive to win games or push yourself forward (lots of boys are scared of pushy girls). Lose games with a good-natured smile, stick around and help clear up the debris afterwards. He'll soon cotton on.

3. A nice sincere smile and a friendly "hello" without angling for more talk will relax him, make him think he must get to know you.

4. Don't cling to a girl-friend for courage, it'll put him off. Being on your own with a slightly lost look (but not hidden at the back of the crowd) encourages him to get things started.

5. Find a nice, unmanageable, preferably large dog and take it for walks where you'll find your other dumb friend and leave the rest to nature!

6. At a crowded social do, wear something that makes you stand out. A plain, clear colour is often better than patterns from the eye-catching point of view. Or an all-white trouser-suit. Or a mini when the rest have gone below-the-knee (especially if you have good legs!).

7. Perfume. Lots of girls don't bother. Make yours always the same and he will recognise you before he sees you. But make sure it's a subtle one, nothing overpowering!

THE DIRECT INVITATION, BUT NICELY . . .

8. Ask him the time (but hide your watch first).

9. Request change for the phone, the bus, the fruit machine.

10. Ask him the way somewhere. If you're suitably dense he may even take you there himself!

11. Carry a large (empty) parcel everywhere. Ask him to hold it while you get your purse out of your bag . . .

12. . . . and if necessary, leave the parcel behind, beside him. Of course, you'll have your address on it in large block capitals.

13. In the coffee bar ask him to pass you the sugar, the salt, the vinegar, tomato sauce, mustard, more sugar and the menu. As you've only ordered an orangeade, that should get him interested!

14. On the bus or train, ask him the best stop to get off for the swimming baths (or whatever you like).

IF ALL ELSE FAILS . . .

15. Look the other way and walk right into him.

16. Drop the ice-cream you're licking all over his sleeve. Then you have to clean it off, don't you!

17. Offer him a chip, crisp or sweet.

18. Ask if he'll sponsor you for a charity walk. Make sure you get his address, to collect what he owes, later.

19. Pretend you think he's a friend of someone you know and chatter away nonstop before you discover he isn't.

20. "Faint" in front of him.

21. Ask him for a date!

WHAT? You've honestly worked your way through and he still hasn't noticed you? Are you sure he's still breathing? Maybe you should try your fatal charms on another bloke. Good luck!

HOW DO YOU PICTURE YOURSELF?

HOW much do you know about your inner self? You probably imagine you know all about yourself and are aware of a your particular personality traits — but there may be lots more for you to discover! The true secrets of your person ality lie hidden in our psycho-picture, which may look just like a pretty picture to you, but in fact, it's full of deep meaning and hidden significance!

To unlock the secrets of the picture — and the secrets of your personality — do our fun quiz and find out all about you true self!

1. Do you think the artist who painted this picture is —
(b) a young, handsome, successful artist,
(c) married with three kids,
(d) starving in a Parisian garret,
(a) an idealistic art student with a lot of talent but no success?

2. Do you think this picture was inspired by —
(d) an ancient Greek legend,
(b) a traditional European fairy story,
(a) an obscure Russian folk story,
(c) an old Irish nursery rhyme?

3. What is the river called?
(a) The River of Boundlessness.
(d) River-Bird Springs.
(c) Little-Snodmarsh Waterway.
(b) The Great Northern Boundary Canal.

4. Are the boy and girl —
(a) orphans on a voyage of discovery,
(c) a couple in the throes of a super holiday romance,
(d) desperately in love and eloping secretly,
(b) travelling to seek fame and fortune in the big city?

5. Are they going to —
(c) cross the bridge to visit the cottage,
(a) cross the bridge and head for the mountains,
(b) take the lowland road,
(d) take a boat and sail down the river?

6. Who lives in the cottage?
(c) A farm worker.
(d) A dear little old lady.

(a) No-one — it's a wayfarer's cottage open to all who pass by.
(b) A millionaire who uses it for fishing at weekends.

7. Where do you think the boy and girl have just come from?
(a) They've just escaped from the dark, brooding castle of an evil witch.
(b) They've just left their little country village because nothing ever happened there.
(c) They've just come from their hotel, where they're on holiday with their parents.
(d) They've just come from taking food to a poor, lonely old woodcutter.

8. What are the birds flying overhead?
(b) Kestrels.
(c) Swallows.
(d) Skylarks.
(a) Hawks.

9. What are the mountains like?
(d) They're full of mountain goats and rare wild flowers.
(c) They're dotted with holiday villas and ski slopes.
(a) They're volcanic and pitted with caves.
(b) They're lush with vegetation and olive groves.

10. What do the clouds in the sky mean?
(a) Evil.
(d) Doubt and uncertainty.
(c) Pain.
(b) A terrible, dramatic, electric storm brewing.

11. How would you sum up the gen mood and atmosphere of the pictu
(d) Beautiful and dreamlike.
(b) An amusing, fairly normal in of childhood.
(a) Rather strange and mysteriou
(c) Very nice and pretty.

12. What do you think that dragon's d in the middle of this peaceful r scene?
(c) It's not a real dragon, it's or stone-carving!
(a) It's symbolic of all the hards and problems facing the yo couple.
(b) The artist put the dragon into wrong picture by mistake.
(d) The dragon is one of the cer characters in the story of the and girl.

13. Is there anything which isn't in picture which you'd like to see in
(b) A few witches and broomst a couple of gnomes and an ele kettle in case the poor old dr runs out of steam.
(a) A really dark, dense myste forest on the foothills of mountains for added dra atmosphere.
(c) A big red double-decker bus g over the bridge 'cos the boy girl are getting awfully tire walking.
(d) A beautiful fairytale ca swarms of rare butterflies exotic birds of paradise, a ga ing white horse and a golden l

Now count your score, mainly (a), (b or (d) and turn to the conclusions.

IF YOUR ANSWERS WERE:

Mostly (a) — You have a creative mind, and are fascinated by unusual, complicated and mind-boggling thoughts and ideas! You enjoy working things out for yourself, and the harder the puzzle the more of a challenge it is for you. You have a great deal of nervous energy and your mind is very alive, constantly ticking over and aware. Sometimes you tend to take this a bit too far, though, reading far too much into situations and crediting people with motives and feelings which are often non-existent. The point is that, rather than accepting things at face value, you always look for a reason. No wonder your relationships tend to be difficult and more complicated than they need to be! You look for friends on your own special wavelength, people you can talk to and confide in, but your emotions tend to chop and change where people are concerned. The danger is that you go overboard on friendships, building the other person up in your mind, and then you tend to be disillusioned when they fail to live up to your expectations of them.

However, you tend to favour close friendships and once you have found a deep and trusting relationship, you're an interesting, lively companion. You're a bit moody at times, though, and you tend to be a bit over-emotional. You're a real character, an individual, and if you are mixed up sometimes, this is just part and parcel of being rather a special, interesting person!

Mostly (b) — You're quick witted and lively, often hot tempered and impatient, quite aggressive but able to look after yourself. Although you're friendly and sociable, and at ease with all kinds of people, you never lose sight of yourself or your own feelings and opinions.

Perhaps your biggest fault is that you refuse

Sometimes you take this quality to extremes and become self-willed and obstinate, refusing to take criticism or advice, but at other times it simply means that you're self-confident, self-reliant and capable. You usually know what you're doing and it's within your powers to be calculating when you have to be. You're ambitious, you cope well with responsibility and you find challenges exciting. You need an active life, you enjoy meeting people, and if you ever feel shy you're good at hiding it and controlling it. Money and power are attractive to you and you're more inclined to go for a sophisticated lifestyle than to be content with the simple life. You want to travel far and pack a lot of experience into your life. You're attracted to people who are successful, and even if the boy next door is a very nice guy, you'll turn your back on him and go for the more impressive stranger. You have a great deal of energy — and you'll need all of it to embark on your journey up the dizzy ladder of success!

Mostly (c) — The thing that really comes across about your character is your sense of humour and your sheer bubbling enjoyment of life. You're like champagne — fizzy, extro-vert, quite zany and even a little bit wicked sometimes! You're a boaster and a bit of a show-off, though, and you'll grab the lime-light and sail through life without much thought for other people's feelings. But if you blunder into awkward situations and crash into catastrophes, there's usually someone on hand to bail you out.

Your fantastic but zany and uncontrolled personality is the sort which makes others protective towards you. You're like a refresher course and a stimulant to those around you! You get on well with people, not always going in for deep friendships, but you have a spontaneous warmth which attracts people.

Perhaps your biggest fault is that you refuse

Mostly (d) — You're a warm, genuine person with warm, genuine feelings for other people, you live on your emotions and your heart always rules your head. Your impulsive feelings live on your emotions and your heart rule your head. You have true feminine instincts which enables you to float through life, in to the whim of the moment, acting on instinct and getting deeply involved with people.

All this helps you to get a lot of satisfaction from life, but it also sometimes causes pain and heartache when things go wrong. But, however many times you are let emotionally by people, you will carry on trusting them, because that's your nature. Hardness and cynicism doesn't come to you, and you try to live out your romantic day-dreams in real life. So whatever happens, your life is always emotionally rich during good patches your happiness is unequalled.

You also have a rich imagination and a self-confident philosophy of life. You're disappointed and depressed sometimes to make up for the bad times you are capable of experiencing real joy. You're inclined to the past, you enjoy past memories, but also have a sense of hope and excitement about the future.

to face problems because you can convince yourself they don't exist! always easy to get on to be emotional you tend to dismiss emotion, and although may feel things very deeply, you're loth to share your real heart-felt with others. But on the bonus side, you're a naturally cheerful and optimistic approach life, bags of confidence and enough for ten people! So be grateful for mercies!

PHOTO FINISH!

Here we are, at the end of another Jackie annual! But we can't say goodbye without a special thank-you to all the lovely people who've brought us a lot of happiness over the past few months. They've all got that extra something which makes them very special!

THE BEE GEES
It's lovely to see The Bee Gees back! Robin, Maurice and Barry were around 60's, but they're even more lovely no they look fantastic in their Sergeant outfits? Then, of course, there was great music for "Saturday Night Fe terrific, talented trio . . .

LAURA
The Jackie face of 1978, Laura Letham, is bang up to the minute with fashion, and her own gentle Punk looks. She's one of our very favourite models, so keep your eyes open for her in 1979!

DAVID SOUL
Soul-searching time again. This page just wouldn't be complete without David. Just one smile and we all go ga-ga. Wonder what it is about that sexy smile, blond hair and long legs? Sigh . . .

PAUL MICHAEL GLASER
Unglaze those glasered eyes! It's lovely P.M. himself, pastrami-on-rye lover extraordinaire! If we ate that stuff he got through as Starsky, we'd all be like balloons. Still, he needs lots of energy — to keep running from all his fans!

MISS PIGGY
A firm favourite, but what can you say about a pig with class . . . (We couldn't get hold of Kermit for a photograph. He was last seen hot-webbing it through Outer Mongolia. Rumour has it Miss Piggy finally got that kissie, kissie, and Kermit hasn't looked back since . . .)

THE PROFESSIONALS
What a team — they should have won the Wo for looks! It's Martin Shaw and Lewis of "The Professionals" of course, w the most exciting TV partnership for Bet they've got hearts of gold under grim exteriors!

MARK HAMILL
None of us will ever forget "Star Wars," nor will we forget the lovely Mark Hamill who played Luke Skywalker. He's out of this world — a real heavenly body, and long may he shine among the stars.

THE FONZ
Hey-y-y! It's thumbs up to Henry "The Fonz" Winkler, who's shown us how it was in the 50's when everything was so Daddy Cool. Thanks for all those "happy days," Fonzie!

DEBBIE HARRY
Grrr . . . The lovely Debbie Harry of Blondie shot on to the scene early in 1978 with "Denis" Boys swooned, grandfathers gaped, and girls, well, let's face it . . . weren't we all a teeny, weeny bit jealous?

JOHN TRAVOLTA
Reports started coming in at the beginning of last year about the new Fred Astaire. "Oh, yeah?" we all said — until we saw John Travolta in action for ourselves, in "Saturday Night Fever." And, well, what can you say? Except that he was incredible. Mr Superstar himself . . .

SANDY
. . . and this little fella just trotted along to stardom, as Annie's dog in the musical. He's become loved by thousands, and no wonder, he's so cute. A shaggy dog story, if ever there was one!

ANDREA McARDLE
Andrea McArdle hit Britain in May 1978 as the star of the musical "Annie." She's a great actress, a great singer, and she won lots of hearts on stage. Keep your eyes and ears open for Andrea. She's got a big future ahead of her.

KATE BUSH
1978 was Kate Bush's year, when she made us all Cathys looking for our own Heathcliffes. She's brought a new dimension to the pop world with her lovely voice and looks and now she's reached the "Heights" let's hope she'll stay there.

NCE ANDREW
t year a certain boy w up and started get himself noticed girls all over the rld. Yes, Prince Andrew, d isn't he gorgeous? til he finds his own cial princess, we'd just him to know that we're available!

JOHN LLOYD
If you're wondering who the deuce this is, then shame on you, and score love all! It's John Lloyd, and he's the dishiest thing around in tennis shorts. Roll on next summer, for another glimpse of those golden thighs!

BOOMTOWN RATS
One of the nicest packs around — of rats, that is. The Boomtown Rats have given us so much — from their great music, to Johnny Fingers, who's certainly "struck a chord" in those crazy pyjamas!

NICHOLAS BALL
As 'Azell, 'e really 'ad us all 'anging on 'is every word!

GARRETT
t favourite of ours, is Leif Garrett. He into our lives on a skateboard, and d us out with his singing. Long may his keep turning!

Jackie **PIN-U**
ROBERT POWEL

YOUR DATES ARE NUMBERED

HIM ▶	1	2	3	4
YOU ▼ 1	Different personalities, but the same tastes. G.P. sense of humour B.P. Selfishness.	You'll discover long before he does that it's a dead-end.	He likes you . . . and half a dozen others. Don't let him know you care so much.	He likes you ... than you like
2	Be the first to forgive, the last to forget.	A romance that's going places! G.P. generosity B.P. temper.	Things buck up after a disappointing first date.	Let him be the ... you take the ...
3	Mean what you say with this bloke!	A few hearts have been broken by this one and you won't change the pattern.	Row over a TV programme leads to a temporary split.	More like a wre... contest. G.P. Se... fun. B.P. selfish...
4	Don't put him on a pedestal or there could be a nasty bump.	He'll make you so glad to be alive G.P. enthusiasm B.P. roving eye.	Fun while it lasts G.P. coolness B.P. unpunctuality.	Young love d... last, but it c... wonderful...
5	This one's someone special. G.P. knack of making friends B.P. wanderlust.	Changing your hairstyle, interests, skirt-length, accent won't help. He doesn't think of you that way.	The fourth-last boy before you meet your One-and-Only.	The more you s... him, the less yo... him.
6	After three weeks you'll wonder what you ever saw in him.	A bumpy journey, and you'll meet jealousy along the way. But the good times will more than make up.	A separation will lead to a change of heart. G.P. self-reliance B.P. intolerance.	Keep your ... crossed for the ... week.
7	Let him be the first to mention love. G.P. faithfulness B.P. over-caution.	Join the fan club if you want, but the subscription fee is a chunk out of your heart.	Loving and giving, though he wasn't born on a Friday.	When he tells ... secret, you'll h... tussle with ... conscience...
8	Infuriating but magical. Look on it as good experience even if it doesn't lead anywhere.	Some "friends" will wonder what he sees in you. And so, secretly, will you.	Fears, tears, then cheers! He improves with knowing.	You two will l... hate each oth...
9	He'll do crazy things to your heart, then break it. G.P. charm B.P. unreliability.	You may never win a beauty title, but you'll have many boy-friends better than him.	One to remember, maybe with regret. G.P. his feelings for you. B.P. jealousy.	Who's chasing ... G.P. imaginatio... conceit.

WANT to know the prospects for your love life? All you have to do is find out the zodiac sign of your current boy (or the one you fancy) and locate it at the top of the page. Check yours from those at the side. Where the two cross is the verdict of the stars.

You don't know his birthday? Don't despair! We've another angle for you on page 94.

...ART

...ANCER 21-July 22	LEO July 23-Aug. 22	VIRGO Aug. 23-Sept. 22	LIBRA Sept. 23-Oct. 22	SCORPIO Oct. 23-Nov. 21	SAGITTARIUS Nov. 22-Dec. 21	CAPRICORN Dec. 22-Jan. 19
...nd has al-...let him know ...feelings.	He'll make his exit before the current No. 1 leaves the Top Thirty.	A girl has hurt him badly and he's unsure of himself.	Happy - go - lucky dating. No strings, no strain.	Sheep in sheep's clothing.	Only one tiny cloud in the sky.	So close, he's the only one you can really confide in.
...moment he's ...nterested in ...al relation-ship.	A female relative of his will make mischief between you.	His impudent sense of humour could give you a red face.	Some of his habits will irritate you.	He'll two-time and lie so plausibly, you'll feel YOU should apologise.	If you're not possessive, it could last as long as you want.	If at first you don't succeed, try someone else.
reach the ...s and the ...s and have a decision to make.	You won't make progress until the shadow of an old flame disappears.	Your loves and hates have a lot in common.	A slow starter, but watch out after a few weeks!	You'll wonder how you ever existed without him.	He's Nearly-Mr-Right. You won't meet the real thing for years.	Fate has dealt you some good cards. Be thankful.
...ot as tough ...pretends. ...tell all to ...r mates.	Revenge is sweet—but is that the real reason you want to date him?	Clinging to a girl-friend for courage will put him off.	Right fella, wrong time.	Don't confuse the image for the real boy.	Both of you are putting on an act. Your true selves would hit it off better.	Overconfidence is a mask for his basic shyness.
...you believe ...ared of you?	Wolf in wolf's clothing.	He's scared of pushy girls, so you don't need to put on an act.	He'll bring you out of your shell and you'll surprise yourself.	There are just too many difficulties in the way.	Too alike—that's why it won't last long.	Your tastes couldn't be farther apart.
...friends will ...reen when ...see you to-gether.	Don't neglect your best friend—you could need her sympathy.	When you hit it off, someone else is going to be hurt.	He has a mind of his own and your views don't always match.	You'll leave your mark on him.	Wolf in sheep's clothing.	He feels dating you would prove expensive.
..., yes-no, ...The guy ...n't make up ...is mind.	With your temperament, steer clear of Fire sign boys.	A charmer who could get uppity if he thinks he's your one and only.	Poor lad—he won't know what hit him!	An animal will bring you closer together.	You're more attractive than he'd have you believe.	Don't let a misunderstanding ruin a promising friendship.
...rt-lived af-...unless you ...er your pos-...ve instinct.	Strike a light — the perfect match!	Wear asbestos-lined gloves if you don't want your fingers burned.	When you outgrow him, you'll find he's a clinger.	He thinks you conceited.	Another year and you'll be able to pick and choose.	His persistence will annoy, then please you.
...mum would ...him—is that ...iss of death?	Life is dull, but very peaceful when you're apart.	You're two of a kind. Could be boring.	Take your time. He'll be around for a while.	He can't afford a steady girlfriend.	He'll be the first of seven men in your life.	He's not as unconcerned as you thought.
...destiny lies ...an Air sign ...a high-flier, too!	You'll forget all about him when a stranger comes into your life.	All signals at go!	A boy with a Fire or Earth birth sign would make you a better partner.	You're reading too much into his light-hearted offer.	Every date gets better.	Are you tolerant enough to put up with him?
...s more ex-...when he's ...d, but it's a ...turvy ro-mance.	At the moment he feels you're too young for him.	He's scared in case you get too serious.	With a bit of practice you can twist him round your finger.	There will be a chance to become better acquainted on a Tuesday.	You'll be put off his type for life.	You're a different type from his other girlfriends.
...quarrels, but ...agic either.	Beneath it all, he's a very ordinary, likeable boy.	He's not known as Mr Love 'em and Leave 'em for nothing.	If at first you don't succeed—leave him be.	Get to the back of the queue.	Two friends would just love to be in your shoes.	Your Saturdays will be the happiest you've known.